D1592166

Farm Journal's
CREAM OF THE CROP
COOKBOOK

300 Classic Dishes Picked From
Farm Journal's Famous Test Kitchens
Plus! Fat-Skimming Options With Each Recipe

Edited by Karen Freiberg and M.J. Smith, RD

Published by Farm Journal, Inc.

Farm Journal's Cream of the Crop Cookbook
© 1998 by Farm Journal, Inc.
Decheros Reservados
All rights reserved. Except for brief passages for review purposes,
no part of this publication may be reproduced, stored in a retrieval system
or transmitted, in any form or by any means, without the prior written
permission of Farm Journal, Inc.

Library of Congress Catalog Number: 98-73274

ISBN 0-89795-999-X

EDITED BY: Karen Freiberg and M.J. Smith, RD
COVER DESIGN: Joe Tenerelli
TEXT DESIGN: Al Casciato
PHOTOGRAPHS: Front cover: Farm scene by Grant Heilman Photography; Breakfast Berry Pizza by M. Jensen Photography. Back cover (left to right): Curried Smoked Turkey in a Pocket, Chicken and Double-Corn Dumplings, Harvest Lasagne by M. Jensen Photography.

Printed in the United States of America

Published by
Farm Journal, Inc.
Centre Square West
1500 Market Street
Philadelphia, PA 19102-2181

INTRODUCTION

The country cook's fat-fighter manual

Farm Journal is the Magazine of American Agriculture and the stonghold of America's most treasured country recipes. When country cooks make a meal, whether it's for company or for the kids, for one or for a crowd, Farm Journal recipes are part of the action.

Our recipes have been a staple of dependable, delicious country food for generations. That's because they come from the best sources—country cooks themselves. For decades, Farm Journal has solicited recipes from farm folks who grow our food and know its importance to the health of our families.

Through the years, teams of editors and home economists chose the best of those offerings and developed many new ones. Then they taste-tested and double-checked each recipe in Farm Journal's Test Kitchens. The result: hundreds of mouthwatering dishes. This book represents 300 of these recipes, handpicked from the more than 1,300 published in the pages of Farm Journal since 1970.

Much has changed, both on the farm and in the concepts of good nutrition, since the first of these recipes came to be. Farmers now raise livestock that produces meat so lean and tasty no one would have recognized it 25 years ago. And nutritionists have clearly mounted a wholesale war against fat in food. In 1989, studies show

fewer than 30% of consumers worried about dietary fat. By 1995, that percentage more than doubled to 65%.

This emphasis on fat-as-the-enemy in the American diet need not impair your love of country cooking, however. Master fat-fighter M.J. Smith took on the original recipes in this book as a personal challenge. A registered dietitian, M.J. has spent her entire career teaching people how to control fat in their diets. Along the way, she has authored 10 cookbooks, including *All-American Low-Fat Meals in Minutes, Daily Bread* and *Diabetic Low Fat/No Fat Meals in Minutes.*

Side by side with the classic Farm Journal recipes in this volume, M.J. has configured fat-skimming options and added full nutritional analysis for both methods. You can now choose your own country cooking style between traditional or reduced-fat recipes—or mix and match dishes within the same meal.

Country cooking has come a long way since the days of lard cake and potatoes fried in bacon fat. *Farm Journal's Cream of the Crop Cookbook* forges this fat-skimming path into the new millennium.

Karen Freiberg
Managing Editor
Farm Journal

Sifting through culinary history

I got hooked the first time I heard the title *Cream of the Crop*. Even dietitians love the sound of something rich. I may be a busy author, but there is no project that I love more than working with "the best of the best."

I have written 10 cookbooks over the past 15 years. My days in the kitchen and at the computer have been joyful ones, taking fat out of brownies and lasagne (*All- American Low-Fat Meals in Minutes*), planning holiday menus for the diabetic Aunt Louise's of the world (*Diabetic Low Fat/No Fat Meals in Minutes*) and encouraging readers to view food as a blessing (*Daily Bread*).

But this project would be different. The recipes were already developed, even tested! What was needed were my fat-lowering secrets and tricks. I know fat-free cream cheese never really blends, and you can't take every drop of oil out of a vegetable marinade. Preserving taste and appeal is priority one in my own books and would be with this one too.

We started out with a stack of 1,300 original documents. It might as well have been a Tuesday in 1972 with a pile of ironing too big to ever get done. But like the last time you retrieved your metal sifter to make that perfect cake, results of thoughtful sorting are worth the effort.

This collection boils out, distills down and captures the culinary history of Farm Journal, tracing recipes like Danish Pot Roast and Molasses Drop Cookies from the '70s, to Miniature Quiches in the '80s, ending with Smoked Turkey Stuffed Shells in the '90s.

FARM MADE
The penny-pinching, use-what-you-have nature of farm cooks graces this work. You'll love knowing how to prepare All Purpose Baking Mix for Country Pancakes or a Quick Coffee Cake. Just like mom said, it costs less and tastes better than store-bought.

YIELD DATA
You will notice small differences in recipe style over three decades. With those early classics, for instance, few people worried about yield and portion size, so there is a range of serving sizes at the top of the page. As the readership grew interested in calories per serving, measurements became more precise.

SIZED FOR LOW FAT
The nutrition analysis puts the original recipe version side by side with the fat-skimming options. If you watch calories, a few of those original counts will scare you. But like all honest farmers, we simply didn't fudge the numbers. Here's

how we figured the analysis: We used the largest number of servings in a range and omitted optional garnishes or toppings. If there is a measurement before an ingredient, such as "1 prepared pie crust," it is included in the count.

This tedious effort is because dietitians, magazine editors and livestock producers will all agree on one thing: reducing obesity and, specifically, saturated fat in the American diet is a way to beat heart disease and cancer. And we are all partners in that national mission to give people informed nutrition choices and to help them prepare good food in healthy ways.

VOICES FROM THE PAST . . .

To capture the stories that accompanied recipes, chapter division pages reveal voices from the kitchen. I tracked down readers from the '70s like Jennifer Sechler Bennett who was 9 years old when her family served in the Farm Journal Family Test Group. And I found Georgia Engelby, nearly 70, still cooking dinner for her husband and three grown sons during harvest time. The loyalty and familiarity between long-time readers and this Magazine of American Agriculture was felt in every call.

. . . INTO THE FUTURE

So now, please go on and turn the pages, and remember the smell of cinnamon rolls on Saturday morning. Explore the potluck salads and desserts family reunions are remembered by. Dig into the eggs and meat and milk and grains and vegetables grown from your lands: The cream of the crop is here.

M.J. Smith
Registered Dietitian

Consult your physician or registered dietitian: Readers are asked to seek the guidance of a licensed physician or registered dietitian before making diet changes. This book is intended for informational purposes only and is not for use as an alternative to appropriate medical care. Exchange diet information is based on the system developed in 1995 by the American Dietetic Association and the American Diabetes Association.

DEDICATION

This book is dedicated to the thousands of
Farm Journal readers who have preserved
the goodness of country cooking within the
revolution of a fast, fat-free American food-style.

———————————————

ACKNOWLEDGMENTS
Thank You!

• Stanford Erickson for sharing our vision and backing our enterprise.

• Dorothy Snell and Laura Redfield for transforming the original recipes from three decades of magazines speedily and accurately into manuscript.

• Jean Tracy for her eagle-eyed proofing and conceptualization of the printed words.

• Susan Heath, a banker and nutrition analyst, who counted dimes by day and fat grams by night.

• The food editors who staffed Farm Journal's test kitchens over the past 30 years, developing and presenting recipes with great delight and flair for farm cooks across the nation, including: Joanne G. Fullan, Mary Gunderson, Elise W. Manning, Alice Joy Miller, Nell Nichols and Patricia A. Ward.

• The farm women and men who graciously shared their cooking secrets and favorite recipes with us over these many years.

CONTENTS

Chapter

1   APPETIZERS, SNACKS AND BEVERAGES 1

2   BREADS 25

3   DESSERTS 57

4   EGGS, CHEESE AND LEGUMES 105

5   FISH AND SHELLFISH 119

6   PASTA, RICE AND GRAINS 127

7   POULTRY 139

8   PRESERVED FOODS.. 159

9   RED MEATS 169

10 SALADS 203

11 SOUPS, STEWS AND SANDWICHES....................................... 231

12 VEGETABLES 259

    INDEX 287

CHAPTER ONE

APPETIZERS, SNACKS AND BEVERAGES

Oh, please let's pull over!

Who doesn't remember sighting a roadside watermelon stand from the back seat of the family car? "Oh, let's stop" was the kids' chorus as you pressed your nose to the window and wondered, "Will Dad pull over?"

What's it like to live on a watermelon farm? Texas producer William Watson admits you get pretty good at picking out prize-winning specimens. His three-step method for selecting the best melon in the bin goes like this:
• The melon's appearance is free of cuts, bruises and dents.
• The melon feels heavy for its size when you lift it.
• The melon is ripe when the underside is a pale creamy yellow and the skin has a healthy sheen.

Watermelon consumption has increased 50% since 1980, as the American palate has peaked for fruit. Slice it up for a snack, cube it for salads or desserts or throw it in the back seat for the family reunion. As you bite into the sweetness of this all-American favorite, consider the Vitamins A, C, B_6 and potassium it provides at just 50 calories per cup. This first chapter features newfangled Watermelon Grapefruit Fiesta, a sweet and tangy slush prepared in just 10 minutes.

To discover more ways to celebrate watermelon, be sure to visit the National Watermelon Promotion Board on the Internet at *http://www.watermelon.org* for recipes.

Asparagus Roll-ups
Yield: 24 appetizers

12 thin slices white bread
2 (3 ounce) packages cream cheese, softened
1 tablespoon milk
8 slices bacon, cooked, drained and crumbled
12 cooked asparagus spears, chilled
2 tablespoons butter or margarine, melted

> *Fat-skimming options: Substitute light (50% reduced fat) cream cheese.*
> *With options, exchange diets count: 1 vegetable, 1 fat.*

• Trim crusts from bread. With a rolling pin, roll each slice to flatten.
• Beat cream cheese and milk until smooth; blend in crumbled bacon. Spread on flattened bread slices.
• Place an asparagus spear on one end of each bread slice; roll up. Cut each roll in half crosswise.

• Place seamside down on greased baking sheet. Brush rolls with melted butter. Cover and refrigerate until ready to bake.
• Bake in 400 degree F oven 5 minutes, then broil several minutes until lightly browned.

Nutrition Analysis Per Serving: As Originally Published/With Fat-Skimming Options

Calories: 82/73
Protein: 3 g/3 g
Carbohydrate: 7 g/7 g
Fat: 5 g/4 g

Saturated Fat: 3 g/2 g
Cholesterol: 12 mg/7 mg
Sodium: 137 mg/156 mg
Dietary Fiber: 0 g/0 g

Chicken Salsa Dip

Yield: 4 cups or 16 ($^1/_4$ cup) servings

1$^1/_2$ cups finely diced tomato
1 cup finely diced cooked chicken
$^1/_2$ medium cucumber, peeled, seeded and finely diced
$^1/_2$ medium green pepper, finely diced
3 tablespoons finely chopped onion
3 tablespoons finely chopped parsley
2 tablespoons vinegar
1 tablespoon olive oil or vegetable oil
$^1/_2$ teaspoon salt
$^1/_4$ teaspoon sugar
$^1/_8$ teaspoon pepper
Tortilla chips for dippers

Fat-skimming options: none. Exchange diets, count: 1 lean meat.

• In bowl, mix together first 11 ingredients.
Refrigerate until ready to serve.

Nutrition Analysis Per Serving: As Originally Published	
Calories: 46	Saturated Fat: 0 g
Protein: 5 g	Cholesterol: 16 mg
Carbohydrate: 1 g	Sodium: 83 mg
Fat: 2 g	Dietary Fiber: 0 g

Double Cheese Fondue

Yield: 4 cups or 16 (¹/₄ cup) servings

2 tablespoons minced celery
¹/₄ cup butter
¹/₄ cup flour
1 cup milk
1 cup light cream
³/₄ pound Swiss cheese, shredded
¹/₄ pound Brick cheese, shredded
1 teaspoon Worcestershire sauce
¹/₄ teaspoon dry mustard
¹/₄ teaspoon onion salt
¹/₁₆ teaspoon cayenne pepper

> *Fat-skimming options: Replace butter with 2 tablespoons soft margarine.*
> *Substitute evaporated skim milk for cream and select reduced-fat Swiss and Brick cheese.*
> *With options, exchange diets count: 1 lean meat, 2 fat.*

• Sauté celery in melted butter in 3-quart heavy saucepan until tender. Stir in flour. Gradually stir in milk and cream. Cook, stirring, until thick.

• Slowly add cheeses; stir until melted. Add remaining ingredients.
• Pour into fondue pot and keep warm. If mixture gets too thick, stir in some hot milk.

Nutrition Analysis Per Serving: As Originally Published/With Fat-Skimming Options

Calories: 176/149	Saturated Fat: 9 g/6 g
Protein: 9 g/9 g	Cholesterol: 45 mg/31 mg
Carbohydrate: 4 g/5 g	Sodium: 142 mg/92 mg
Fat: 14 g/10 g	Dietary Fiber: 0 g/0 g

Ham and Broccoli Loaves

Yield: 2 loaves, 3 to 4 servings each, or 8 servings total

1 recipe White Bread Dough
1 (10 ounce) package frozen chopped broccoli, thawed and well drained
1½ cups diced cooked ham
4 hard-cooked eggs, peeled and coarsely chopped
2 cups shredded mozzarella cheese (8 ounces)
¼ cup grated Parmesan cheese
¼ teaspoon salt
¼ teaspoon pepper

> *Fat-skimming options: Use whites of egg only. Use part-skim mozzarella cheese.*
> *With options, exchange diets count: 3 starch, 2 vegetable, 3 lean meat.*

• Prepare White Bread Dough. Roll out each dough half to a 14x9 inch rectangle.
• In bowl, mix together broccoli, ham, hard-cooked eggs, mozzarella cheese, Parmesan cheese, salt and pepper.
• Spoon broccoli mixture in a 3-inch-wide strip down center of each rectangle to ½ inch from short sides.
• Make 2½-inch-long cuts at 1 inch intervals on long sides of each rectangle. Twist each strip twice; fold strips crisscross fashion over filling on each rectangle.
• Place loaves 3 inches apart on greased large baking sheet.
• Cover and let rise in warm place until doubled, about 30 minutes.
• Bake in 375 degree F oven 20 to 25 minutes or until golden brown. Serve warm.
• Baked loaves may be frozen up to 2 months. Thaw before reheating in 325 degree F oven 15 minutes.

White Bread Dough

4 teaspoons (2 packages) active dry yeast
1 tablespoon granulated sugar
1 teaspoon salt
4 to 4½ cups sifted all-purpose flour
1⅓ cups milk
2 tablespoons margarine or butter
1 large egg

• In large bowl, stir together yeast, sugar, salt and 1½ cups flour.
• Heat milk and margarine to 120-130 degrees F. Add to yeast mixture. With mixer at medium speed, beat 2 minutes. Add egg; blend well.
• Stir in enough remaining flour to make a stiff dough. Turn out onto lightly floured surface. Knead until smooth and elastic, 5 minutes.
• Cover dough with inverted bowl; let rest 30 minutes.
• Punch down dough; divide dough in half.

Nutrition Analysis Per Serving: As Originally Published/With Fat-Skimming Options

Calories: 500/461
Protein: 29 g/28 g
Carbohydrate: 54 g/54 g
Fat: 18 g/14 g

Saturated Fat: 9 g/7 g
Cholesterol: 192 mg/78 mg
Sodium: 1,169 mg/1,232 mg
Dietary Fiber: 2 g/2 g

Hot Spinach-Bacon Dip

Yield: 2¹/₄ cups or 9 (¹/₄ cup) servings

1 (8 ounce) package cream cheese, cubed
1 (5 ounce) jar sharp pasteurized process cheese spread
¹/₄ cup milk
¹/₄ teaspoon garlic powder
¹/₈ teaspoon hot pepper sauce
1 (10 ounce) package frozen chopped spinach, thawed and drained
6 slices bacon, cooked, drained and crumbled

Fat-skimming options: Substitute light (50% reduced fat) cream cheese and skim milk. With options, exchange diets count: 1 very lean meat, 1 vegetable, 2 fat.

• In 2-quart microwave-safe bowl, place first 5 ingredients. Microwave on high (100% power) 3 minutes, stirring after each minute until melted and smooth.

• Stir in spinach and bacon. Microwave 1 minute or until hot.
• Serve hot with bread cubes or raw vegetables.

Nutrition Analysis Per Serving: As Originally Published/With Fat-Skimming Options

Calories: 189/148
Protein: 7 g/8 g
Carbohydrate: 4 g/5 g
Fat: 16 g/11 g

Saturated Fat: 9 g/6 g
Cholesterol: 44 mg/24 mg
Sodium: 489 mg/559 mg
Dietary Fiber: 0 g/0 g

Reuben Loaves
Yield: 2 loaves, 3 to 4 servings each, or 8 servings total

1 recipe Rye Bread Dough
8 ounces thinly sliced corned beef
$\frac{1}{2}$ cup Russian dressing
2 pounds fresh or canned sauerkraut, drained and squeezed dry
2 cups shredded Swiss cheese (8 ounces)
1 large egg, beaten
1 teaspoon caraway seed

Fat-skimming options: Use low-fat Russian dressing. Use reduced-fat Swiss cheese.
With options, exchange diets count: 3 lean meat, 2 vegetable, 3 starch, 1 skim milk.

• Prepare Rye Bread Dough. Roll out each dough half to a 14x9 inch rectangle.
• Arrange corned beef in a 4-inch-wide strip down center of each rectangle to 1 inch of short sides. Spread with Russian dressing. Top with sauerkraut and Swiss cheese.
• Brush edges of rectangles with some of the beaten egg. Fold long sides of each rectangle over filling, overlapping long sides 2 inches. Pinch seams to seal.
• Place loaves seamside down, 3 inches apart, on greased large baking sheet, tucking the ends under.
• Cover and let rise in warm place until doubled, about 30 minutes.
• Cut 3 shallow diagonal slashes in top of each loaf.
• Brush loaves with remaining beaten egg; sprinkle with caraway seed.
• Bake in 375 degree F oven 20 to 25 minutes or until golden brown. Serve warm.

• Baked loaves may be frozen up to 2 months. Thaw before reheating in 325 degree F oven 15 minutes.

Rye Bread Dough
2 packages active dry yeast
2 tablespoons packed brown sugar
1 teaspoon salt
$1\frac{1}{2}$ cups stirred medium rye flour
3 cups sifted all-purpose flour
$1\frac{1}{3}$ cups milk
2 tablespoons margarine or butter
1 large egg

• In large bowl, stir together yeast, sugar, salt and $1\frac{1}{2}$ cups flour.
• Heat milk and margarine to 120-130 degrees F. Add to yeast mixture. With mixer at medium speed, beat 2 minutes. Add egg; blend well.
• Stir in enough remaining flour to make a stiff dough. Turn out onto lightly floured surface. Knead until smooth and elastic, 5 minutes.
• Cover dough with inverted bowl; let rest 30 minutes.
• Punch down dough; divide dough in half.

Nutrition Analysis Per Serving: As Originally Published/With Fat-Skimming Options	
Calories: 602/532	Saturated Fat: 11 g/8 g
Protein: 24 g/26 g	Cholesterol: 121 mg/116 mg
Carbohydrate: 64 g/67 g	Sodium: 2,023 mg/2,027 mg
Fat: 27 g/17 g	Dietary Fiber: 4.5 g/4.5 g

Salami and Sweet Pepper Loaves

Yield: 2 loaves, 3 to 4 servings each, or 8 servings total

1 recipe White Bread Dough
1 large sweet green pepper, quartered, seeded and sliced
1 cup chopped onion
8 ounces thinly sliced hard salami
2 cups shredded mozzarella cheese (8 ounces)
1 teaspoon dried oregano leaves, crushed
1 large egg, beaten
2 tablespoons grated Parmesan cheese

Fat-skimming options: Substitute lean ham for salami. Use ¼ cup liquid egg substitute for egg. Substitute reduced-fat mozzarella cheese. With options, exchange diets count: 3 starch, 1 vegetable, 3 lean meat.

• Prepare White Bread Dough.
• Place green pepper and onion in microwave-safe bowl; cover with paper towel. Microwave on high 4 minutes or until barely tender. (Or sauté green pepper and onion in 2 teaspoons oil in skillet over medium heat.) Drain on paper towels.
• Roll out each dough half to a 14x9 inch rectangle.
• Arrange salami in a 4-inch-wide strip down center of each rectangle to ½ inch from short sides. Top salami with green pepper and onion. Sprinkle with mozzarella cheese and oregano.
• Make 2½-inch-long cuts at 1 inch intervals on long sides of each rectangle. Fold strips crisscross fashion over filling on each rectangle.
• Place loaves 3 inches apart on greased large baking sheet.
• Cover and let rise in warm place until doubled, about 30 minutes.
• Brush loaves with beaten egg; sprinkle with Parmesan cheese.

Bake in 375 degree F oven 20 to 25 minutes or until golden brown. Serve warm.
• Baked loaves may be frozen up to 2 months. Thaw before reheating in 325 degree F oven 15 minutes.

White Bread Dough

2 packages active dry yeast
1 tablespoon granulated sugar
1 teaspoon salt
4 to 4½ cups sifted all-purpose flour
1⅓ cups milk
2 tablespoons margarine or butter
1 large egg

• In large bowl, stir together yeast, sugar, salt and 1½ cups flour.
• Heat milk and margarine to 120-130 degrees F. Add to yeast mixture. With mixer at medium speed, beat 2 minutes. Add egg; blend well.
• Stir in enough remaining flour to make a stiff dough. Turn out onto lightly floured surface. Knead until smooth and elastic, 5 minutes.
• Cover dough with inverted bowl; let rest 30 minutes.
• Punch down dough; divide dough in half.

Nutrition Analysis Per Serving: As Originally Published/With Fat-Skimming Options

Calories: 440/422	Saturated Fat: 8 g/6 g
Protein: 19 g/22 g	Cholesterol: 95 mg/63 mg
Carbohydrate: 55 g/55 g	Sodium: 649 mg/722 mg
Fat: 16 g/12 g	Dietary Fiber: 2.5 g/2.5 g

Salmon-Parsley Log

Yield: 1 log (2½ cups) or 10 (¼ cup) servings

1 (14½ to 15½ ounce) can salmon, drained, and skin and bones removed
1 (8 ounce) package cream cheese, softened
1 teaspoon lemon juice
1 teaspoon grated onion
1 teaspoon prepared horseradish
¼ teaspoon liquid smoke
½ cup chopped fresh parsley
⅓ cup chopped pecans

> *Fat-skimming options: Substitute light (50% reduced fat) cream cheese.*
> *With options, exchange diets count: ½ skim milk, 1 lean meat, 1 fat.*

• Beat together first 6 ingredients until well blended. Shape into a 9-inch log; wrap in plastic wrap. Refrigerate several hours or overnight.

• On sheet of waxed paper, mix together parsley and pecans. Roll log in parsley mixture to coat; wrap. Refrigerate until ready to serve. Serve with cucumber slices or crackers.

Nutrition Analysis Per Serving: As Originally Published/With Fat-Skimming Options

Calories: 163/137
Protein: 9 g/9 g
Carbohydrate: 2 g/3 g
Fat: 14 g/10 g

Saturated Fat: 5 g/3 g
Cholesterol: 21 mg/6 mg
Sodium: 253 mg/303 mg
Dietary Fiber: 1 g/1 g

Savory Potted Cheese
Yield: 3 cups or 12 (¹/₄ cup) servings

1 pound sharp Cheddar cheese
1 (3 ounce) package cream cheese
1 teaspoon dry mustard
1 teaspoon garlic salt
1 teaspoon Worcestershire sauce
2 tablespoons vegetable oil
1 tablespoon milk

Fat-skimming options: Substitute reduced-fat Cheddar cheese and light (50% reduced fat) cream cheese. Omit oil. With options, exchange diets count: 1 lean meat, 1 fat.

• Grate Cheddar cheese into large mixer bowl. Let grated and cream cheeses stand at room temperature just long enough to soften.

• Add remaining ingredients. Beat at low speed until blended thoroughly.
• Pack into jar, cover and refrigerate at least 24 hours before using.

Nutrition Analysis Per Serving: As Originally Published/With Fat-Skimming Options

Calories: 198/113
Protein: 10 g/13 g
Carbohydrate: 1 g/2 g
Fat: 17 g/7 g

Saturated Fat: 10 g/4 g
Cholesterol: 48 mg/27 mg
Sodium: 260 mg/298 mg
Dietary Fiber: 0 g/0 g

Spinach-Cheese Loaves

Yield: 2 loaves, 3 to 4 servings each, or 8 servings total

1 recipe Whole Wheat Bread Dough
2 (10 ounce) packages frozen chopped spinach, thawed and squeezed dry
1 (15 ounce) container ricotta cheese
2 cups shredded Cheddar cheese (8 ounces)
1 large egg
2 cloves garlic, minced
1 teaspoon dried basil leaves, crushed
$1/4$ teaspoon salt

> *Fat-skimming options: Substitute nonfat ricotta cheese, $1/4$ cup liquid egg substitute and reduced-fat Cheddar cheese.*
> *With options, exchange diets count: 3 starch, 2 vegetable, 4 lean meat.*

• Prepare Whole Wheat Bread Dough. Roll out each dough half to a 14x9 inch rectangle.
• In bowl, mix together spinach, ricotta cheese, Cheddar cheese, egg, garlic, basil, salt.
• Spread spinach mixture in a 3-inch-wide strip down center of each rectangle to $1/2$ inch from short sides.
• Make $2^1/2$-inch-long cuts at 1 inch intervals on long sides of each rectangle. Fold strips crisscross fashion over filling.
• Place loaves 3 inches apart on greased large baking sheet.
• Cover and let rise in warm place until doubled, about 30 minutes.
• Bake in 375 degree F oven 20 to 25 minutes or until golden brown. Serve warm.
• Baked loaves may be frozen up to 2 months. Thaw before reheating in 325 degree F oven 15 minutes.

Whole Wheat Bread Dough

4 teaspoons (2 packages) active dry yeast
1 tablespoon granulated sugar
1 teaspoon salt
2 cups stirred whole wheat flour
2 to $2^1/2$ cups sifted all-purpose flour
$1^1/3$ cups milk
2 tablespoons margarine or butter
1 large egg

• In large bowl, stir together yeast, sugar, salt and $1^1/2$ cups flour.
• Heat milk and margarine to 120-130 degrees F. Add to yeast mixture. With mixer at medium speed, beat 2 minutes. Add egg; blend well.
• Stir in enough remaining flour to make a stiff dough. Turn out onto lightly floured surface. Knead until smooth and elastic, 5 minutes.
• Cover dough with inverted bowl; let rest 30 minutes.
• Punch down dough; divide dough in half.

Nutrition Analysis Per Serving: As Originally Published/With Fat-Skimming Options	
Calories: 635/497	Saturated Fat: 20 g/9 g
Protein: 33 g/38 g	Cholesterol: 155 mg/83 mg
Carbohydrate: 54 g/58 g	Sodium: 830 mg/902 mg
Fat: 33 g/16 g	Dietary Fiber: 5 g/5 g

Sweet-Spiced Shrimp

Yield: 8 servings

1½ cups water
3 tablespoons mixed pickling spice
1 tablespoon seafood boiling spice
1 tablespoon vinegar
½ teaspoon salt
1½ pounds large shrimp (about 50), shells and tails left on but legs removed

Fat-skimming options: none. Exchange diets count: 1½ very lean meat.

• In 10 inch skillet over high heat, bring first 5 ingredients to a boil. Add shrimp; cover and cook 3 minutes, or until shrimp are opaque.

• Pour shrimp and cooking liquid into flat baking dish. Refrigerate until chilled.

Nutrition Analysis Per Serving: As Originally Published

Calories: 45
Protein: 9 g
Carbohydrate: 1 g
Fat: 1 g

Saturated Fat: 0 g
Cholesterol: 65 mg
Sodium: 196 mg
Dietary Fiber: 0 g

Fruit-Nut Mix

Yield: 3¼ pounds or 44 (¼ cup) servings

1 pound unsalted dry-roasted peanuts (3 cups)
1 (15 ounce) box seedless raisins
½ pound dates, cut up (1¼ cups)
¼ pound unroasted cashew pieces (1 cup)
¼ pound walnut pieces (1 cup)
1 (3½ ounce) can flaked coconut
3 ounces dried apricots, cut in half (½ cup)

Fat-skimming options: Use just ½ pound peanuts. Reduce cashews to ¼ cup. Add 1½ cups dried apple chips. With options, exchange diets count: 1 starch, ½ fat.

• Combine all ingredients in large bowl; toss to mix. Place in airtight container or plastic bags and store in refrigerator.

Nutrition Analysis Per Serving: As Originally Published/With Fat-Skimming Options

Calories: 130/97
Protein: 4 g/2 g
Carbohydrate: 13 g/13 g
Fat: 8 g/4 g

Saturated Fat: 1 g/1 g
Cholesterol: 0 mg/0 mg
Sodium: 105 mg/54 mg
Dietary Fiber: 1.5 g/1.0 g

Spicy Holiday Brew

Yield: 3 quarts or 12 (1 cup) servings

2 quarts water
2½ cups sugar
2 cinnamon sticks
2 tablespoons chopped crystallized ginger
2 whole cloves
2 cups apple juice
2 cups strong tea
2 cups fresh orange juice
⅓ cup lemon juice
Lemon slices

Fat-skimming options: Reduce sugar to ½ cup. With options, exchange diets count: 1 fruit.

• Combine water, sugar, cinnamon sticks, ginger and cloves in a saucepan. Bring mixture to a boil; boil 15 minutes. Remove from heat. Let stand in refrigerator overnight.

• Strain mixture. Add apple juice, tea, orange juice and lemon juice. Heat to serve. Garnish with lemon slices.

Nutrition Analysis Per Serving: As Originally Published/With Fat-Skimming Options

Calories: 201/72	Saturated Fat: 0 g/0 g
Protein: 0 g/0 g	Cholesterol: 0 mg/0 mg
Carbohydrate: 51 g/18 g	Sodium: 3 mg/2 mg
Fat: 0 g/0 g	Dietary Fiber: 0 g/0 g

Spicy Tea
Yield: 4¹/₃ cups mix or 60 servings

³/₄ cup instant tea
2 cups orange-flavored instant breakfast drink
1 (3 ounce) package lemonade mix
1¹/₂ cups sugar
2 teaspoons cinnamon
1 teaspoon cloves
¹/₄ teaspoon salt

*Fat-skimming options: Use sugar-free instant breakfast drink and reduce sugar to ¹/₂ cup.
With options, exchange diets count: free.*

• Combine all the above ingredients.
• Store in tightly sealed container.

• To serve, stir 2 heaping teaspoonfuls of mix into 1 cup of boiling water.

Nutrition Analysis Per Serving: As Originally Published/With Fat-Skimming Options

Calories: 29/6
Protein: 0 g/0 g
Carbohydrate: 7 g/2 g
Fat: 0 g/0 g

Saturated Fat: 0 g/0 g
Cholesterol: 0 mg/0 mg
Sodium: 10 mg/9 mg
Dietary Fiber: 0 g/0 g

Citrus Slush

Yield: 2 gallons or 32 (1 cup) servings

2½ cups sugar
3 cups water
1 (12 ounce) can frozen orange juice concentrate
1 (12 ounce) can frozen lemonade concentrate
1 (46 ounce) can pineapple juice
3 cups cold water
4 quarts lemon-lime soda or ginger ale, chilled
Lime slices

Fat-skimming options: Reduce sugar to ½ cup. Substitute sugar-free lemon-lime soda or ginger ale. With options, exchange diets count: 1½ fruit.

• In 6-quart Dutch oven over high heat, bring sugar and 3 cups water to a boil, stirring until sugar dissolves; remove from heat.
• Stir in frozen orange juice and lemonade concentrates until melted. Stir in pineapple juice and 3 cups cold water until well blended.

• Pour into 2 (13x9x2 inch) baking pans. Cover and freeze overnight until juice mixture is firm.
• Cut each panful of frozen juice mixture into 24 squares. Place squares in 2-gallon punch bowl or Thermos jug.
• Slowly pour chilled soda over squares; stir until punch is slushy. Ladle into glasses. Garnish each glass with a lime slice.

Nutrition Analysis Per Serving: As Originally Published/With Fat-Skimming Options

Calories: 177/78	Saturated Fat: 0 g/0 g
Protein: 0 g/0 g	Cholesterol: 0 mg/0 mg
Carbohydrate: 45 g/19 g	Sodium: 17 mg/2 mg
Fat: 0 g/0 g	Dietary Fiber: 0 g/0 g

Cranberry-Apple Cooler
Yield: 1 gallon or 16 (8 ounce) servings

6 tea bags
4 cups boiling water
2 (32 ounce) bottles cranberry juice cocktail
1 (32 ounce) bottle apple juice
2 tablespoons lemon juice
3 tablespoons light corn syrup
1 lemon, sliced

Fat-skimming options: none. Exchange diets count: 1 fruit.

• Steep tea bags in water 5 minutes. Remove tea bags. Cool.
• Add cranberry juice, apple juice, lemon juice and corn syrup; mix well. Pour into cold beverage container or pitcher with ice cubes. Add lemon slices.

Nutrition Analysis Per Serving: As Originally Published

Calories: 78
Protein: 0 g
Carbohydrate: 20 g
Fat: 0 g

Saturated Fat: 0 g
Cholesterol: 0 mg
Sodium: 11 mg
Dietary Fiber: 0 g

Frosty Pineapple Spritzers

Yield: 8 servings

1 (20 ounce) can crushed pineapple
3 tablespoons lemon juice
2 cups pineapple juice
$^1/_3$ cup water
$^3/_4$ cup sugar
About 1$^1/_2$ quarts seltzer
Fresh mint leaves for garnish

Fat-skimming options: Reduce sugar to $^1/_4$ cup. Replace seltzer with sparkling mineral water. With options, exchange diets count: 1$^1/_2$ fruit.

• Purée undrained pineapple and lemon juice in blender until smooth.
• In 2-quart saucepan over medium heat, heat pineapple juice, water and sugar to a simmer; simmer 10 minutes. Stir into puréed pineapple. Pour into ice cube trays; freeze overnight.

• To serve, let frozen cubes stand at room temperature 10 minutes. Divide cubes among 8 (12 ounce) glasses. Add about $^3/_4$ cup seltzer to each glass; muddle with spoon. Top each drink with mint leaves.

Nutrition Analysis Per Serving: As Originally Published/With Fat-Skimming Options

Calories: 134/85	Saturated Fat: 0 g/0 g
Protein: 0 g/0 g	Cholesterol: 0 mg/0 mg
Carbohydrate: 34 g/22 g	Sodium: 30 mg/1 mg
Fat: 0 g/0 g	Dietary Fiber: 0 g/0 g

Piña Colada Flip

Yield: 3 quarts or 12 (1 cup) servings

1 (46 ounce) can pineapple juice, chilled
1 (16 ounce) can cream of coconut
1 quart vanilla ice cream
1 (28 ounce) bottle club soda, chilled

Fat-skimming options: Substitute vanilla ice milk.
With options, exchange diets count: 1 fruit, 1 starch, 2 fat.

• Combine pineapple juice and cream of coconut in punch bowl; mix well. Spoon in ice cream. Slowly pour in club soda.

Nutrition Analysis Per Serving: As Originally Published/With Fat-Skimming Options

Calories: 259/227	Saturated Fat: 11 g/9 g
Protein: 3 g/3 g	Cholesterol: 13 mg/6 mg
Carbohydrate: 32 g/31 g	Sodium: 75 mg/65 mg
Fat: 14 g/11 g	Dietary Fiber: 0 g/0 g

Sparkling Citrus Punch
Yield: 1 gallon or 25 (5 ounce) servings

Lemon-Lime Ice Ring
1 (6 ounce) can frozen orange juice concentrate
1 (6 ounce) can frozen grapefruit juice concentrate
1 (6 ounce) can frozen tangerine juice concentrate
1 (6 ounce) can frozen lemonade concentrate
½ cup fresh or bottled lime juice
6 cups water
2 (28 ounce) bottles club soda, chilled

Fat-skimming options: none. Exchange diets, count: 1 fruit.

•Prepare Lemon-Lime Ice Ring.
•Combine remaining ingredients in punch bowl; mix well. To unmold ice ring, dip mold into hot water until ice ring slips out. Float in punch.

Lemon-Lime Ice Ring
1 cup water
3 lemons
3 limes

•Pour 1 cup water into 6-cup ring mold. Freeze. Slice lemons and limes. Alternately arrange lemon and lime slices on top of ice in ring mold, overlapping edges. Add enough water to just barely cover fruit slices. Freeze until solid.

Nutrition Analysis Per Serving: As Originally Published

Calories: 52
Protein: 0 g
Carbohydrate: 13 g
Fat: 0 g
Saturated Fat: 0 g
Cholesterol: 0 mg
Sodium: 13 mg
Dietary Fiber: 0 g

Summer Sparkle Punch

Yield: 1 gallon or 32 (4 ounce) servings

2 (3 ounce) packages strawberry-flavored gelatin
2 cups boiling water
2 (12 ounce) cans frozen lemonade, slightly thawed
3 (28 ounce) bottles ginger ale
Ice cubes

*Fat-skimming options: Substitute sugar-free gelatin and gingerale.
With options, exchange diets count: 1 fruit.*

• Dissolve gelatin in water. Cool. Stir in
lemonade. Add ginger ale and ice cubes.

Nutrition Analysis Per Serving: As Originally Published/With Fat-Skimming Options

Calories: 85/65	Saturated Fat: 0 g/0 g
Protein: 0 g/0 g	Cholesterol: 0 mg/0 mg
Carbohydrate: 21 g/0 17 g	Sodium: 22 mg/8 mg
Fat: 0 g/0 g	Dietary Fiber: 0 g/0 g

Tropical Fruit Shake

Yield: 2 (1 cup) servings

1 cup orange juice
1 banana, cut in chunks
1 cup vanilla ice cream

*Fat-skimming options: Substitute vanilla ice milk.
With options, exchange diets count: 2 fruit, ½ skim milk, 1 fat.*

• Combine ingredients in blender container.
Cover and whirl just until smooth.

Nutrition Analysis Per Serving: As Originally Published/With Fat-Skimming Options

Calories: 248/208	Saturated Fat: 4 g/2 g
Protein: 3 g/4 g	Cholesterol: 20 mg/10 mg
Carbohydrate: 42 g/42 g	Sodium: 52 mg/42 mg
Fat: 8 g/4 g	Dietary Fiber: 1 g/1 g

Watermelon Grapefruit Fiesta

Yield: 1 serving

2 tablespoons frozen pink grapefruit juice concentrate (1 ounce)
2 cups cubed watermelon (about 1 inch cubes), seeds removed
Dash of hot red pepper sauce

Fat-skimming options: none. Exchange diets count: 2½ fruit.

• Place grapefruit juice concentrate, watermelon and pepper sauce in electric blender. Cover and blend until puréed.
• Pour into glasses and serve.

• **For a slushy drink:** Freeze 1 cup of the cubed watermelon. Blend grapefruit juice concentrate and remaining 1 cup cubed watermelon until puréed. Add frozen cubed watermelon and pulse until mixture is slushy. Serve immediately.

Nutrition Analysis Per Serving: As Originally Published

Calories: 152	Saturated Fat: 0 g
Protein: 2 g	Cholesterol: 0 mg
Carbohydrate: 35 g	Sodium: 6 mg
Fat: 1 g	Dietary Fiber: 1 g

Zippy Tomato Lemon Cocktail
Yield: 12 (4 ounce) servings

1 (46 ounce) can tomato juice
2 tablespoons lemon juice
1½ tablespoons Worcestershire sauce
1 teaspoon grated lemon rind
Thin lemon slices

Fat-skimming options: none. Exchange diets, count: 1 vegetable.

• Combine all ingredients in large pitcher.
Cover with plastic wrap. Chill at least 2
hours in refrigerator.

Nutrition Analysis Per Serving: As Originally Published

Calories: 24	Saturated Fat: 0 g
Protein: 1 g	Cholesterol: 0 mg
Carbohydrate: 6 g	Sodium: 440 mg
Fat: 0 g	Dietary Fiber: 0 g

CHAPTER TWO

BREADS

Thanks to 4-H, she learned how to make bread

Any excuse for a coffeecake, and Mary Thompson will bake it. Growing up on a farm near Vinton, Iowa, she spent her Saturdays kneading dough for rolls and tea rings. If her two older brothers were home, the whole batch didn't last the weekend. Eggs and milk were always on hand, and her love for baking was inherited from a paternal grandmother who whipped out a fresh pie every morning of the year, just as routine as making her bed.

Mary's mother, Eleanor Thompson, was a farm wife who worked during the day as a hospital dietitian and credits 4-H leaders and a wonderful home-economics teacher for teaching Mary how to bake yeast bread, long before bread machines were invented. Those sweaty hours on demonstration days gave young women the confidence and experience to make everything from yeast dough to white sauce from scratch at home.

Today, as features editor of Farm Journal, Mary bakes at holiday and vacation time. You'll find recipes for traditional Golden Crunch Coffeecake, Orange Sugar Ring (starts with refrigerator biscuit dough), Quick Coffeecake (starts with baking mix) and Strawberry Swirl Coffeecake in this chapter.

Banana Lemon Loaf

Yield: 1 loaf or 15 slices

2 cups sifted flour
3 teaspoons baking powder
1/2 teaspoon salt
1/2 cup shortening
1 cup sugar
2 eggs
1 cup mashed bananas (approximately 3 medium)
2 tablespoons lemon juice
1 cup chopped walnuts
1 teaspoon grated lemon rind

Fat-skimming options: Replace shortening with 1/4 cup corn oil plus 1/4 cup nonfat sour cream.
Substitute 1/2 cup liquid egg substitute for eggs. Reduce walnuts to 1/3 cup.
With options, exchange diets count: 2 starch, 1/2 fat.

• Sift together flour, baking powder and salt.
• Cream together shortening and sugar until light and fluffy. Add eggs, one at a time, beating well after each addition. Beat in bananas and lemon juice.

• Gradually add dry ingredients; mix just until moistened. Stir in walnuts and lemon rind. Turn batter into greased 9x5x3 inch loaf pan.
• Bake at 350 degrees F for 50 minutes or until bread tests done. Cool for 10 minutes. Remove from pan. Cool.

Nutrition Analysis Per Serving: As Originally Published/With Fat-Skimming Options

Calories: 275/199
Protein: 6 g/4 g
Carbohydrate: 32 g/32 g
Fat: 16 g/7 g

Saturated Fat: 3 g/1 g
Cholesterol: 0 mg/0 mg
Sodium: 80 mg/92 mg
Dietary Fiber: 1.5 g/1.0 g

Banana Walnut Bread

Yield: 1 loaf or 16 slices

¹/₃ cup shortening
¹/₂ cup sugar
2 eggs
1³/₄ cups unsifted flour
1 teaspoon baking powder
¹/₂ teaspoon baking soda
¹/₂ teaspoon ground cinnamon
1 cup mashed ripe bananas (3 medium)
¹/₂ cup chopped walnuts

> *Fat-skimming options: Omit shortening and use 2 tablespoons oil plus 3 tablespoons nonfat sour cream. Use ¹/₂ cup liquid egg substitute and reduce walnuts to ¹/₄ cup. With options, exchange diets count: 1¹/₂ starch, ¹/₂ fat.*

• Choose the cooking method that suits you—oven, range top or slow cooker— and grease the appropriate container.
• Cream together shortening and sugar in mixing bowl, using electric mixer at medium speed. Add eggs, one at a time, beating well after each addition.
• Stir together flour, baking powder, baking soda and cinnamon. Add to creamed mixture alternately with mashed bananas, blending well. Stir in walnuts.
• **Oven baking (45 to 50 minutes):** Turn mixture into a well-greased 9x5x3 inch loaf pan. Bake in 350 degree F oven 45 to 50 minutes or until bread tests done. Remove from pan immediately. Cool on rack.

•**Range top cooking (2 hours):** Turn batter into well-greased 2 pound coffee can. Cover tightly with aluminum foil. Place can on rack in Dutch oven. Pour in boiling water to depth of an inch. (Add more water during cooking if necessary.) Cover and steam over low heat 2 hours or until done. Remove from coffee can immediately. Cool on rack.
• **Slow cooker (2 hours):** Turn batter into well-greased 2 pound coffee can. Cover tightly with aluminum foil. Place can in 3¹/₂-quart slow cooker. (No water is needed.) Cover and cook on high setting 2 hours or until done. Remove from coffee can immediately. Cool on rack.

Nutrition Analysis Per Serving: As Originally Published/With Fat-Skimming Options

Calories: 180/140	Saturated Fat: 3 g/0 g
Protein: 4 g/3 g	Cholesterol: 53 mg/0 mg
Carbohydrate: 23 g/23 g	Sodium: 96 mg/57 mg
Fat: 9 g/4 g	Dietary Fiber: 2 g/1 g

Orange Walnut Bread
Yield: 1 loaf or 15 slices

2 cups sifted flour
1 teaspoon baking powder
$^1/_2$ teaspoon baking soda
$^1/_2$ teaspoon salt
$^3/_4$ cup orange juice
1 cup sugar
1 egg, slightly beaten
2 tablespoons melted butter
$^3/_4$ cup finely chopped dates
$^3/_4$ cup coarsely chopped walnuts
$1^1/_2$ teaspoons grated orange rind
1 tablespoon flour

Fat-skimming options: Reduce walnuts to $^1/_4$ cup. With options, exchange diets count: $1^1/_2$ starch, 1 fruit.

• Sift together 2 cups flour, baking powder, baking soda and salt into bowl.
• Combine orange juice, sugar, egg and butter; mix well. Gradually add to flour mixture; stir well.

• Combine remaining ingredients; stir into batter. Turn into greased $8^1/_2$x$4^1/_2$x$2^1/_2$ inch loaf pan.
• Bake in 350 degree F oven $1^1/_4$ hours or until done.

Nutrition Analysis Per Serving: As Originally Published/With Fat-Skimming Options

Calories: 223/177
Protein: 5 g/3 g
Carbohydrate: 33 g/32 g
Fat: 9 g/4 g

Saturated Fat: 1 g/1 g
Cholesterol: 18 mg/18 mg
Sodium: 134 mg/134 mg
Dietary Fiber: 1 g/1 g

Popovers
Yield: 8 popovers

3 eggs
1½ cups sifted flour
1½ cups milk
¾ teaspoon salt
1½ tablespoons cooking oil

*Fat-skimming options: Use ¾ cup liquid egg substitute for eggs. Use skim milk.
With options, exchange diets count: 1½ starch, ½ fat.*

• Combine eggs, flour, milk and salt. Beat with electric mixer at low speed 1½ minutes. Add oil. Beat ½ minute more. Pour into 8 well-greased (6 ounce) custard cups.
• Bake in 450 degree F oven 15 minutes. Reduce oven temperature to 350 degrees F. Bake 35 minutes more.
• Slit tops with sharp knife to let steam escape. Turn oven off. Let popovers stand in oven 10 minutes.

• Popovers are best enjoyed fresh out of the oven, but if you want to preserve them for later try this method: Cool on rack. Wrap in aluminum foil. Freeze up to 4 weeks.
• To reheat, place frozen popovers on baking sheet. Bake in 350 degree F oven 8 minutes or until hot.

Nutrition Analysis Per Serving: As Originally Published/With Fat-Skimming Options

Calories: 159/144
Protein: 6 g/7 g
Carbohydrate: 20 g/20 g
Fat: 6 g/4 g

Saturated Fat: 1 g/0 g
Cholesterol: 83 mg/1 mg
Sodium: 247 mg/266 mg
Dietary Fiber: 1 g/1 g

Banana Nut Muffins

Yield: 18 muffins

2 cups sifted flour
3 teaspoons baking powder
½ teaspoon salt
½ cup shortening
1 cup sugar
2 eggs
1⅓ cups mashed bananas (approximately 3 medium)
1 cup chopped walnuts

Fat-skimming options: Omit shortening and substitute ¼ cup corn oil plus ¼ cup nonfat sour cream. Replace eggs with ½ cup liquid egg substitute. Reduce walnuts to ¼ cup. With options, exchange diets count: 1½ starch, 1 fat.

• Sift together flour, baking powder and salt.
• Cream together shortening and sugar in a bowl until light and fluffy. Beat in eggs, one at a time, blending well after each addition.
• Stir in mashed bananas.
• Add dry ingredients, stirring just enough to moisten. Do not overbeat. Batter will be lumpy.
• Gently mix in chopped nuts.
• Fill greased 3 inch muffin-pan cups two-thirds full.
• Bake in 350 degree F oven for 20 minutes until muffins are golden brown.

Nutrition Analysis Per Serving: As Originally Published/With Fat-Skimming Options

Calories: 247/170
Protein: 5 g/3 g
Carbohydrate: 28 g/28 g
Fat: 14 g/6 g

Saturated Fat: 2 g/0 g
Cholesterol: 24 mg/0 mg
Sodium: 67 mg/72 mg
Dietary Fiber: 1 g/1 g

Refrigerator Bran Muffins
Yield: 60 muffins

5 cups sifted flour
5 teaspoons baking soda
2 teaspoons salt
2 cups boiling water
2 cups All-Bran or any flaked bran cereal
2 cups sugar
1 cup shortening
4 eggs, well beaten
1 quart buttermilk
4 cups Bran Buds or any crunchy nugget bran cereal

Fat-skimming options: Replace shortening with ½ cup corn oil plus ½ cup nonfat sour cream. With options, exchange diets count: 1 starch, 1 fat.

• Sift together first 3 ingredients.
• Pour boiling water over All-Bran; set aside.
• Cream together sugar and shortening in a 6-quart bowl until light and fluffy. Add eggs; beat well. Blend in buttermilk, Bran Buds and soaked All-Bran. Add sifted dry ingredients; mix well.

• Batter can be stored in refrigerator in covered container up to 6 weeks. When needed, fill greased muffin tins two-thirds full and bake at 400 degrees F for 20 minutes or until brown.

Nutrition Analysis Per Serving: As Originally Published/With Fat-Skimming Options

Calories: 126/114	Saturated Fat: 1 g/0 g
Protein: 3 g/3 g	Cholesterol: 15 mg/15 mg
Carbohydrate: 21 g/22 g	Sodium: 248 mg/250 mg
Fat: 4 g/3 g	Dietary Fiber: 2.5 g/2.5 g

Cranberry Muffins
Yield: 12 muffins

2¼ cups sifted flour
¼ cup sugar
¾ teaspoon baking soda
¼ teaspoon salt
1 egg, slightly beaten
¾ cup buttermilk
¼ cup cooking oil
1 cup chopped raw cranberries
½ cup sugar

*Fat-skimming options: Use ¼ cup liquid egg substitute for egg.
With options, exchange diets count: 1 starch, 1 fruit, 1 fat.*

• Sift together flour, ¼ cup sugar, baking soda and salt into bowl.
• Combine egg, buttermilk and oil in small bowl; blend well. Add all at once to dry ingredients, stirring just enough to moisten.
• Combine cranberries and ½ cup sugar; stir into batter.
• Spoon the batter into greased 2½ inch muffin-pan cups, filling two-thirds full.
• Bake in 400 degree F oven 20 minutes or until golden brown.

Nutrition Analysis Per Serving: As Originally Published/With Fat-Skimming Options

Calories: 191/189
Protein: 3.5 g/3.5 g
Carbohydrate: 32 g/32 g
Fat: 6 g/5 g

Saturated Fat: 1 g/0 g
Cholesterol: 18 mg/1 mg
Sodium: 145 mg/149 mg
Dietary Fiber: 1 g/1 g

Date Nut Bran Muffins

Yield: 60 muffins

5 cups sifted flour
2 cups sugar
5 teaspoons baking soda
1 teaspoon salt
2 cups All-Bran or any flaked bran cereal
2 cups wheat germ
2 cups 40% Bran flakes or any 40% flaked bran cereal
2 cups chopped dates
2 cups coarsely chopped walnuts
1 cup cooking oil
4 eggs, slightly beaten
2 cups water
1 quart buttermilk

Fat-skimming options: Replace ½ cup oil with ½ cup nonfat sour cream.
Use 1 cup liquid egg substitute for eggs and reduce walnuts to ½ cup.
For exchange diets, count: 1 starch, 1 fat.

• Sift together flour, sugar, baking soda and salt; set aside.
• Combine remaining ingredients in 6-quart mixing bowl; mix well. Add dry ingredients, stirring just enough to moisten.
• Store in covered container in refrigerator up to 6 weeks.
• To bake: Fill greased 3 inch muffin-pan cups two-thirds full. Bake in 400 degree F oven 20 minutes or until done.

Nutrition Analysis Per Serving: As Originally Published/With Fat-Skimming Options

Calories: 187/131
Protein: 5 g/4 g
Carbohydrate: 23 g/21 g
Fat: 9 g/4 g

Saturated Fat: 1 g/0 g
Cholesterol: 15 mg/0 mg
Sodium: 192 mg/198 mg
Dietary Fiber: 2 g/2 g

Heirloom Raisin Muffins

Yield: 12 muffins

1 cup raisins
1 cup water
$^1/_2$ cup butter, softened
$^3/_4$ cup sugar
2 eggs
1$^1/_2$ cups sifted flour
1 teaspoon baking powder

*Fat-skimming options: Omit butter and substitute $^1/_4$ cup soft margarine plus $^1/_4$ cup nonfat sour cream. Use $^1/_2$ cup liquid egg substitute for eggs.
With options, exchange diets count: 2 starch, $^1/_2$ fat.*

• Combine raisins and water in saucepan. Bring to a boil; reduce heat and cover. Simmer 20 minutes. Drain raisins, reserving liquid. Add enough water to reserved liquid to make $^1/_2$ cup. Cool well.
• Cream together butter and sugar in bowl until fluffy, using electric mixer at medium speed. Add eggs; beat 2 more minutes.

• Sift together flour and baking powder. Add flour mixture alternately with $^1/_2$ cup raisin liquid, beating well after each addition. Stir in raisins. Spoon into greased 3-inch muffin pan cups, filling two-thirds full.
• Bake in 400 degree F oven 18 minutes or until golden brown. Muffins are best when served warm with soft butter.

Nutrition Analysis Per Serving: As Originally Published/With Fat-Skimming Options

Calories: 227/194
Protein: 3 g/4 g
Carbohydrate: 36 g/37 g
Fat: 9 g/4 g

Saturated Fat: 5 g/1 g
Cholesterol: 56 mg/0 mg
Sodium: 91 mg/59 mg
Dietary Fiber: 1 g/1 g

Just-in-Trails Coconut-Topped Chocolate-Orange Muffins
Yield: 24 muffins

1 cup granulated sugar
²/₃ cup vegetable oil
1 cup orange juice
2 eggs
3 cups all-purpose flour
1 tablespoon baking powder
1 teaspoon salt
1 (11 ounce) can mandarin orange segments, drained
²/₃ cup chocolate chips
1 cup shredded coconut
¹/₃ cup granulated sugar
2 tablespoons melted butter

Fat-skimming options: Replace ¹/₃ cup of the oil with ¹/₃ cup nonfat sour cream. Use ¹/₂ cup liquid egg substitiute for eggs. Reduce chocolate chips to ¹/₃ cup. Reduce coconut to ¹/₃ cup. With options, exchange diets count: 1 starch, 1 fruit, ¹/₂ fat.

• In medium bowl, beat together sugar and oil. Stir in orange juice and eggs.
• In small bowl, combine flour, baking powder, baking soda and salt. Blend into sugar-egg mixture just until mixed.
• Stir in orange slices and chocolate chips just until mixed.
• Spoon batter into greased or paper-lined muffin tins to two-thirds full.
• In small bowl, combine shredded coconut, ¹/₃ cup granulated sugar and melted butter or margarine. Sprinkle over tops of muffins.
• Bake at 375 degrees F 15 to 20 minutes, or until wooden pick inserted in center comes out clean and muffins are golden brown.

Nutrition Analysis Per Serving: As Originally Published/With Fat-Skimming Options

Calories: 216/165
Protein: 3 g/2 g
Carbohydrate: 30 g/27 g
Fat: 10 g/5 g

Saturated Fat: 3 g/2 g
Cholesterol: 14 mg/3 mg
Sodium: 116 mg/115 mg
Dietary Fiber: 1 g/1 g

Pumpkin Oat Muffins
Yield: 12 muffins

1 cup sifted flour
2 teaspoons baking powder
1 teaspoon pumpkin pie spice
$^1/_2$ teaspoon salt
$^1/_4$ teaspoon baking soda
$^3/_4$ cup canned mashed pumpkin
$^1/_2$ cup brown sugar, packed
1 egg, slightly beaten
$^1/_4$ cup milk
$^1/_4$ cup cooking oil
1 cup quick-cooking oats
$^1/_2$ cup raisins
Topping for Muffins

*Fat-skimming options: Use $^1/_4$ cup liquid egg substitute for egg. Use skim milk.
With options, exchange diets count: 2 starch, $^1/_2$ fruit, 1 fat.*

• Sift together dry ingredients.
• Combine remaining ingredients in bowl; blend well. Add dry ingredients; stir just enough to moisten. Fill greased 3-inch muffin pan cups two-thirds full. Sprinkle with Topping for Muffins.
• Bake in 400 degree F oven 18 to 20 minutes or until done.

Topping for Muffins
$^1/_2$ cup packed brown sugar
1 tablespoon flour
$^1/_4$ teaspoon pumpkin pie spice
2 tablespoons butter

• Combine brown sugar, flour, pumpkin pie spice and butter; mix well. Sprinkle on top of muffins before baking.

Nutrition Analysis Per Serving: As Originally Published/With Fat-Skimming Options

Calories: 229/226
Protein: 3 g/3 g
Carbohydrate: 38 g/38 g
Fat: 8 g/7 g

Saturated Fat: 2 g/1 g
Cholesterol: 23 mg/5 mg
Sodium: 152 mg/156 mg
Dietary Fiber: 1 g/1 g

Apple Pancakes
Yield: 18 pancakes

1½ cups sifted flour
1½ teaspoons baking powder
¾ teaspoon salt
1 tablespoon sugar
1 egg, beaten
1¼ cups milk
2 tablespoons oil
¾ cup grated peeled apples

Fat-skimming options: Use ¼ cup liquid egg substitute for egg.
Use skim milk and reduce oil to 1 teaspoon. With options, exchange diets count: 1 starch.

• Sift together the flour, baking powder, salt and sugar.
• Combine egg, milk and oil. Add gradually to dry ingredients, stirring only until batter is smooth. Fold in apples.

• Drop by spoonfuls onto hot greased griddle. Cook slowly until the surface is covered with bubbles. Turn and cook until the bottom is a delicate brown.

Nutrition Analysis Per Serving: As Originally Published/With Fat-Skimming Options

Calories: 71/61
Protein: 2 g/2 g
Carbohydrate: 11 g/11 g
Fat: 2 g/1 g

Saturated Fat: 0 g/0 g
Cholesterol: 13 mg/0 mg
Sodium: 101 mg/104 mg
Dietary Fiber: 0.5 g/0.5 g

Country Pancakes
Yield: 16 (4 inch) pancakes

2 cups All-Purpose Baking Mix
1 egg
1½ cups milk
½ teaspoon vanilla

> *Fat-skimming options: In baking mix omit shortening and use ¾ cup soft margarine. With options, exchange diets count: 1 starch.*

• Combine above 4 ingredients. Beat until smooth.
• Bake on lightly greased hot griddle, using scant ¼ cup batter for each pancake.

All-Purpose Baking Mix
Yield: 12 cups or 6 (2 cup) batches

10 cups sifted flour
1¾ cups sifted confectioners sugar
1⅓ cups instant nonfat dry milk
¼ cup baking powder
2 tablespoons salt
1 cup shortening

• Combine dry ingredients in very large mixing bowl. Cut in shortening with pastry blender or two knives until mixture resembles cornmeal.
• Store mix in airtight containers in a cool place.
• **To use:** Stir mix with large spoon before measuring. Spoon lightly into measuring cup and level off.

Nutrition Analysis Per Serving: As Originally Published/With Fat-Skimming Options

Calories: 91/91
Protein: 3 g/3 g
Carbohydrate: 14 g/14 g
Fat: 3 g/3 g

Saturated Fat: 1 g/0 g
Cholesterol: 2 mg/2 mg
Sodium: 65 mg/65 mg
Dietary Fiber: 0 g/0 g

Dutch Pancake With Orange Sauce

Yield: 2 to 3 breakfast servings

$\frac{1}{2}$ cup unsifted flour
$\frac{1}{2}$ cup milk
2 eggs
$\frac{1}{4}$ teaspoon salt
1 teaspoon vanilla
1 tablespoon vegetable oil
$\frac{1}{2}$ cup packed brown sugar
$\frac{1}{4}$ cup orange juice
3 tablespoons butter or regular margarine
1 teaspoon grated orange rind

*Fat-skimming options: Omit butter. Use skim milk and $\frac{1}{2}$ cup liquid egg substitute.
With options, exchange diets count: 2 starch, 1$\frac{1}{2}$ fruit, 1 very lean meat.*

- In bowl using mixer at medium speed, beat flour, milk, eggs and salt 2 minutes until smooth.
- In 450 degree F oven on lowest rack, heat 10 inch round casserole pan or oven-safe 10 inch skillet 5 minutes.
- Add vegetable oil to hot pan, tilting pan to coat bottom and side. Pour batter into pan.
- Bake 10 minutes. Reduce temperature to 350 degrees F and bake 10 minutes more or until pancake is puffy and brown. (As pancake bakes, it rises like a popover; as it cools, it will shrink slightly.)

- Meanwhile, in small saucepan stir together brown sugar and remaining ingredients. Over medium heat bring mixture to a boil. Reduce heat to medium low and simmer 5 minutes.
- Remove from heat. Cool slightly.
- Cut pancake into wedges and serve sauce over wedges.

Nutrition Analysis Per Serving: As Originally Published/With Fat-Skimming Options

Calories: 382/272	Saturated Fat: 8 g/0 g
Protein: 8 g/8 g	Cholesterol: 172 mg/1 mg
Carbohydrate: 56 g/56 g	Sodium: 358 mg/288 mg
Fat: 15 g/2 g	Dietary Fiber: 0 g/0 g

Golden Delight Pancakes

Yield: 20 (4 inch) pancakes

1 cup cream-style cottage cheese
6 eggs
$1/2$ cup sifted flour
$1/4$ teaspoon salt
$1/4$ cup oil
$1/4$ cup milk
$1/2$ teaspoon vanilla

Fat-skimming options: Substitute nonfat cottage cheese and 1 cup liquid egg substitute. Reduce oil to 1 tablespoon, then increase skim or 1% milk to $1/2$ cup. With options, exchange diets count: $1/2$ starch.

• Put all ingredients into a blender. Cover. Blend at high speed for 1 minute, stopping to stir down once.

• Bake pancakes on a greased griddle, using $1/4$ cup batter for each.

Nutrition Analysis Per Serving: As Originally Published/With Fat-Skimming Options

Calories: 71/40
Protein: 4 g/3 g
Carbohydrate: 3 g/3 g
Fat: 5 g/1 g

Saturated Fat: 1 g/0 g
Cholesterol: 66 mg/2 mg
Sodium: 90 mg/92 mg
Dietary Fiber: 0 g/0 g

Honey-Baked French Toast

Yield: 6 servings

1½ cups skim milk
4 large eggs
½ teaspoon ground cinnamon
4 tablespoons honey
12 (1 inch thick) diagonally cut slices French bread
3 tablespoons packed brown sugar
2 tablespoons margarine or butter, melted

> *Fat-skimming options: Use 1 cup liquid egg substitute for eggs. Omit margarine.*
> *With options, exchange diets count: 2 starch, ½ fruit.*

• In large bowl, beat together milk, eggs, cinnamon and 2 tablespoons honey.
• Dip bread into egg mixture, allowing egg mixture to be absorbed into both sides of each slice.
• Arrange bread, overlapping slices, in greased 2-quart shallow baking dish. Pour any remaining egg mixture over bread. (May be covered and refrigerated overnight at this point.) Sprinkle with brown sugar. Drizzle with melted margarine and remaining 2 tablespoons honey.

• Bake in 350 degree F oven 30 minutes, or until golden brown and knife inserted into center of bread comes out clean.

Nutrition Analysis Per Serving: As Originally Published/With Fat-Skimming Options

Calories: 314/265
Protein: 10 g/11 g
Carbohydrate: 48 g/47 g
Fat: 9 g/3 g

Saturated Fat: 3 g/0 g
Cholesterol: 153 mg/1 mg
Sodium: 416 mg/409 mg
Dietary Fiber: 1.5 g/1.5 g

Golden Crunch Coffeecake

Yield: 12 servings

3 cups sifted flour
1/2 teaspoon salt
3 teaspoons baking powder
1/2 cup butter
1 1/2 cups sugar
1 teaspoon vanilla
4 eggs
1 cup milk
1 cup brown sugar, firmly packed
2 tablespoons butter
2 tablespoons flour
1 teaspoon ground cinnamon
1 cup chopped walnuts

> *Fat-skimming options: Replace butter with 1/4 cup corn oil plus 1/4 cup nonfat sour cream.*
> *Substitute 1 cup liquid egg substitute for eggs. Use skim milk. Reduce walnuts to 1/4 cup.*
> *Reduce portion size to yield 24 servings. With options, exchange diets count: 2 starch, 1/2 fruit.*

• Sift together dry ingredients.
• Cream together 1/2 cup butter and sugar until light and fluffy. Add vanilla and eggs, beating well. Add dry ingredients alternately with milk, blending well after each addition.

• Spread half of batter in greased 13x9x2 inch baking pan. Combine remaining ingredients. Sprinkle half of mixture over batter. Spread with remaining batter, and top with remaining crumbs.
• Bake in 350 degree F oven 45 minutes or until done.

Nutrition Analysis Per Serving: As Originally Published/With Fat-Skimming Options

Calories: 520/194
Protein: 11 g/4 g
Carbohydrate: 72 g/35 g
Fat: 23 g/4 g

Saturated Fat: 8 g/1 g
Cholesterol: 98 mg/1 mg
Sodium: 227 mg/76 mg
Dietary Fiber: 2 g/1 g

Orange Sugar Ring
Yield: 12 servings

2 (8 ounce) packages refrigerator biscuits
$\frac{1}{4}$ cup butter, melted
2 tablespoons orange juice
$\frac{1}{2}$ cup sugar
$\frac{1}{2}$ cup brown sugar, firmly packed
1 teaspoon grated orange rind
$\frac{1}{4}$ teaspoon nutmeg

Fat-skimming options: Substitute reduced-fat biscuits. Replace butter with low-fat margarine. With options, exchange diets count: 1 starch.

• Separate biscuits. Combine butter and orange juice. Mix remaining ingredients in separate bowl. Dip biscuits in butter then sugar mixture. Stand upright in well-greased 1$\frac{1}{2}$ quart ring mold. Bake at 450 degrees F for 12 to 15 minutes. Turn out on plate.

Nutrition Analysis Per Serving: As Originally Published/With Fat-Skimming Options

Calories: 92/70
Protein: 0 g/0 g
Carbohydrate: 16 g/14 g
Fat: 3 g/2 g

Saturated Fat: 2 g/0 g
Cholesterol: 8 mg/0 mg
Sodium: 72 mg/52 mg
Dietary Fiber: 0 g/0 g

Quick Coffeecake
Yield: 9 servings

2 cups All-Purpose Baking Mix
¾ cup sugar
1 beaten egg
3 tablespoons shortening
¾ cup milk
1 teaspoon vanilla
½ cup firmly packed brown sugar
1 tablespoon flour
1 tablespoon butter
½ teaspoon cinnamon

Fat-skimming options: Use ¼ cup liquid egg substitute for egg. Use skim milk.
In baking mix omit shortening and use ¾ cup soft margarine.
With options, exchange diets count: 3 starch 1½ fat.

• Combine first 6 ingredients. Beat with electric mixer at medium speed 4 minutes. Spread batter in greased 9 inch square pan.
• Combine brown sugar, flour, butter and cinnamon; mix until crumbly. Sprinkle over batter.
• Bake in 350 degree F oven for 30 minutes or until done.

All-Purpose Baking Mix
Yield: 12 cups or 6 (2 cup) batches

10 cups sifted flour
1¾ cups sifted confectioners sugar
1⅓ cups instant nonfat dry milk
¼ cup baking powder
2 tablespoons salt
1 cup shortening

• Combine dry ingredients in very large mixing bowl. Cut in shortening with pastry blender or two knives until mixture resembles cornmeal.
• Store mix in airtight containers in a cool place.
• **To use:** Stir mix with large spoon before measuring. Spoon lightly into measuring cup and level off.

Nutrition Analysis Per Serving: As Originally Published/With Fat-Skimming Options

Calories: 321/305	Saturated Fat: 3 g/2 g
Protein: 4 g/4 g	Cholesterol: 29 mg/4 mg
Carbohydrate: 53 g/53 g	Sodium: 125 mg/164 mg
Fat: 11 g/9 g	Dietary Fiber: 1 g/1 g

Strawberry Swirl Coffeecake

Yield: 8 to 10 servings

3¹/₂ cups biscuit mix
¹/₄ cup sugar
1 egg, beaten
1 teaspoon vanilla
Milk
2 tablespoons melted butter
²/₃ cup strawberry preserves
¹/₂ cup chopped nuts
¹/₂ cup confectioners sugar
1 tablespoon milk

> *Fat-skimming options: Substitute reduced fat baking mix.*
> *Use ¹/₄ cup liquid egg substitute for egg. Reduce nuts to ¹/₄ cup.*
> *With options, exchange diets count: ¹/₂ fruit, 1 starch, 1 fat.*

• Blend biscuit mix and sugar.
• Add enough milk to egg and vanilla to make 1 cup; add to dry mixture. Stir with fork into a soft dough; beat vigorously 20 strokes until stiff and slightly sticky.
• Knead on well-floured board ¹/₂ minute. Roll into a 7x18 inch rectangle. Leaving 1 inch uncovered on long sides for sealing, spread with butter and ¹/₂ cup of preserves. Sprinkle with nuts; moisten edge. Roll like jelly roll; let rest on sealed side 1 minute, then turn seam to side.

• Cut roll in half lengthwise. Cut 5 inches from one strip; form loosely into circle on center of greased baking sheet, keeping cut surfaces up. Coil remainder of strip loosely in circle around it. Make outer circle with second strip; seal end. Spoon remaining jam between strips. Bake in moderate oven (375 degrees F) for 25 to 30 minutes, until lightly browned.
• Combine confectioners sugar and milk; brush evenly over surface of hot coffee cake. Serve warm.

Nutrition Analysis Per Serving: As Originally Published/With Fat-Skimming Options	
Calories: 206/164	Saturated Fat: 2 g/2 g
Protein: 4 g/2 g	Cholesterol: 8 mg/8 mg
Carbohydrate: 10 g/6 g	Sodium: 75 mg/55 mg
Fat: 10 g/6 g	Dietary Fiber: 0.5 g/0 g

Glazed Potato Doughnuts

Yield: 42 doughnuts

2 teaspoons (1 package) active dry yeast
¼ cup warm water
1 cup milk, scalded
¼ cup shortening
¼ cup sugar
1 teaspoon salt
¾ cup mashed potatoes (instant may be used)
2 eggs, beaten
5 to 6 cups sifted flour
1 pound confectioners sugar
6 tablespoons water
1 tablespoon vanilla

Fat-skimming options: Use skim milk and ½ cup liquid egg substitute.
With options, count: 1½ starch, 1 fat.

• Dissolve yeast in warm water.
• Combine milk, shortening, sugar and salt. Cool until lukewarm. Stir in yeast, potatoes and eggs. Gradually add enough flour to make soft dough. Turn onto floured surface; knead until smooth and satiny. Place in lightly greased bowl; turn over to grease top. Cover. Let rise in a warm place until doubled, about 1 to 1½ hours.

• Roll to ½ inch thickness; cut with 3 inch doughnut cutter. Cover; let rise until doubled (about 30 minutes).
• Meanwhile, stir confectioners sugar, water and vanilla together. (Mixture will look like very thick cream.)
• Fry in deep hot fat (375 degrees F). Drain on absorbent paper. Drop hot doughnuts into glaze. Cool on rack until glaze is set.

Nutrition Analysis Per Serving: As Originally Published/With Fat-Skimming Options

Calories: 157/150	Saturated Fat: 0.5 g/0.5 g
Protein: 2 g/2 g	Cholesterol: 11 mg/1 mg
Carbohydrate: 21 g/21 g	Sodium: 293 mg/295 mg
Fat: 7 g/6 g	Dietary Fiber: 0 g/0 g

Bread Machine Kulich

Yield: 12 servings

¹/₂ cup water, plus 1 tablespoon if necessary
1 egg
¹/₄ cup softened butter or margarine
2³/₄ cups bread flour
1 teaspoon salt
2 teaspoons (1 package) active dry yeast
¹/₄ cup currants or mixed dried fruit
¹/₄ cup sliced almonds
1 teaspoon grated lemon peel
Icing
Multicolored candies

Fat-skimming options: none. Exchange diets count: 2 starch, 1 fat.

• Place first six ingredients in bread machine in the order suggested by your bread machine manufacturer. Begin knead cycle. If dough appears dry add additional 1 tablespoon water. Run knead cycle, adding currants, almonds and lemon peel during last minute.
• Remove dough from bread machine. Place in greased bowl, cover and let rise in warm place until doubled. Meanwhile, grease well 2 (1 pound 2 ounce) cans.
• Punch down dough and divide into two portions. Shape each into a slightly oval ball and place one ball in each prepared can.
• Cover and let rise 45 minutes.
• Bake at 350 degrees F for about 30 to 35 minutes or until well browned. Remove from cans at once and cool on wire rack about 10 minutes.
• While still warm, drizzle with Icing. Decorate with multicolored candies.

Icing
¹/₂ cup confectioners sugar
2 teaspoons milk or water

• Combine confectioners sugar and milk or water.

Nutrition Analysis Per Serving: As Originally Published

Calories: 196	Saturated Fat: 3 g
Protein: 5 g	Cholesterol: 29 mg
Carbohydrate: 31 g	Sodium: 216 mg
Fat: 6 g	Dietary Fiber: 1.5 g

Crusty Brown Rolls

Yield: 36 rolls

4 teaspoons (2 packages) active dry yeast
1¾ cups lukewarm water (110 to 115 degrees F)
4 teaspoons sugar
2 teaspoons salt
2 tablespoons melted shortening
6½ to 7 cups sifted flour
3 egg whites, beaten stiff
1 egg white
1 tablespoon water

Fat-skimming options: Substitute 1 tablespoon soft margarine for shortening.
With options, exchange diets count: 1 starch.

• Sprinkle yeast on lukewarm water in bowl; stir to dissolve. Add sugar, salt, shortening and 2 cups flour; beat well. Add the beaten egg whites. Stir in enough remaining flour to make a soft dough that leaves sides of bowl.
• Turn out on lightly floured surface. Knead dough until smooth and elastic with tiny blisters showing on the surface (about 5 minutes).
• Place in a lightly greased bowl; turn dough over to grease top. Cover with a damp cloth.
• Let rise in a warm place until doubled, about 1 hour. Punch down.

• You may shape the dough at this point. But for superior results, let the dough rise again until doubled, then punch down and shape.
• Shape raised dough in 3-inch balls. Place rolls on greased baking sheets sprinkled lightly with cornmeal. Beat slightly 1 egg white with 1 tablespoon water. Brush on rolls. Let rise until doubled; brush again with egg mixture.
• Bake in 425 degree F oven 20 minutes or until brown and crusty. Place a large shallow pan of boiling water on the bottom of oven to provide steam while the rolls bake. This makes the rolls crusty.

Nutrition Analysis Per Serving: As Originally Published/With Fat-Skimming Options

Calories: 99/96
Protein: 3 g/3 g
Carbohydrate: 19 g/19 g
Fat: 1 g/0 g

Saturated Fat: 0 g/0 g
Cholesterol: 0 mg/0 mg
Sodium: 125 mg/128 mg
Dietary Fiber: 1 g/1 g

French Rolls

Yield: 36 rolls

4 teaspoons (2 packages) active dry yeast
1³/4 cups lukewarm water (110 to 115 degrees F)
4 teaspoons sugar
2 teaspoons salt
2 tablespoons melted shortening
6½ to 7 cups sifted flour
3 egg whites, beaten stiff
1 egg white
1 tablespoon water
Poppy or sesame seeds

> *Fat-skimming options: Substitute 1 tablespoon soft margarine for shortening.*
> *With options, exchange diets count: 1 starch.*

• Sprinkle yeast on lukewarm water in bowl; stir to dissolve. Add sugar, salt, shortening and 2 cups flour; beat well. Add the beaten egg whites. Stir in enough remaining flour to make a soft dough that leaves sides of bowl.
• Turn out on lightly floured surface. Knead dough until smooth and elastic with tiny blisters on the surface (about 5 minutes).
• Place in a lightly greased bowl; turn dough over to grease top. Cover with a damp cloth.
• Let rise in a warm place until doubled, about 1 hour. Punch down.
• You may shape the dough at this point. For superior results, let the dough rise again until doubled, then punch down and shape.

• Shape raised dough in 3-inch balls. Flatten to make 4-inch circles or 6-inch tapered oblongs ³/4 inch thick. Use a very sharp knife or razor to make shallow cuts about ¹/4 inch deep on top.
• Place rolls on greased baking sheets sprinkled lightly with cornmeal. Beat slightly 1 egg white with 1 tablespoon water. Brush on rolls. Sprinkle with poppy or sesame seeds. Let rise until doubled; brush again with egg mixture.
• Bake in 425 degree F oven 20 minutes or until brown and crusty. Place a large shallow pan of boiling water on the bottom of oven to provide steam while the rolls bake. This makes the rolls crusty.

Nutrition Analysis Per Serving: As Originally Published/With Fat-Skimming Options

Calories: 99/96
Protein: 3 g/3 g
Carbohydrate: 19 g/19 g
Fat: 1 g/0 g

Saturated Fat: 0 g/0 g
Cholesterol: 0 mg/0 mg
Sodium: 125 mg/128 mg
Dietary Fiber: 1 g/1 g

Onion Rolls

Yield: 36 rolls

4 teaspoons (2 packages) active dry yeast
1³/₄ cups lukewarm water (110 to 115 degrees F)
4 teaspoons sugar
2 teaspoons salt
2 tablespoons melted shortening
6¹/₂ to 7 cups sifted flour
3 egg whites, beaten stiff
3 tablespoons instant minced onion
3 tablespoons cold water
1 tablespoon poppy seeds
1 egg white
1 tablespoon water

> *Fat-skimming options: Substitute 2 tablespoons soft margarine for shortening.*
> *With options, exchange diets count: 1 starch.*

• Sprinkle yeast on lukewarm water in bowl; stir to dissolve. Add sugar, salt, shortening and 2 cups flour; beat well. Add the beaten egg whites. Stir in enough remaining flour to make a soft dough that leaves sides of bowl.
• Turn out on lightly floured surface. Knead dough until smooth and elastic and tiny blisters show on surface (about 5 minutes).
• Place in a lightly greased bowl; turn dough over to grease top. Cover with a damp cloth.
• Let rise in a warm place until doubled, about 1 hour. Punch down.
• You may shape the dough at this point. For superior results, let the dough rise again until doubled, then punch down and shape.

• Shape raised dough in 3-inch round rolls ¹/₂ inch thick. Make hollow in center of each roll with fingers. Fill with an onion mixture made from the instant minced onions soaked in 3 tablespoons cold water, then drained and mixed with poppy seeds.
• Place rolls on greased baking sheets sprinkled lightly with cornmeal. Beat slightly 1 egg white with 1 tablespoon water. Brush on rolls. Let rise until doubled; brush again with egg mixture.
• Bake in 425 degree F oven 20 minutes or until brown and crusty. Place a large shallow pan of boiling water on the bottom of oven to provide steam while the rolls bake. This makes the rolls crusty.

Nutrition Analysis Per Serving: As Originally Published/With Fat-Skimming Options	
Calories: 99/96	Saturated Fat: 0 g/0 g
Protein: 3 g/3 g	Cholesterol: 0 mg/0 mg
Carbohydrate: 19 g/19 g	Sodium: 125 mg/128 mg
Fat: 1 g/0 g	Dietary Fiber: 1 g/1 g

Freeze Ahead White Bread Dough

Yield: 4 loaves or 60 slices

12$\frac{1}{2}$ to 13$\frac{1}{2}$ cups unsifted flour
$\frac{1}{2}$ cup sugar
2 tablespoons salt
$\frac{2}{3}$ cup instant nonfat dry milk solids
4 packages active dry yeast
$\frac{1}{4}$ cup softened butter or margarine
4 cups very warm water (120 to 130 degrees F)

Fat-skimming options: none. Exchange diets count: 1$\frac{1}{2}$ starch.

• In a large bowl thoroughly mix 4 cups flour, sugar, salt, dry milk solids and undissolved active dry yeast. Add butter.
• Gradually add water to dry ingredients and beat 2 minutes at medium speed of electric mixer, scraping bowl occasionally. Add 1$\frac{1}{2}$ cups flour. Beat at high speed 2 minutes, scraping bowl occasionally. Stir in enough additional flour to make a stiff dough. Turn out onto lightly floured board; knead until smooth and elastic, about 15 minutes. Cover with a towel; let rest 15 minutes.
• Divide dough into 4 equal parts. Form each piece into a smooth round ball. Flatten each ball into a mound 6 inches in diameter. Place on greased baking sheets. Cover with plastic wrap. Freeze until firm. Transfer to plastic bags. Freeze up to 4 weeks.

• **To use:** Remove dough from freezer; place on ungreased baking sheet. Cover; let stand at room temperature until fully thawed, about 4 hours.
• For round bread, let thawed dough rise on ungreased baking sheet in warm place, free from draft, until doubled in bulk, about 1 hour. Or for loaf shape, roll each ball to 12x8 inches. Shape into loaf. Place in greased 8$\frac{1}{2}$x4$\frac{1}{2}$x2$\frac{1}{2}$ inch loaf pan. Let rise in warm place, free from draft, until doubled in bulk, about 1$\frac{1}{2}$ hours.
• Bake at 350 degrees F about 35 minutes, or until done. Remove from pans and cool on wire racks.

Nutrition Analysis Per Serving: As Originally Published

Calories: 118	Saturated Fat: 0 g
Protein: 3 g	Cholesterol: 2 mg
Carbohydrate: 23 g	Sodium: 229 mg
Fat: 1 g	Dietary Fiber: 1 g

Golden Pecan Cinnamon Buns

Yield: 30 buns

1⅓ cups golden raisins
2 cups boiling water
3 cups stirred whole wheat flour
4 teaspoons (2 packages) active dry yeast
1¼ teaspoons salt
1 egg
⅓ cup shortening
⅓ cup honey
2 cups sifted all-purpose flour
4 tablespoons butter, melted
Cinnamon Filling
Browned Butter Icing

Fat-skimming options: Omit shortening and substitute 2 tablespoons soft margarine. Omit butter and substitute 2 tablespoons soft margarine. Reduce pecans to ½ cup. With options, exchange diets count: 2 starch, ½ fruit, 1 fat.

• Soak raisins in boiling water 5 minutes. Drain, reserving liquid. (If necessary, add enough water to make 1⅔ cups). Cool to very warm (120 to 130 degrees F).
• Stir together 2 cups of the whole wheat flour, yeast and salt in a bowl. Add egg, shortening, honey and reserved liquid. Beat until smooth, using electric mixer. Stir in raisins, remaining 1 cup whole wheat flour and enough all-purpose flour to make a soft dough. Knead on floured surface until smooth, about 10 minutes. Place in greased bowl. Cover; let rise until doubled, about 1 hour.
• Punch down dough; divide in half. Roll out each half to 15x10 inch rectangle. Brush each with 2 tablespoons melted butter and sprinkle with half the Cinnamon Filling. Starting at wide end, roll up one rectangle. Pinch edges. Repeat with other piece. Cut each roll into 15 slices. Place in 2 greased 13x9x2 inch baking pans, 15 slices to a pan.

Cover; let rise until doubled, about 45 minutes.
• Bake in 375 degree F oven 25 minutes or until golden brown. Drizzle warm rolls with Browned Butter Icing.

Cinnamon Filling

1¼ cups packed brown sugar
⅓ cup wheat germ
4 teaspoons ground cinnamon
1 cup pecan halves

• Combine brown sugar, wheat germ, cinnamon and pecan halves. Mix well.

Browned Butter Icing

3 tablespoons butter
2 cups sifted confectioners sugar
3 tablespoons milk

• Heat butter in saucepan until lightly browned. Remove from heat. Add confectioners sugar and milk, stirring until smooth. If icing is too thick, add a little more milk.

Nutrition Analysis Per Serving: As Originally Published/With Fat-Skimming Options

Calories: 271/227	Saturated Fat: 2.5 g/1 g
Protein: 4 g/4 g	Cholesterol: 14 mg/10 mg
Carbohydrate: 43 g/42 g	Sodium: 123 mg/128 mg
Fat: 10 g/6 g	Dietary Fiber: 2.5 g/2.2 g

Hot Cross Buns

Yield: 18 buns

6 to 6½ cups sifted flour
½ cup sugar
¾ teaspoon salt
2 teaspoons ground cinnamon
4 teaspoons (2 packages) active dry yeast
1½ cups milk
6 tablespoons butter
3 eggs
1¼ cups currants
1 egg yolk
2 tablespoons cold water
Icing

> *Fat-skimming options: Use skim milk. Use ¾ cup liquid egg substitute for eggs.*
> *With options, exchange diets count: 3 starch, ½ fat.*

• Combine 2 cups flour, sugar, salt, cinnamon and undissolved yeast in mixing bowl; mix thoroughly.
• Combine milk and butter in saucepan. Heat until very warm (120 to 130 degrees F). Add to dry ingredients, beating with electric mixer at medium speed 2 minutes. Add 3 eggs and 1 cup flour; beat 2 minutes. Stir in currants and enough additional flour to make a soft dough.
• Turn dough out on lightly floured surface. Knead until smooth and elastic, about 10 minutes. Place in greased bowl, turning to grease top. Cover; let rise until doubled, about 1 hour.
• Punch down dough. Shape into 18 balls. Place in greased 13x9x2 inch baking pan. Combine egg yolk and water, and brush buns with mixture. Cover; let rise until doubled, about 45 minutes.
• Bake in 375 degree F oven 20 to 25 minutes or until golden brown. Remove from pan; cool on rack. Frost with icing before serving. Buns are best served warm.

Icing
1 cup sifted confectioners sugar
1 tablespoon milk
½ teaspoon vanilla

• Combine sugar, milk and vanilla; beat until smooth.
• Drip icing from spoon over center of each bun, both lengthwise and crosswise, to form a cross.

Nutrition Analysis Per Serving: As Originally Published/With Fat-Skimming Options

Calories: 266/259
Protein: 7 g/7 g
Carbohydrate: 46 g/46 g
Fat: 6 g/5 g

Saturated Fat: 3 g/2.5 g
Cholesterol: 59 mg/23 mg
Sodium: 150 mg/159 mg
Dietary Fiber: 1 g/1 g

Herb Garden Bread

Yield: 1 (1½ pound) loaf or 24 slices

2 teaspoons (1 package) active dry yeast
3 cups bread flour
2 tablespoons granulated sugar
1 teaspoon salt
1½ teaspoons dried chives
1½ teaspoons dried oregano
1½ teaspoons dried thyme
1½ teaspoons dried basil
1½ tablespoons butter or margarine
1¼ cups water

Fat-skimming options: none. Exchange diets count: 1 starch.

• Place all ingredients in bread machine, according to manufacturer's directions. If using fresh herbs, double the amounts.

• Select mode and press Start. The recipe can be made with regular, rapid or delayed-time bake cycles.

Nutrition Analysis Per Serving: As Originally Published

Calories: 68
Protein: 2 g
Carbohydrate: 13 g
Fat: 1 g

Saturated Fat: 0 g
Cholesterol: 2 mg
Sodium: 94 mg
Dietary Fiber: 1 g

Pizza Dough

Yield: 8 slices or servings

2 teaspoons (1 package) active dry yeast
1 teaspoon sugar
1 cup warm water (105 to 115 degrees F)
2 tablespoons vegetable oil
1 teaspoon salt
3 to 3$^{1}/_{4}$ cups sifted all-purpose flour

Fat-skimming options: Reduce oil to 1 tablespoon. With options, exchange diets count: 2 starch.

• In large bowl, sprinkle yeast and sugar over warm water; stir until dissolved. Stir in oil, salt and enough flour to make a soft dough.
• Turn dough out onto lightly floured surface. Knead until dough is smooth and elastic, about 5 minutes.
• Place in greased large bowl, turning dough over to grease top. Cover; let rise in warm place 30 minutes.
• Punch down dough; turn out onto lightly floured surface. Knead until no longer sticky, about 30 seconds. Cover; let rest 5 minutes.
• To bake: Divide dough in half. Pat and stretch each half into a greased 12-inch round pizza pan. Add your favorite pizza sauce, toppings and cheese. Bake, on lowest rack, at 400 degrees F for 20 minutes, or until bottom of crust is browned.
• **Whole Wheat Pizza Dough:** Add 1$^{1}/_{2}$ cups stirred whole wheat flour to liquid ingredients. Use only 1$^{1}/_{2}$ to 1$^{3}/_{4}$ cups sifted all-purpose flour to make a soft dough.

• **Food Processor Method:** In small bowl, sprinkle yeast and sugar over warm water; stir until dissolved.
• Place salt and 3 cups sifted flour (or 1$^{1}/_{2}$ cups sifted all-purpose flour and 1$^{1}/_{2}$ cups stirred whole wheat flour) in processor bowl with metal blade. While processor is running, pour yeast mixture through feed tube. Process until soft dough forms that leaves side of bowl, about 45 seconds.
• Add oil; process 1 minute. If dough sticks to side of bowl, add additional flour, 1 tablespoon at a time, processing 10 seconds after each addition.
• **Refrigerated Pizza Dough:** Prepare and knead dough. Cover with plastic wrap and refrigerate 2 to 24 hours. Punch down dough; turn out onto lightly floured surface. Knead until no longer sticky, about 30 seconds. Cover and let rest 5 minutes.

Nutrition Analysis Per Serving: As Originally Published/With Fat-Skimming Options

Calories: 206/191
Protein: 5 g/5 g
Carbohydrate: 37 g/37 g
Fat: 4 g/2 g

Saturated Fat: 0 g/0 g
Cholesterol: 0 mg/0 mg
Sodium: 267 mg/267 mg
Dietary Fiber: 1.5 g/1.5 g

CHAPTER THREE

DESSERTS

Find a cow pumpkin for the best pie

Joyce Sapp of Columbia, Mo., has introduced homemade pumpkin pie to literally hundreds of customers who visit her at Strawberry Hill Farms. She recommends the beige-colored (similar to butternut squash) thick-fleshed "Cow" or "Buckskin" pumpkins for the best-tasting pies. Every fall, families from Columbia flock to her farm to sit on hay bales, roll in the clover and pick out pumpkins for painting. Joyce cheers for jack-o-lantern painting, instead of carving, so families can discover the wonderful food inside this thing that sits on the porch, once Halloween passes.

During the summer months, Joyce and her family stake out their spot at the Columbia farmers market, where over a hundred growers sell produce. Thirty-somethings from the city get pretty excited about the taste of her "fresh-dug" potatoes.

Back home in her kitchen, Joyce follows doctor's orders to limit fat and sugar in her family's diet as her husband must manage his diabetes. You will find her recipe for Fresh Pumpkin Pie in this chapter with options for evaporated skim milk and egg substitute.

Carrot Cake With Cream Cheese Frosting
Yield: 8 servings

2 cups flour
2 teaspoons ground cinnamon
1 teaspoon baking powder
$^1/_4$ teaspoon salt
$^1/_4$ cup soft margarine
$^1/_3$ cup nonfat sour cream
1 cup sugar
$^3/_4$ cup liquid egg substitute
$^2/_3$ cup skim milk
3 medium carrots, grated
2 tablespoons chopped walnuts
Frosting
Topping

Fat-skimming options: none.
Exchange diets count: 2 starch, 2 fruit, 1 fat.

• Preheat oven to 350 degrees F. Spray a 9 inch round cake pan with nonstick cooking spray, dust with flour and tap out excess.
• Mix together flour, cinnamon, baking powder and salt.
• Beat together margarine, sour cream and sugar at medium speed until fluffy. Add egg substitute; beat smooth. At low speed, alternately beat flour mixture and milk into sugar mixture. Fold in carrots and nuts. Pour batter into pan.
• Bake until top springs back when touched and toothpick inserted in center comes out clean, about 35 to 40 minutes. Cool 10 minutes, then turn out onto rack to cool.
• Frost cake; sprinkle with Topping.

Frosting
1 tablespoon soft margarine
4 ounces 50% reduced fat cream cheese, softened
1 teaspoon vanilla
2 cups confectioner's sugar

• Prepare the icing by beating the margarine and cream cheese smooth. Beat in vanilla, then beat in confectioner's sugar until smooth.

Topping
2 tablespoons chopped walnuts
2 tablespoons firmly packed brown sugar

• Combine ingredients.

Nutrition Analysis Per Serving: As Originally Published

Calories: 425
Protein: 9 g
Carbohydrate: 119 g
Fat: 15 g

Saturated Fat: 3 g
Cholesterol: 7 mg
Sodium: 413 mg
Dietary Fiber: 3 g

Glorious Golden Fruitcake

Yield: 1 (5 pound) fruitcake or 24 slices

4 cups sifted flour
1½ teaspoons baking powder
½ teaspoon salt
2 cups butter
2½ cups sugar
6 eggs
¼ cup milk
4 cups chopped walnuts
1 cup golden raisins
½ cup chopped candied pineapple
½ cup chopped red candied cherries
½ cup chopped green candied cherries
1 tablespoon grated lemon rind
Pineapple Glaze
Pecan halves

Fat-skimming options: Replace butter with 1 cup corn oil plus 1 cup nonfat sour cream. Reduce walnuts to 1 cup. With options, exchange diets count: 3 starch, 2 fruit.

• Sift together flour, baking powder and salt; reserve ¼ cup.
• Cream together butter and sugar until fluffy. Add eggs, one at a time, beating well. Add dry ingredients alternately with milk, beating well after each addition.
• Combine walnuts, raisins, pineapple, candied cherries, lemon rind and ¼ cup flour. Stir into batter. Spread batter in greased and waxed-paper-lined 10 inch tube pan.
• Bake in 275 degree F oven 2 hours 45 minutes or until done. Cool in pan 30 minutes. Remove from pan; cool on rack.

• Wrap fruitcake tightly in foil. Store in refrigerator up to 4 weeks. (Fruitcake keeps better if stored unfrosted).
• To serve, prepare Pineapple Glaze. Frost top of cake, letting glaze drip down sides. Decorate with pecan halves.

Pineapple Glaze

1 cup sifted confectioners sugar
2 tablespoons pineapple juice

• Combine confectioners sugar and pineapple juice; mix until smooth.

Nutrition Analysis Per Serving: As Originally Published/With Fat-Skimming Options	
Calories: 573/361	Saturated Fat: 10 g/1 g
Protein: 12 g/6 g	Cholesterol: 40 mg/0 mg
Carbohydrate: 54 g/53 g	Sodium: 308 mg/75 mg
Fat: 36 g/ 16 g	Dietary Fiber: 3 g/1 g

Lemon Chiffon Cake

Yield: 16 servings

1½ cups flour
¾ cup granulated sugar
2 teaspoons baking powder
¼ teaspoon salt
½ cup corn oil
½ cup fresh lemon juice
1 teaspoon lemon extract
Grated zest of 2 lemons, about 3½ tablespoons
6 large egg whites at room temperature
2 tablespoons sifted confectioners sugar
Lemon Glaze

> *Fat-skimming options: Substitute ¼ cup nonfat sour cream for half of oil.*
> *With options, exchange diets count: 1 starch, 1 fruit, ½ fat.*

• Coat 9 inch Bundt pan with nonstick cooking spray. Dust pan with flour.
• Sift flour, sugar, baking powder and salt into a large bowl. Make a well in the center and add oil, lemon juice, lemon extract and 3 tablespoons of lemon zest, reserving remainder for garnish. Set aside before mixing.
• In another large bowl, beat egg whites until foamy. Add confectioners sugar and whip until whites are stiff, but not dry. Set whites aside. Return beaters to mixer without washing.
• With mixer on medium low, beat the flour-oil mixture until well blended. In several additions, gently fold batter into whites.
• Turn batter into prepared pan and smooth top with rubber spatula. Rap pan sharply on counter once to remove any large air bubbles. Bake in 350 degree F oven for about 35 minutes, or until top of cake is golden brown and springy to touch and wooden pick inserted in center comes out clean.
• Cool cake in pan on wire rack for 10 minutes. With a long, thin knife, loosen the cake from sides of center tube of pan. Top cake with rack, invert and lift off pan.
• Make Lemon Glaze.
• Spread glaze over top of warm cake, letting it drip down sides. Sprinkle reserved lemon zest on top of glaze.

Lemon Glaze
1½ cups confectioners sugar
2 tablespoons fresh lemon juice

• Combine sugar and lemon juice in bowl. Beat until smooth. Adjust consistency by adding more sugar or juice if needed. Glaze should be thick, but pourable.

Nutrition Analysis Per Serving: As Originally Published/With Fat-Skimming Options

Calories: 194/167
Protein: 2 g/2 g
Carbohydrate: 31 g/32 g
Fat: 7 g/3 g

Saturated Fat: 0.5 g/0 g
Cholesterol: 0 mg/0 mg
Sodium: 55 mg/60 mg
Dietary Fiber: 0 g/0 g

Oatmeal Spice Cake

Yield: 16 servings

1 cup quick-cooking oats
$^1\!/_2$ cup butter, cut in small pieces
1$^1\!/_2$ cups boiling water
1$^1\!/_2$ cups sifted flour
1 cup sugar
1 teaspoon baking soda
$^1\!/_2$ teaspoon salt
1 teaspoon ground cinnamon
$^1\!/_2$ teaspoon ground allspice
$^1\!/_2$ teaspoon ground nutmeg
2 eggs
1 cup firmly packed brown sugar
Coconut Topping

Fat-skimming options: Omit butter and use $^1\!/_4$ cup corn oil plus $^1\!/_4$ cup nonfat sour cream. Use $^1\!/_2$ cup liquid egg substitute for eggs. Reduce coconut in topping to $^1\!/_2$ cup and walnuts to $^1\!/_4$ cup. With options, exchange diets count: 2 starch, 1$^1\!/_2$ fruit, 1 fat.

• Combine oats, butter and boiling water in bowl. Cool.
• Sift together flour, sugar, baking soda, salt, cinnamon, allspice and nutmeg; set aside.
• Add eggs to oat mixture; beat well. Add dry ingredients and brown sugar to oat mixture; beat at medium speed 2 minutes. Pour batter into greased 13x9x2 inch baking pan.
• Bake in 350 degree F oven 30 to 35 minutes or until cake tests done.
• Spread with Coconut Topping. Place under the broiler for 2 to 3 minutes or until golden brown. Cool in pan on rack.

Coconut Topping

1 cup coconut
1 cup brown sugar, firmly packed
1 cup chopped walnuts
$^1\!/_2$ cup milk

Combine coconut, brown sugar, walnuts and milk in bowl; mix well.

Nutrition Analysis Per Serving: As Originally Published/With Fat-Skimming Options	
Calories: 386/292	Saturated Fat: 6 g/1 g
Protein: 7 g/4 g	Cholesterol: 43 mg/0 mg
Carbohydrate: 56 g/54 g	Sodium: 239 mg/185 mg
Fat: 16 g/7 g	Dietary Fiber: 1.5 g/1 g

Old-Fashioned Jelly Roll
Yield: 2 jelly rolls or 28 small slices

³/₄ cup plus 2 tablespoons sifted flour
1 teaspoon baking powder
¹/₈ teaspoon salt
3 eggs (²/₃ cup)
1 cup granulated sugar
1 teaspoon vanilla
¹/₃ cup water
Confectioners sugar
¹/₃ cup apricot or peach preserves
¹/₃ cup raspberry or strawberry jam

*Fat-skimming options: Use ³/₄ cup liquid egg substitute for eggs.
With options, exchange diets count: 1 starch.*

• Grease a 15¹/₂x10¹/₂x1 inch jelly roll pan. Line bottom of pan with waxed paper; grease waxed paper. Set aside.
• Sift together flour, baking powder and salt; set aside.
• In small bowl with mixer at high speed, beat together eggs, granulated sugar and vanilla until thick and lemon colored, 5 minutes.
• Reduce speed to low; blend in water.
• Add dry ingredients; beat just until blended.
• Pour batter into prepared jelly roll pan; spread batter evenly.

• Bake in 350 degree F oven 15 minutes, or until top springs back when touched lightly.
• Meanwhile, sift confectioners sugar over linen dish towel.
• Loosen edges of cake and immediately invert onto towel. Trim stiff edges from cake. Cut cake crosswise in half.
• Place one cake half on another towel sprinkled with confectioners sugar.
• Starting at long side, tightly roll up each cake half, together with towel. Cool on rack.
• Unroll cake halves. Spread one half with apricot preserves and the other with raspberry jam to within ¹/₂ inch of edges. Reroll and cut each into 14 slices.

Nutrition Analysis Per Serving: As Originally Published/With Fat-Skimming Options

Calories: 72/70
Protein: 1 g/1 g
Carbohydrate: 16 g/16 g
Fat: 0 g/0 g

Saturated Fat: 0 g/0 g
Cholesterol: 23 mg/0 mg
Sodium: 17 mg/22 mg
Dietary Fiber: 0 g/0 g

Pineapple Upside-Down Cake
Yield: 10 servings

¹/₃ cup plus 1 tablespoon firmly packed dark brown sugar
3 tablespoons light corn syrup
1¹/₂ tablespoons fresh lemon juice
2 cups pineapple tidbits
¹/₂ cup granulated sugar
¹/₂ cup liquid egg substitute
¹/₃ cup corn oil
¹/₃ cup nonfat sour cream
¹/₃ cup pineapple juice
1 teaspoon vanilla extract
1¹/₂ cups flour
1 teaspoon baking powder
¹/₂ teaspoon cinnamon
¹/₂ teaspoon nutmeg
¹/₄ teaspoon baking soda
¹/₈ teaspoon salt

Fat-skimming options: none. Exchange diets count: 1¹/₂ starch, 2 fruit.

• Prepare topping by spraying a 10-inch cake pan with nonstick cooking spray.
• Add brown sugar, corn syrup and lemon juice; stir. Place pan over low heat for about 1 minute, stirring with wooden spoon to partially melt sugar.
• Remove pan from heat. Add pineapple in a single layer. Set aside.
• In large bowl, combine sugar, egg substitute, corn oil, nonfat sour cream, pineapple juice and vanilla extract. Whisk lightly.

• Stir in flour, baking powder, cinnamon, nutmeg, baking soda and salt. Beat until well blended, but don't overmix.
• Pour batter evenly over fruit. Bake in 325 degree F oven for 30 to 35 minutes or until wooden pick comes out clean.
• Cool cake in pan on wire rack for 3 to 4 minutes, until fruit stops bubbling.
• Top pan with large flat serving platter. Holding plate and pan together with potholders, invert.

Nutrition Analysis Per Serving: As Originally Published

Calories: 235	Saturated Fat: 0 g
Protein: 3 g	Cholesterol: 0 mg
Carbohydrate: 51 g	Sodium: 91 mg
Fat: 3 g	Dietary Fiber: 0 g

Pumpkin-Nut Cake Roll

Yield: 8 to 10 servings

³/₄ cup sifted flour
1 teaspoon baking powder
1 teaspoon ground cinnamon
¹/₂ teaspoon salt
¹/₂ teaspoon ground ginger
¹/₄ teaspoon ground nutmeg
3 eggs
1 cup granulated sugar
²/₃ cup mashed, cooked pumpkin
1 teaspoon lemon juice
1 cup finely chopped walnuts
¹/₃ cup confectioners sugar
Cheese Filling

*Fat-skimming options: Use ³/₄ cup liquid egg substitute for eggs. Reduce walnuts to ¹/₄ cup.
In Cheese Filling, omit butter and use light (50% reduced fat) cream cheese.
With options, exchange diets count: 2 starch, ¹/₂ skim milk, 1 fat.*

• Sift together first 6 ingredients; set aside.
• In large bowl using mixer at high speed, beat eggs 5 minutes. Beat in sugar, 1 tablespoon at a time, until thick.
• Stir in pumpkin and lemon juice. Fold in flour mixture until blended.
• Spread batter evenly into a well-greased and floured 15¹/₂x10¹/₂x1 inch jelly roll pan. Sprinkle nuts evenly over top. Bake in 375 degree F oven 15 minutes, or until top springs back when lightly touched.
• Meanwhile, sift confectioners sugar over linen dish towel.
• Immediately invert cake onto towel. Starting with one short side, roll up cake and towel; cool on rack. Prepare Cheese Filling.

• Unroll cake and spread filling almost to edge. Reroll cake, using towel to help make a tight roll. Place roll seamside down. Refrigerate at least 4 hours.

Cheese Filling

2 (3 ounce) packages cream cheese, softened
¹/₂ cup sifted confectioners sugar
¹/₄ cup butter, softened
¹/₂ teaspoon vanilla

• In small bowl, using mixer at low speed, beat cream cheese, confectioners sugar, butter, and vanilla until smooth and fluffy.

Nutrition Analysis Per Serving: As Originally Published/With Fat-Skimming Options

Calories: 414/240
Protein: 10 g/7 g
Carbohydrate: 41 g/40 g
Fat: 25 g/7 g

Saturated Fat: 8 g/2 g
Cholesterol: 95 mg/6 mg
Sodium: 224 mg/237 mg
Dietary Fiber: 1 g/0.5 g

Spicy Applesauce Cake

Yield: 9 servings

1½ cups sifted flour
1 teaspoon baking soda
1 teaspoon salt
1 teaspoon ground cinnamon
¼ teaspoon ground cloves
½ cup shortening
1 cup sugar
2 eggs
1 cup applesauce
1 cup raisins
1 cup chopped pecans
1 tablespoon flour

> *Fat-skimming options: Omit shortening and use ¼ cup oil plus ¼ cup nonfat sour cream.*
> *Use ½ cup liquid egg substitute for eggs. Reduce pecans to ¼ cup.*
> *With options, exchange diets count: 2 starch, 2 fruit, 2 fat.*

• Sift together 1½ cups flour, baking soda, salt, cinnamon and cloves.
• Cream together shortening and sugar in bowl until light and fluffy. Add eggs, one at a time, beating well after each addition.
• Add dry ingredients alternately with applesauce, beating well after each addition. Combine raisins, pecans and 1 tablespoon flour. Stir into batter. Pour batter into greased 9-inch square baking pan.

• Bake in 350 degree F oven for 55 minutes or until cake tests done. Cool in pan on rack. If you wish, serve cake slightly warm with a dollop of whipped cream.

Nutrition Analysis Per Serving: As Originally Published/With Fat-Skimming Options	
Calories: 527/357	Saturated Fat: 4 g/1 g
Protein: 6 g/5 g	Cholesterol: 47 mg/0 mg
Carbohydrate: 64 g/61 g	Sodium: 394 mg/414 mg
Fat: 30 g/11 g	Dietary Fiber: 3.5 g/2 g

Light Chocolate Brownie Cupcakes
Yield: 24 cupcakes

4 squares semisweet chocolate
1 cup butter
1 cup chopped walnuts
1 teaspoon vanilla
1 cup sifted flour
1³/₄ cups sugar
4 eggs

Fat-skimming options: Omit butter and substitute ¹/₂ cup low-fat margarine and ¹/₂ cup nonfat sour cream. Use 1 cup liquid egg substitute for eggs. Reduce walnuts to ¹/₄ cup. With options, exchange diets count: 1 starch, 1 fat.

• Melt chocolate and butter over very low heat. Remove from heat. Add walnuts and vanilla.
• Sift together flour and sugar into bowl. Add eggs; beat until blended. Stir in chocolate mixture. Pour into paper-lined 2¹/₂-inch muffin pan cups, filling half full.

• Bake in 325 degree F oven 35 minutes or until cupcakes test done.

Nutrition Analysis Per Serving: As Originally Published/With Fat-Skimming Options

Calories: 213/121
Protein: 4 g/3 g
Carbohydrate: 15 g/15 g
Fat: 17 g/6 g

Saturated Fat: 7 g/2 g
Cholesterol: 56 mg/0 mg
Sodium: 89 mg/63 mg
Dietary Fiber: 1 g/1 g

Chocolate-Covered Turtle Cookies
Yield: 40 cookies

1¹/₂ cups sifted flour
¹/₄ teaspoon baking soda
¹/₄ teaspoon baking powder
¹/₂ cup butter
¹/₂ cup packed brown sugar
2 eggs
1 teaspoon vanilla
160 large pecan halves (about 8 ounces)
Chocolate Icing

> *Fat-skimming options: In cookies, substitute ¹/₄ cup corn oil plus ¹/₄ cup nonfat sour cream for the butter. Use ¹/₂ cup liquid egg substitute for the eggs. With options, exchange diets count: 1 fruit, 1 fat.*

• Sift together flour, baking soda and baking powder; set aside.
• Cream together butter and brown sugar in bowl until light and fluffy, using electric mixer at medium speed. Add eggs, one at a time, beating well after each addition. Beat in vanilla.
• Gradually stir dry ingredients into creamed mixture, mixing well. Place pecan halves in clusters of 4, about 2 inches apart, on ungreased baking sheets, arranging halves in each cluster in the form of a cross. Drop a rounded teaspoonful of dough in the center of each cross.

• Bake in 350 degree F oven 10 minutes, or until golden brown. Remove from baking sheets; cool on racks. Prepare Chocolate Icing. Frost center of each cookie with Chocolate Icing.

Chocolate Icing
1 cup sifted confectioners sugar
1 tablespoon soft butter
1¹/₂ (1 ounce) squares unsweetened chocolate
3 tablespoons milk

• Melt and cool chocolate.
• Combine confectioners sugar, butter, chocolate and milk in bowl. Stir until well blended.

Nutrition Analysis Per Serving: As Originally Published/With Fat-Skimming Options

Calories: 110/102
Protein: 1 g/1 g
Carbohydrate: 11 g/11 g
Fat: 7 g/6 g

Saturated Fat: 2 g/1 g
Cholesterol: 18 mg/1 mg
Sodium: 39 mg/20 mg
Dietary Fiber: 0.5 g/0.5 g

Classic Chocolate Chip Cookies
Yield: 40 cookies

2½ cups sifted flour
1 teaspoon baking soda
½ teaspoon salt
1 cup margarine or butter
1 cup packed light brown sugar
¾ cup granulated sugar
1 teaspoon vanilla
2 large eggs
2½ cups semisweet chocolate pieces
2 cups coarsely chopped walnuts

Fat-skimming options: Omit butter and use ½ cup low-fat margarine plus ½ cup nonfat sour cream. With options, exchange diets count: 1½ starch, 2 fat.

• Sift together flour, baking soda and salt; set aside.
• In large bowl, using mixer at medium speed, beat margarine, brown sugar, granulated sugar and vanilla until light. Add eggs; blend well.
• Reduce speed to low. Add dry ingredients; beat just until blended. Stir in chocolate pieces and walnuts.

• With damp hands, shape dough into 1½-inch balls; place on waxed-paper-covered baking sheet. Using back of teaspoon dipped in water, flatten balls to ¾ inch thickness. Freeze 15 minutes, or refrigerate 6 hours or overnight.
• Remove from waxed paper; place 3 inches apart on greased baking sheets.
• Bake in 375 degree F oven 12 to 14 minutes or until golden. Cool 2 minutes; remove from baking sheets. Cool on racks.

Nutrition Analysis Per Serving: As Originally Published/With Fat-Skimming Options

Calories: 228/200
Protein: 4 g/4 g
Carbohydrate: 23 g/24 g
Fat: 14 g/11 g

Saturated Fat: 5 g/2 g
Cholesterol: 23 mg/11 mg
Sodium: 112 mg/91 mg
Dietary Fiber: 1 g/1 g

Coconut-Date Mounds

Yield: 24 cookies

3½ cups cornflakes
1 cup chopped, pitted dates
¾ cup sugar
2 eggs, beaten
1 cup chopped walnuts
1 teaspoon vanilla
1⅓ cups flaked coconut
12 candied cherries, cut into halves

Fat-skimming options: Use ½ cup liquid egg substitute.
Reduce walnuts and coconut each to ⅓ cup. With options, exchange diets count: 1 starch.

• Crush cornflakes slightly with hands; set aside.
• Combine dates, sugar and eggs in 10 inch skillet. Cook over medium heat, stirring constantly, until mixture pulls away from the sides of the pan, about 5 minutes. Remove from heat.

• Stir walnuts and vanilla into date mixture. Gently stir in cornflakes. Cool slightly, about 5 minutes.
• Shape mixture into 1½-inch balls. Roll each in flaked coconut. Place on waxed-paper-lined baking sheets. Press a candied cherry half in each ball, flattening slightly.

Nutrition Analysis Per Serving: As Originally Published/With Fat-Skimming Options

Calories: 137/90	Saturated Fat: 2 g/1 g
Protein: 3 g/2 g	Cholesterol: 18 mg/0 mg
Carbohydrate: 17 g/15 g	Sodium: 55 mg/54 mg
Fat: 7 g/3 g	Dietary Fiber: 0.5 g/0.5 g

Double Chocolate Caramel Bars

Yield: 48 bars

1 (14 ounce) bag caramels (about 48)
$^2/_3$ cup evaporated milk, divided
1 (18$^1/_4$ ounce) box devil's food cake mix
$^3/_4$ cup butter or margarine, melted
1 cup semisweet chocolate chips
1 cup chopped walnuts

Fat-skimming options: Use evaporated skim milk. Substitute low-fat margarine. Substitute reduced-fat chocolate chips. Reduce nuts to $^1/_4$ cup.

• In top of double boiler over boiling water, stir caramels and $^1/_3$ cup evaporated milk until caramels are melted and mixture is smooth. Keep warm over hot water. Or place caramels and $^1/_3$ cup evaporated milk in microwave-safe bowl. Microwave on medium 6 to 7 minutes, stirring after 3 minutes and then after each 1 minute, until caramels are melted and mixture is smooth.

• In large bowl, using mixer at medium speed, beat cake mix, melted butter and remaining $^1/_3$ cup evaporated milk 2 minutes.

• Spread half the batter in greased 13x9x2 inch baking pan.

• Bake in 350 degree F oven 8 minutes. Cool on rack 2 minutes.

• Pour caramel mixture evenly over baked layer; tilt pan to cover completely. Sprinkle with chocolate chips.

• Stir $^1/_2$ cup walnuts into remaining batter. Drop by spoonfuls evenly over chocolate chip layer. Sprinkle with remaining $^1/_2$ cup walnuts.

• Bake in 350 degree F oven 20 minutes. Cool on rack. If necessary, chill before cutting into 2x1 inch bars.

Nutrition Analysis Per Serving: As Originally Published/With Fat-Skimming Options

Calories: 155/112
Protein: 3 g/1 g
Carbohydrate: 17 g/16 g
Fat: 10 g/5 g

Saturated Fat: 2 g/1 g
Cholesterol: 10 mg/9 mg
Sodium: 148 mg/149 mg
Dietary Fiber: 0 g/0 g

Ginger Thins

Yield: 96 cookies

³/₄ cup sugar
¹/₃ cup butter or regular margarine, softened
¹/₃ cup shortening
¹/₄ cup molasses
1 egg
2¹/₂ cups sifted flour
1 tablespoon ground ginger
2 teaspoons baking soda
1 teaspoon ground cinnamon
1 teaspoon ground cloves
¹/₄ teaspoon pepper

Fat-skimming options: Choose margarine instead of butter. Substitute ¹/₄ cup oil for shortening. Use ¹/₄ cup liquid egg substitute for egg. With options, exchange diets count: ¹/₂ starch.

• Beat first 5 ingredients for 2 minutes, using mixer at medium speed.
• Reduce speed to low. Add dry ingredients; beat until well mixed.
• Shape dough into 2 (12 inch) rolls; wrap in waxed paper. Place rolls in plastic bag; seal.
• Chill rolls 4 hours or until firm. (You can refrigerate up to 1 week or freeze up to 3 months.)

• **To bake:** Cut each roll into ¹/₄ inch thick slices. (Let frozen rolls stand at room temperature a few minutes for easier slicing.) Place slices 2 inches apart on ungreased baking sheets. Flatten each slice using bottom of drinking glass, greased and dipped in sugar.
• Bake in 375 degree F oven 8 to 10 minutes, or until cookies are lightly browned. Remove from baking sheets; cool on racks.

Nutrition Analysis Per Serving: As Originally Published/With Fat-Skimming Options	
Calories: 33/32	Saturated Fat: 1 g/0 g
Protein: 0 g/0 g	Cholesterol: 2 mg/0 mg
Carbohydrate: 5 g/5 g	Sodium: 33 mg/33 mg
Fat: 1 g/1 g	Dietary Fiber: 0 g/0 g

Golden Carrot Cookies

Yield: 48 cookies

¾ cup sugar
¾ cup shortening
1 egg
1¼ cups grated raw carrots
2 cups sifted flour
2 teaspoons baking powder
½ teaspoon salt
1 teaspoon vanilla
½ teaspoon lemon extract

*Fat-skimming options: Replace shortening with ⅓ cup oil and ⅓ cup nonfat sour cream.
With options, exchange diets count: ½ starch.*

• Cream together sugar and shortening until light and fluffy. Add egg; beat well. Stir in carrots.
• Sift together dry ingredients. Stir into creamed mixture. Add vanilla and lemon extract. Drop by teaspoonfuls on greased baking sheets.
• Bake in 375 degree F oven 15 minutes or until golden.

Nutrition Analysis Per Serving: As Originally Published/With Fat-Skimming Options

Calories: 62/48
Protein: 1 g/1 g
Carbohydrate: 7 g/8 g
Fat: 3 g/1 g

Saturated Fat: 1 g/0 g
Cholesterol: 4 mg/4 mg
Sodium: 24 mg/26 mg
Dietary Fiber: 0 g/0 g

Hand-Painted Lemon Butter Cookies

Yield: 72 cookies

1½ cups butter
1 cup sugar
2 eggs
1 teaspoon grated lemon rind
4½ cups sifted flour
¼ teaspoon salt
Food coloring

> *Fat-skimming options: Substitute ¾ cup soft margarine and ¾ cup nonfat sour cream for butter. Substitute ½ cup liquid egg substitute for eggs. With options, exchange diets count: 1 starch.*

• Cream together butter and sugar. Add eggs and rind; beat well. Sift together flour and salt; add gradually to creamed mixture. Chill dough 3 to 4 hours.
• Roll out on lightly floured surface ⅛ inch thick and cut in desired shapes. Place on greased baking sheet and bake at 400 degrees F for 6 to 8 minutes or until golden.
• Remove cookies from oven. Using a toothpick, twist a small hole in the top of each cookie. Cool slightly. Remove cookies from baking sheet.

• **To decorate the cookies,** pour food coloring in small saucers. Add a few drops of water. You can make many beautiful colors by mixing the basic colors. Use narrow brushes for fine lines and wider brushes for large areas. Rinse brush out in water when you change colors so that your colors will be clear and not murky. With colors of your choice, paint your own original designs on the cookies.
• To hang cookies on Christmas tree, draw narrow colored cord through the hole in each cookie.

Nutrition Analysis Per Serving: As Originally Published/With Fat-Skimming Options

Calories: 75/60	Saturated Fat: 2 g/0 g
Protein: 1 g/1 g	Cholesterol: 16 mg/6 mg
Carbohydrate: 9 g/9 g	Sodium: 48 mg/28 mg
Fat: 4 g/2 g	Dietary Fiber: 0 g/0 g

Amish Oatmeal Cookies

Yield: 54 cookies

1½ cups raisins
1 cup salted peanuts
6 cups sifted flour
3 teaspoons baking powder
1 teaspoon salt
1 teaspoon ground nutmeg
1 teaspoon ground cinnamon
1½ cups lard or shortening
3 cups sugar
2 cups quick-cooking oats
3 teaspoons baking soda
1 cup buttermilk
½ cup dark molasses
4 eggs

Fat-skimming options: Omit shortening and use low-fat margarine.
Substitute 1 cup liquid egg substitute for eggs.
With options, exchange diets count: 1 fruit, 1 starch, 1 fat.

• Grind raisins and peanuts through food grinder using medium blade; set mixture aside.
• Sift together flour, baking powder, salt, nutmeg and cinnamon into very large bowl or dishpan. Cut in lard using pastry blender or two knives until mixture forms fine crumbs. Add ground raisin mixture, sugar and quick-cooking oats; mix well, using hands if necessary.

• Dissolve baking soda in buttermilk in small bowl. Add molasses and 3 of the eggs; beat with rotary beater until blended. Add to flour mixture; mix well with spoon. Drop by heaping tablespoonfuls or small ice cream scoop, about 3 inches apart, on greased baking sheets. With floured bottom of drinking glass, flatten each to 2½ inch round.
• Beat remaining egg in bowl until blended. Brush tops of rounds with egg.
• Bake in 375 degree F oven 8 to 10 minutes or until golden brown.

Nutrition Analysis Per Serving: As Originally Published/With Fat-Skimming Options	
Calories: 208/178	Saturated Fat: 1 g/0 g
Protein: 4 g/4 g	Cholesterol: 16 mg/0 mg
Carbohydrate: 30 g/30 g	Sodium: 122 mg/174 mg
Fat: 8 g/5 g	Dietary Fiber: 1 g/1 g

Oatmeal-Fruit Cookies
Yield: 40 Cookies

1 cup sifted flour
1 teaspoon baking soda
1 cup water
$^1/_2$ cup chopped, pitted dates
$^1/_2$ cup chopped, peeled apple
$^1/_2$ cup raisins
$^1/_2$ cup regular margarine or butter
1 cup quick-cooking oats
2 eggs, beaten
1 teaspoon vanilla
$^3/_4$ cup chopped walnuts

Fat-skimming options: Reduce walnuts to $^1/_4$ cup.
With options, exchange diets count: $^1/_2$ fat, $^1/_2$ starch.

• On sheet of waxed paper, sift together flour and baking soda; set aside.
• In 2-quart saucepan over medium-high heat, bring water, dates, apple and raisins to a boil. Reduce heat to low; simmer 3 minutes. Remove from heat. Add margarine; stir until melted.
• Pour into large bowl; cool slightly.
• Stir in flour mixture, oats, beaten eggs, vanilla and chopped walnuts until well blended. Cover and refrigerate overnight.
• Drop by heaping teaspoonfuls, 2 inches apart, on greased baking sheets.
• Bake in 350 degree F oven 12 to 14 minutes. Remove from baking sheets; cool on racks. Store in refrigerator in airtight container.

Nutrition Analysis Per Serving: As Originally Published/With Fat-Skimming Options

Calories: 81/64
Protein: 2 g/1 g
Carbohydrate: 7 g/7 g
Fat: 5 g/3 g

Saturated Fat: 0 g/0 g
Cholesterol: 11 mg/11 mg
Sodium: 56 mg/56 mg
Dietary Fiber: 1 g/0.5 g

Peanut Cookie Balls
Yield: 48 cookies

⅔ cup shortening
½ cup peanut butter
½ teaspoon salt
½ cup sifted confectioners sugar
1½ teaspoons vanilla
2½ cups sifted flour
¾ cup finely chopped salted peanuts
Sifted confectioners sugar

Fat-skimming options: Replace shortening with ⅓ cup corn oil plus ⅓ cup nonfat sour cream. With options, exchange diets count: ½ starch and ½ fat.

• Cream together shortening, peanut butter and salt until mixture is light and fluffy. Gradually add ½ cup confectioners sugar. Blend in vanilla, then flour. Mix in peanuts.

• Shape dough into balls. Place 1½ inch apart on ungreased baking sheet. Bake in 375 degree F oven about 12 minutes, until golden brown. Cool 5 minutes. Roll in sifted confectioners sugar.

Nutrition Analysis Per Serving: As Originally Published/With Fat-Skimming Options

Calories: 71/62
Protein: 2 g/2 g
Carbohydrate: 7 g/7 g
Fat: 4 g/3 g

Saturated Fat: 1 g/0 g
Cholesterol: 0 mg/0 mg
Sodium: 42 mg/45 mg
Dietary Fiber: 1 g/1 g

Soft Molasses Drops

Yield: 72 cookies

³/₄ cup butter
1¹/₂ cups brown sugar
3 eggs
1 teaspoon vanilla
2 tablespoons molasses
1 teaspoon baking soda
3 cups sifted flour
1 cup raisins

> *Fat-skimming options: Replace butter with ¹/₂ cup corn or soybean oil plus ¹/₄ cup nonfat sour cream.*
> *With options, exchange diets count: 1 starch.*

• Cream butter and sugar until light and fluffy. Add eggs and vanilla; beat well.
• Combine molasses and baking soda. Add to creamed mixture. Gradually stir in flour. Add raisins.

• Drop by teaspoonfuls onto greased baking sheets. Bake at 350 degrees F for 8 minutes or until brown.

Nutrition Analysis Per Serving: As Originally Published/With Fat-Skimming Options

Calories: 79/77
Protein: 1.5 g/1.5 g
Carbohydrate: 16 g/16 g
Fat: 2 g/2 g

Saturated Fat:1.2 g/0.2 g
Cholesterol: 14 mg/9 mg
Sodium: 42 mg/24 mg
Dietary Fiber: 0 g/0 g

Breakfast Berry Pizza

Yield: 10 servings

Crust:
1 cup all-purpose flour
¼ cup powdered sugar
½ cup butter or margarine
¼ cup finely chopped walnuts

Filling:
1 cup granulated sugar, divided
1 (8 ounce) package cream cheese, softened
1 egg
1 quart mixed fresh berries, rinsed and drained*
¼ cup water
2 tablespoons cornstarch

Choose from strawberries, blackberries, raspberries, boysenberries, or blueberries. Or use one kind of berries. Or substitute 1 quart mixed sliced peaches, apricots and kiwi fruit.

> *Fat-skimming options: Use low-fat margarine. Reduce sugar to ½ cup.*
> *Use light (50% reduced fat) cream cheese. Reduce walnuts to 1 tablespoon.*
> *With options, exchange diets count: 1 starch, 1 fruit, 1 fat.*

• For crust: In medium bowl with pastry blender or 2 knives, combine crust ingredients and spread in an ungreased 12 inch pizza pan. Bake at 350 degrees F for about 10 minutes, just until lightly browned. Don't overbake.
• For filling: In medium bowl, mix ⅓ cup sugar, cream cheese and egg. Pour over slightly cooled shell and return to 250 degree F oven for 10 to 12 minutes or until filling is set. Cool.

• In food processor or blender, purée half of berries with ⅔ cup sugar.
• In medium saucepan, mix water and cornstarch. Add puréed berries and bring to boiling, stirring often, until clear bubbles appear and mixture is glossy. Cool, and spread on cooled filling.
• Arrange whole and sliced berries on purée.

Nutrition Analysis Per Serving: As Originally Published/With Fat-Skimming Options

Calories: 467/194	Saturated Fat: 12 g/1 g
Protein: 10 g/5 g	Cholesterol: 70 mg/21 mg
Carbohydrate: 42 g/30 g	Sodium: 174 mg/112 mg
Fat: 31 g/6 g	Dietary Fiber: 3 g/2 g

Crunchy Ice Cream Squares

Yield: 8 servings

1 cup firmly packed brown sugar
$\frac{1}{2}$ cup butter
$2\frac{1}{2}$ cups coarsely crushed cornflakes
$\frac{1}{2}$ cup chopped Spanish peanuts
$\frac{1}{2}$ cup flaked coconut
1 quart vanilla ice cream, softened

> *Fat-skimming options: Replace butter with $\frac{1}{4}$ cup soft margarine.*
> *Substitute low-fat vanilla frozen yogurt for ice cream. Reduce portion size to yield 12 servings.*
> *With options, exchange diets count: 2 starch, 1 fruit, 1 fat.*

• Combine brown sugar and butter in small saucepan. Heat until butter melts and sugar is dissolved. Combine with cornflakes, peanuts and coconut.
• Press half of mixture into greased 11x7x1$\frac{1}{2}$ inch baking dish. Spread with ice cream. Top with remaining cornflake mixture. Freeze until firm.

Nutrition Analysis Per Serving: As Originally Published/With Fat-Skimming Options

Calories: 433/261
Protein: 7 g/4 g
Carbohydrate: 55 g/42 g
Fat: 23 g/10 g

Saturated Fat: 12 g/4 g
Cholesterol: 40 mg/10 mg
Sodium: 380 mg/207 mg
Dietary Fiber: 0 g/0 g

Deluxe Cheesecake
Yield: 12 servings

1 cup zwieback crumbs
¼ cup melted butter
5 (8 ounce) packages cream cheese, softened
½ cup milk
6 eggs
1½ cups sugar
1½ teaspoons vanilla
¼ teaspoon salt
1¼ cups dairy sour cream
¼ cup sugar
1 teaspoon vanilla

> *Fat-skimming options: Substitute light cream cheese (50 % reduced fat), nonfat sour cream and 1½ cups liquid egg substitute. With options, exchange diets count: 2 starch, 1 skim milk, 4 fat.*

• Combine zwieback crumbs and butter; mix well. Press mixture into 9 inch spring-form pan.
• Beat together cream cheese and milk. Beat in eggs, one at a time, beating well after each addition. Gradually beat in 1½ cups sugar. Add 1½ teaspoons vanilla and salt; beat well. Pour mixture on crust.
• Bake at 350 degrees F for 1 hour 10 minutes or until set. Remove from oven. Cool 10 minutes.
• Combine sour cream, ¼ cup sugar and 1 teaspoon vanilla. Spread over top of cheesecake. Bake at 475 degrees F for 5 minutes. Cool well. Refrigerate overnight.

Nutrition Analysis Per Serving: As Originally Published/With Fat-Skimming Options

Calories: 599/428
Protein: 11 g/17 g
Carbohydrate: 38 g/46 g
Fat: 46 g/22 g

Saturated Fat: 28 g/13 g
Cholesterol: 242 mg/46 mg
Sodium: 421 mg/728 mg
Dietary Fiber: 0 g/0 g

Minty Fudge Sauce

Yield: 2¹/₃ cups or 20 (2 tablespoon) servings

3 (1 ounce) squares unsweetened chocolate
3 tablespoons butter
1¹/₃ cups sugar
1 (12 ounce) can evaporated milk
¹/₄ teaspoon peppermint extract

> *Fat-skimming options: Omit butter and use 1 tablespoon margarine.*
> *Use evaporated skim milk. With options, exchange diets, count: 1 fruit, 1 fat.*

• In 2-quart saucepan over low heat, heat chocolate and butter until melted.
• Stir in sugar until blended. Gradually stir in evaporated milk.
• Cook over medium heat, stirring constantly, until mixture comes to a boil. Boil 1 minute. Remove from heat; stir in peppermint extract.

• Pour into jars; cover and store in refrigerator (sauce will keep up to 6 weeks).
• Before serving, warm in saucepan over low heat. Serve over ice cream or cake.

Nutrition Analysis Per Serving: As Originally Published/With Fat-Skimming Options

Calories: 114/94	Saturated Fat: 3 g/1 g
Protein: 2 g/2 g	Cholesterol: 10 mg/0 mg
Carbohydrate: 16 g/17 g	Sodium: 38 mg/28 mg
Fat: 5 g/3 g	Dietary Fiber: 1 g/1 g

Orange County Rice Pudding

Yield: 6 servings

3 cups reconstituted nonfat dry milk
¹/₂ cup uncooked rice
¹/₂ cup sugar
¹/₄ teaspoon salt
¹/₂ teaspoon grated orange peel
¹/₂ teaspoon grated lemon peel
1 teaspoon vanilla
³/₄ cup creamed cottage cheese
Orange sections (optional)

Fat-skimming options: Substitute 1% cottage cheese.
With options, exchange diets count: 1 fruit, ¹/₂ starch, 1 skim milk.

• Scald milk in top of double boiler. Stir in rice, sugar and salt. Cover and cook 30 to 40 minutes, until thickened. Remove from heat and add orange and lemon peels and vanilla. Chill.

• Beat cottage cheese. Mix into chilled pudding mixture. Serve garnished with orange sections, if desired.

Nutrition Analysis Per Serving: As Originally Published/With Fat-Skimming Options

Calories: 191/184
Protein: 8 g/8 g
Carbohydrate: 35 g/35 g
Fat: 2 g/1 g

Saturated Fat: 1 g/0 g
Cholesterol: 16 mg/13 mg
Sodium: 259 mg/267 mg
Dietary Fiber: 1 g/1 g

Orange-Coconut Apple Crisp
Yield: 6 servings

6 cups sliced pared apples
2 tablespoons orange juice
$^2/_3$ cup brown sugar, packed
$^1/_3$ cup flour
$^1/_2$ teaspoon grated orange rind
$^1/_3$ cup butter or regular margarine
1 cup flaked coconut
Sweetened whipped cream (optional)

Fat-skimming options: Use $^1/_3$ cup reduced-fat margarine for butter. Reduce coconut to $^1/_3$ cup. With options, exchange diets count: 1 starch, 2 fruit, 1 fat.

• Arrange apples in 8-inch square glass baking dish. Sprinkle with orange juice.
• Combine brown sugar, flour and orange rind in small bowl. Cut in butter with pastry blender or two forks until crumbly. Add coconut and toss. Sprinkle mixture over apples.

• Microwave (high setting) 12 minutes or until apples are tender, rotating dish one-half turn after 6 minutes. Or bake at 400 degrees F for 35 to 40 minutes.
• Cool slightly. Spoon into dessert dishes. Top with whipped cream if desired.

Nutrition Analysis Per Serving: As Originally Published/With Fat-Skimming Options	
Calories: 342/259	Saturated Fat: 10 g/2 g
Protein: 1 g/1 g	Cholesterol: 28 mg/2 mg
Carbohydrate: 55 g/51 g	Sodium: 143 mg/116 mg
Fat: 15 g/7 g	Dietary Fiber: 3 g/3 g

Apple Bread Pudding
Yield: 8 to 10 servings

5 tablespoons margarine or butter, divided
2 large Granny Smith apples, peeled, cored and diced
10 slices firm-textured white bread
$\frac{1}{2}$ cup raisins
4 cups milk
4 large eggs
$\frac{1}{2}$ cup sugar
1 teaspoon ground cinnamon
$\frac{1}{4}$ teaspoon ground nutmeg
Heavy cream (optional)

> *Fat-skimming options: Use low-fat margarine and skim milk.*
> *Use 1 cup liquid egg substitute for eggs.*
> *With options, exchange diets count: 1 starch, 1 fruit, 1 lean meat, 1 fat.*

• In 10 inch skillet over medium heat, melt 2 tablespoons margarine. Add apples and sauté until tender-crisp. Remove from heat, and set aside.
• Spread bread slices on one side with remaining 3 tablespoons margarine. Cut off crusts; dice crusts.
• Line bottom of a greased 12x8x2 inch (2 quart) baking dish with bread slices, margarine-side down. Sprinkle with apples, raisins and diced crusts.
• In bowl, beat together milk, eggs, sugar, cinnamon and nutmeg. Pour over mixture in baking dish; let stand 20 minutes.
• Cover dish with foil. Bake in 325 degree F oven 30 minutes. Uncover and bake 30 minutes more, or until knife inserted in center comes out clean. Serve warm with a pour of heavy cream if desired.

Nutrition Analysis Per Serving: As Originally Published/With Fat-Skimming Options

Calories: 299/251	Saturated Fat: 5 g/3 g
Protein: 8 g/9 g	Cholesterol: 103 mg/12 mg
Carbohydrate: 38 g/38 g	Sodium: 266 mg/289 mg
Fat: 13 g/8 g	Dietary Fiber: 1.5 g/1.5 g

Baked Apples in Caramel Cream

Yield: 4 servings

¼ cup hot water
3 tablespoons packed brown sugar
4 large Rome Beauty apples
12 vanilla caramels, unwrapped
1 tablespoon lemon juice
½ cup heavy cream

Fat-skimming options: Use evaporated skim milk for cream.
With options, exchange diets count: 1½ starch, 2 fruit.

• In 9 inch square baking pan, stir together hot water and brown sugar.
• Core apples; cut peel from top half of each. Stuff each center with 3 caramels. Place in baking pan; sprinkle with lemon juice.
• Bake in 350 degree F oven 1 hour, or until apples are tender, basting with pan juices every 20 minutes.

• Lift apples, letting any caramel in centers drip into pan. Place apples in dessert dishes.
• Slowly stir cream into mixture in pan. Place pan over medium-low heat. Cook, stirring constantly, until mixture is smooth and begins to simmer.
• Remove from heat; spoon sauce over apples and serve.

Nutrition Analysis Per Serving: As Originally Published/With Fat-Skimming Options

Calories: 310/231
Protein: 1 g/3 g
Carbohydrate: 49 g/52 g
Fat: 15 g/3 g

Saturated Fat: 7 g/0 g
Cholesterol: 42 mg/1 mg
Sodium: 92 mg/117 mg
Dietary Fiber: 3 g/3 g

Snowy Glazed Apple Squares

Yield: 24 squares

2¹/₂ cups sifted flour
¹/₂ teaspoon salt
1 cup shortening
2 eggs, separated
¹/₂ cup milk
1¹/₂ cups crushed cornflakes
8 medium-size tart apples, pared and sliced (about 5 cups)
1 cup sugar
1¹/₂ teaspoons cinnamon
Glaze

*Fat-skimming options: Replace shortening with ¹/₄ cup corn
or soybean oil plus ¹/₂ cup nonfat sour cream.
With options, exchange diets count: 2 starch.*

• Combine flour and salt in bowl. Cut in shortening. In a measuring cup, beat egg yolks with enough milk to make ²/₃ cup. Add to mixture; toss lightly.
• Divide dough almost in half. Roll larger portion to fit a 15x9 inch jelly roll pan. Sprinkle with cornflakes. Spread apples over cornflakes. Combine sugar and cinnamon; sprinkle over apples.
• Roll out remaining dough. Place on top; seal edges.

• Beat whites until foamy; spread on crust. Bake at 350 degrees F for 1 hour. Cool slightly; spread with Glaze.

Glaze
1¹/₄ cups sifted confectioners sugar
3 tablespoons water
¹/₂ teaspoon vanilla

Combine confectioners sugar, water and vanilla.

Nutrition Analysis Per Serving: As Originally Published/With Fat-Skimming Options	
Calories: 219/169	Saturated Fat: 2 g/0 g
Protein: 2 g/2 g	Cholesterol: 18 mg/18 mg
Carbohydrate: 33 g/34 g	Sodium: 70 mg/76 mg
Fat: 9 g/3 g	Dietary Fiber: 1 g/1 g

Grandmom's Apricot Squares

Yield: 16 squares

1½ cups sifted flour
1½ cups quick-cooking oats
1 cup firmly packed brown sugar
¾ cup butter, softened
1 (10 ounce) jar apricot preserves (1 cup)

*Fat-skimming options: Substitute low-fat margarine for butter. Use all-fruit preserves.
With options, exchange diets count: 1 fruit, 1 starch, 1 fat.*

• Mix together flour, oats and brown sugar in bowl. Cut in butter with pastry blender or two knives until mixture is crumbly. Press two-thirds of crumb mixture in greased 8 inch square baking pan, building up sides to make a ½ inch rim.

• Spread apricot preserves over crumb layer. Sprinkle remaining crumbs on top; pat down gently.
• Bake in 350 degree F oven 35 minutes or until golden brown. Cool in pan on rack. When completely cool, cut in 2-inch squares.

Nutrition Analysis Per Serving: As Originally Published/With Fat-Skimming Options

Calories: 251/179
Protein: 2.5 g/2.5 g
Carbohydrate: 39 g/33 g
Fat: 9 g/5 g

Saturated Fat: 5 g/1 g
Cholesterol: 23 mg/0 mg
Sodium: 94 mg/103 mg
Dietary Fiber: 1 g/1 g

Creamy Orange Charlotte

Yield: 12 to 16 servings

4 medium oranges
2 (3 ounce) packages orange-flavored gelatin
2 cups boiling water
1 cup cold water
2 cups heavy cream, whipped
Sweetened whipped cream (optional)
Orange sections (optional)

> *Fat-skimming options: Use sugar-free gelatin. Use nonfat whipped topping for cream.*
> *With options, exchange diets count: ½ fruit.*

• Peel oranges with a sharp knife, removing all of white membrane. Cut into sections, catching juice in bowl. Measure juice. Add water, if necessary to make ½ cup. Dice oranges; blot with paper towels.
• Dissolve gelatin in boiling water in bowl. Stir in cold water and reserved ½ cup juice. Chill gelatin until thick and syrupy.

• Fold gelatin into whipped cream. Chill until mixture is thickened, about 10 minutes. Fold in diced oranges. Pour into 3-quart serving bowl. Chill until set. If desired, decorate with puffs of whipped cream and orange sections just before serving.

Nutrition Analysis Per Serving: As Originally Published/With Fat-Skimming Options	
Calories: 162/34	Saturated Fat: 7 g/0 g
Protein: 1 g/0 g	Cholesterol: 43 mg/5 mg
Carbohydrate: 14 g/5 g	Sodium: 40 mg/9 mg
Fat: 11 g/1 g	Dietary Fiber: 1 g/1 g

Frozen Grapes in Lemonade

Yield: 6 servings

3 cups seedless green grapes
1 (6 ounce) can frozen lemonade
Water

Fat-skimming options: none. Exchange diets count: 1 fruit.

• Wash grapes and pack in half-cup clusters in individual freezer-safe cups.

• Mix can of frozen lemonade with 1 can less water than directions specify. Pour over grapes, filling containers to 1 inch from top. Cover. Serve partially thawed.

Nutrition Analysis Per Serving: As Originally Published/With Fat-Skimming Options

Calories: 61	Saturated Fat: 0 g
Protein: 0 g	Cholesterol: 0 mg
Carbohydrate: 16 g	Sodium: 8 mg
Fat: 0 g	Dietary Fiber: 1 g

Georgia Peaches and Cream

Yield: 16 servings

2 cups all-purpose flour
³/₄ cup melted butter or margarine
1 cup chopped pecans
3 cups confectioners sugar
1 (8 ounce) package cream cheese, softened
1 (12 ounce) container whipped topping or 1¹/₂ cups whipped cream
1 cup granulated sugar
3 tablespoons cornstarch
1 cup water
1 (3 ounce) package peach-flavored gelatin
4 cups fresh peaches, peeled and sliced (or substitute 4 cups sliced strawberries)

> *Fat-skimming options: Use reduced-fat margarine.*
> *Use light (50% reduced fat) cream cheese, nonfat whipped topping, and sugar-free gelatin.*
> *With options, exchange diets count: 2 starch, 1 ¹/₂ fruit, 3 fat.*

• In medium bowl, combine flour and butter. Stir in chopped pecans. Press into 9x13 inch baking dish. Bake in 350 degree F oven about 10 minutes or until lightly browned. Cool completely. Set aside.

• Mix confectioners sugar with cream cheese until smooth. Fold in whipped topping. Spoon on top of crust, pushing sides up to make a slight well for peaches. Set aside.

• In medium pan, mix sugar and cornstarch. Over medium heat, slowly stir in water. Bring to boiling, stirring constantly, and cook 1 minute until mixture is bubbly, clear and slightly thickened. Remove from heat and stir in peach gelatin. Cook another 2 minutes. Cool 5 minutes.

• Reserving ¹/₃ cup for peaches, spoon glaze over cream mixture, leaving a 1 inch border of cream visible.

• Stir reserved glaze into peaches and spoon peaches over glaze.

• Refrigerate several hours or overnight.

Nutrition Analysis Per Serving: As Originally Published/With Fat-Skimming Options

Calories: 459/401
Protein: 4 g/4 g
Carbohydrate: 59 g/55 g
Fat: 24 g/17 g

Saturated Fat: 6 g/3 g
Cholesterol: 19 mg/5 mg
Sodium: 141 mg/177 mg
Dietary Fiber: 2 g/2 g

Lemon Cream Puffs

Yield: 36 cream puffs

1/2 cup butter
1 cup water
1 cup sifted flour
1/4 teaspoon salt
4 eggs
Lemon Filling
Lemon Glaze

Fat-skimming options: In cream puffs, substitute low-fat margarine for butter. Use 1 cup liquid egg substitute for eggs. In filling, substitute 1 cup fat-free whipped topping for heavy cream. With options, exchange diets count: 1/2 starch, 1/2 fat.

• Heat butter and water in saucepan over medium heat until water boils and butter melts, stirring occasionally. Reduce heat to low. Add flour and salt, stirring vigorously until mixture forms a ball. Remove from heat. Let stand 5 minutes. Add eggs, one at a time, beating well after each addition. Drop by teaspoonfuls, 2 inches apart, on greased baking sheets.
• Bake in 400 degree F oven 25 minutes or until golden. Remove from baking sheets; cool on racks.
• Prepare Lemon Filling. Slice tops off cream puffs. Fill with Lemon Filling. Replace tops.
• Prepare Lemon Glaze. Drizzle Lemon Glaze over cream puffs. Store in refrigerator until serving.

Lemon Filling

1 (3 1/8 ounce) package vanilla pudding mix
1 1/2 cups milk
2 teaspoons grated lemon rind
1 tablespoon lemon juice
1/2 cup heavy cream, whipped

• Combine pudding mix and milk in saucepan. Cook over medium heat, stirring constantly, until mixture boils. Remove from heat. Stir in lemon rind and lemon juice. Cool completely.
• Fold in whipped cream.

Lemon Glaze

1 cup sifted confectioners sugar
4 teaspoons lemon juice
1 drop yellow food coloring

• Combine confectioners sugar, lemon juice and food coloring. Beat until smooth.

Nutrition Analysis Per Serving: As Originally Published/With Fat-Skimming Options

Calories: 85/61
Protein: 1 g/1 g
Carbohydrate: 9 g/10 g
Fat: 5 g/2 g

Saturated Fat: 2 g/0 g
Cholesterol: 36 mg/0 mg
Sodium: 95 mg/97 mg
Dietary Fiber: 0 g/0 g

Pear Melba

Yield: 12 servings

3 (29 ounce) cans pear halves
3 (10 ounce) packages frozen raspberries, thawed
1 cup heavy cream
¼ cup sugar
1 teaspoon vanilla

Fat-skimming options: Substitute 2 cups fat-free whipped topping for heavy cream, sugar and vanilla. With options, exchange diets count: 2½ fruit.

• **The day before:** Chill pears.
• **Just before serving:** Drain pears and arrange 2 halves in each dessert dish. Spoon raspberries and some of the juice over pears.

• Whip cream with sugar and vanilla until soft peaks form. Spoon over fruit.

Nutrition Analysis Per Serving: As Originally Published/With Fat-Skimming Options

Calories: 231/165
Protein: 1 g/1 g
Carbohydrate: 43 g/42 g
Fat: 8 g/0 g

Saturated Fat: 5 g/0 g
Cholesterol: 28 mg/0 mg
Sodium: 13 mg/5 mg
Dietary Fiber: 0 g/0 g

Raspberry Cheese Cups

Yield: 12 servings

11 ounces cream cheese
2 tablespoons margarine or butter
1 teaspoon vanilla
$^1/_2$ cup sugar
2 tablespoons cornstarch
2 large eggs
$^1/_2$ cup heavy cream
1 tablespoon lemon juice
$^1/_4$ cup raspberry jam
Raspberries and mint leaves for garnish (optional)

> *Fat-skimming options: Use light (50% reduced fat) cream cheese.*
> *Use $^1/_2$ cup liquid egg substitute for eggs. Substitute evaporated skim milk for cream.*
> *With options, exchange diets count: $^1/_2$ starch, $^1/_2$ skim milk, 1 fat.*

• Oil 12 (2 to 2$^1/_2$ ounce) deep individual molds or fluted muffin-pan cups. (Regular muffin-pan cups may be used but, because they are shallower, the jam may show through the tops of the cheese cups after baking.) Set aside.
• In bowl using mixer at medium speed, beat cream cheese, margarine and vanilla 2 minutes. Add sugar; beat 2 minutes. Blend in cornstarch.
• Add eggs, one at a time, beating well after each addition. Add cream and lemon juice; beat 1 minute.

• Fill molds almost to the top with batter. Spoon 1 teaspoon jam on top of batter in each mold. Gently press down jam until *partially* covered with batter.
• Place molds in shallow roasting pan on oven rack. Pour $^1/_2$ inch boiling water into pan around molds.
• Bake in 350 degree F oven 20 minutes or until set. Remove molds from pan; cool on rack 10 minutes. Loosen edges of cheese cups and unmold onto plastic-wrap-lined baking sheet. Cover and refrigerate. Serve cold, garnished with raspberries and mint leaves.

Nutrition Analysis Per Serving: As Originally Published/With Fat-Skimming Options

Calories: 210/133	Saturated Fat: 9 g/3 g
Protein: 3 g/5 g	Cholesterol: 78 mg/10 mg
Carbohydrate: 15 g/15 g	Sodium: 0 mg/0 mg
Fat: 15 g/7 g	Dietary Fiber: 109 g/200 g

Rhubarb Crunch

Yield: 9 servings

4 cups diced (¹/₂ inch) rhubarb
1 cup packed brown sugar
³/₄ cup flour
³/₄ cup quick-cooking oats
1 teaspoon ground cinnamon
¹/₂ cup butter or regular margarine
Vanilla ice cream (optional)

*Fat-skimming options: Subsitute ¹/₃ cup low-fat margarine for butter.
Serve with nonfat ice milk. With options, exchange diets count: 2 starch, 1¹/₂ fruit, 1 fat.*

• In greased 9x9x2 inch baking pan, place rhubarb; set aside.
• In bowl, stir together brown sugar, flour, oats and cinnamon. Using pastry blender, cut in butter until mixture is crumbly. Sprinkle crumb mixture over rhubarb.

• Bake in 375 degree F oven 50 minutes, or until rhubarb is tender and mixture is bubbly around edges. Cool on rack 10 minutes. Serve warm with ice cream, if desired.

Nutrition Analysis Per Serving: As Originally Published/With Fat-Skimming Options

Calories: 390/295
Protein: 5 g/6 g
Carbohydrate: 54 g/55 g
Fat: 18 g/7 g

Saturated Fat: 11 g/3 g
Cholesterol: 57 mg/10 mg
Sodium: 169 mg/113 mg
Dietary Fiber: 1 g/1 g

Sparkling Fruit Cup

Yield: 8 servings

2 (11 ounce) cans mandarin oranges, drained
1 (1 pound 13½ ounce) can pineapple chunks, drained
2 tablespoons lemon juice
½ teaspoon vanilla
1 quart chilled ginger ale

Fat-skimming options: Substitute sugar-free ginger ale or lemon-lime soft drink for ginger ale. With options, exchange diets count: 1½ fruit.

• Combine first 4 ingredients. Cover and refrigerate overnight.
• To serve, place in individual serving dishes. Pour on ginger ale.

Nutrition Analysis Per Serving: As Originally Published/With Fat-Skimming Options

Calories: 144/98
Protein: 1 g/1 g
Carbohydrate: 37 g/25 g
Fat: 0 g/0 g

Saturated Fat: 0 g/0 g
Cholesterol: 0 mg/0 mg
Sodium: 11 mg/2 mg
Dietary Fiber: 2 g/2 g

Strawberries and Cream Spectacular

Yield: 12 servings

1 (18 ounce) package yellow cake mix
1 tablespoon grated orange rind
2 pints strawberries, hulled
2 cups heavy cream
1/4 cup sugar
1 teaspoon vanilla
3/4 cup red currant jelly

Fat-skimming options: Use reduced-fat cake mix and substitute 4 cups nonfat whipped topping for cream. Omit sugar and vanilla. With options, exchange diets count: 2 starch, 2 fruit.

• Prepare yellow cake mix according to package directions, adding orange rind to batter. Bake in 2 greased 9-inch round cake pans as package directs. Cool well.
• Chop enough strawberries to make 1 cup; reserve remaining berries.
• Whip cream until it begins to thicken. Gradually beat in sugar; blend in vanilla. Beat until soft peaks form. Remove 1 cup cream; refrigerate remaining whipped cream. Fold 1 cup strawberries into 1 cup whipped cream.
• Place one cake layer, top-side down, on serving plate. Spread with strawberry-cream filling. Top with other cake layer, top-side up.
• Slice remaining strawberries. Arrange on top of cake, starting at outer edge. (Place berries with point along edge of cake.) After first circle of berries is completed, continue placing berries in this manner until top is covered. Refrigerate 10 minutes.
• Melt currant jelly in small saucepan over low heat, stirring constantly. Carefully spoon or brush jelly over strawberries.
• Spread whipped cream on sides of cake. Using rosette tip No. 190, pipe rosettes between strawberry points along top edge of cake. Fill in spaces with star tip No. 24. Pipe border along bottom edge of cake, using tip No. 71. If you do not wish to use tips, spoon remaining cream in small puffs between strawberries. Refrigerate until serving time.
• **Note:** Cake is best served same day.

Nutrition Analysis Per Serving: As Originally Published/With Fat-Skimming Options

Calories: 424/273
Protein: 4 g/33 g
Carbohydrate: 57 g/60 g
Fat: 21 g/2 g

Saturated Fat: 10 g/0 g
Cholesterol: 93 mg/0 mg
Sodium: 323 mg/318 mg
Dietary Fiber: 1.5 g/1.5 g

Apple Pie
Yield: 8 servings

Pie Shell
1 (6 ounce) can frozen, unsweetened apple juice concentrate, thawed
2 tablespoons flour
1 teaspoon ground cinnamon
6 cups sliced, peeled apples

Fat-skimming options: In shell, use reduced-fat margarine.
With options, exchange diets count: 1 starch, 1½ fruit, ½ fat.

• Prepare Pie Shell; set aside.
• In jar with tight-fitting lid, shake apple juice concentrate, flour and cinnamon until well blended. Pour into 3-quart saucepan.
• Cook over medium-high heat, stirring constantly, until mixture boils and thickens. Remove from heat.
• Add apples to hot mixture; stir until well coated. Spoon into prepared shell.
• Bake in 450 degree F oven 15 minutes. Reduce heat to 350 degrees F and bake 35 minutes, or until apples are tender. (If pie browns too quickly, cover with foil during last 15 minutes of baking.) Cool on rack.

Pie Shell
1 cup sifted flour
¼ teaspoon salt
⅓ cup regular margarine
2 to 3 tablespoons ice water

• In medium bowl combine flour and salt. Using pastry blender, cut in margarine until coarse crumbs form.
• Sprinkle ice water over crumb mixture a little at a time, tossing with fork until dough forms. Press firmly into a ball.
• On floured surface, roll out dough to 13 inch circle; fit loosely into 9 inch pie plate. Trim edge of dough to 1 inch beyond rim of pie plate. Fold under edge and form ridge. Flute ridge.

Nutrition Analysis Per Serving: As Originally Published/With Fat-Skimming Options

Calories: 222/191
Protein: 2 g/2 g
Carbohydrate: 38 g/38 g
Fat: 7 g/4 g

Saturated Fat: 1 g/1 g
Cholesterol: 0 mg/0 mg
Sodium: 139 mg/142 mg
Dietary Fiber: 3 g/3 g

French Apple Pie

Yield: 8 servings

1 unbaked 9 inch pie shell
7 cups sliced, pared apples
²/₃ cup sugar
¹/₂ teaspoon ground cinnamon
1¹/₂ tablespoons butter
Topping

Fat-skimming options: Omit butter and use ¹/₄ cup soft margarine in topping.
With options, exchange diets count: 2 starch, 2¹/₂ fruit, 2 fat.

• Combine apples, sugar and cinnamon. Turn into pie shell. Dot with butter; sprinkle with Topping. Bake in 400 degree F oven 50 minutes or until apples are tender.

Topping for French Apple Pie

1 cup flour
¹/₂ cup firmly packed brown sugar
¹/₄ teaspoon ground cinnamon
¹/₂ cup butter

• Combine flour, sugar and cinnamon. Cut in ¹/₂ cup butter until crumbly.

Nutrition Analysis Per Serving: As Originally Published/With Fat-Skimming Options

Calories: 461/402
Protein: 3 g/3 g
Carbohydrate: 72 g/72 g
Fat: 19 g/12 g

Saturated Fat: 9 g/3 g
Cholesterol: 33 mg/0 mg
Sodium: 277 mg/205 mg
Dietary Fiber: 1 g/1 g

Cranberry-Raspberry Pie

Yield: 6 to 8 servings

2 cups fresh or frozen cranberries, chopped
1 (10 ounce) package frozen raspberries, thawed
1¹/₂ cups sugar
¹/₄ teaspoon salt
2 tablespoons quick-cooking tapioca
¹/₄ teaspoon almond extract
Almond Pastry for Pie
1 tablespoon butter

Fat-skimming options: Reduce sugar to 1 cup. In pastry, omit shortening and substitute ¹/₂ cup soft margarine. With options, exchange diets count: 2 starch, 2¹/₂ fruit, 2 fat.

• Combine cranberries, raspberries, sugar, salt, tapioca and almond extract; mix well.
• Prepare Almond Pastry.
• Spoon cranberry mixture into pastry-lined pie plate. Dot with butter. Roll out remaining dough; cut into ¹/₂ inch strips. Crisscross over filling making lattice top. Trim strips even with pie edge. Turn bottom crust over ends of strips; seal. Flute edge.
• Bake in 425 degree F oven 10 minutes. Reduce to 350 degrees F; bake 40 minutes or until crust is brown and filling is bubbly.

Almond Pastry for Pie

2¹/₄ cups sifted flour
1 teaspoon salt
1 tablespoon sugar
³/₄ cup shortening
1 egg yolk
2 teaspoons almond extract
¹/₄ cup water

• Sift together flour, salt and sugar. Cut in shortening until mixture resembles fine crumbs.
• Beat together egg yolk, almond extract and water; sprinkle over flour mixture. Toss with fork to make a soft dough.
• Divide dough in half. Roll half of dough into 13 inch circle on lightly floured surface. Line 9 inch pie plate with dough.

Nutrition Analysis Per Serving: As Originally Published/With Fat-Skimming Options

Calories: 520/402	Saturated Fat: 5 g/3 g
Protein: 4 g/4 g	Cholesterol: 31 mg/31 mg
Carbohydrate: 79 g/67 g	Sodium: 350 mg/455 mg
Fat: 22 g/14 g	Dietary Fiber: 1 g/1 g

Door County Cherry Pie

Yield: 8 servings

1³⁄₄ cup all-purpose flour, divided
Scant teaspoon salt
¹⁄₂ cup lard
4 to 6 tablespoons ice water
1 cup granulated sugar
5 cups fresh tart red cherries, pitted, or 2 (16 ounce) cans tart red cherries in water, drained
2 teaspoons Kirsch or 2 drops almond extract
1 teaspoon grated lemon rind
1 tablespoon butter or margarine

> *Fat-skimming options: Substitute ¹⁄₂ cup reduced-fat margarine for lard.
> With options, exchange diets count: 3 fruit, 1 starch, 1 fat.*

• In small bowl, place 1¹⁄₂ cups flour and ³⁄₄ teaspoon salt. Cut in half of lard. Add remaining lard and cut in again with pastry blender.
• Sprinkle dough with water, mixing lightly with fork until it just holds together. Chill at least 20 minutes.
• On lightly floured surface, roll out two-thirds of pastry to a generous 12 inch circle, reserving remaining pastry. Line 9 inch pie plate with rolled pastry. Trim edge to ¹⁄₂ inch beyond rim of pie plate.

• In bowl, combine sugar, remaining ¹⁄₄ cup flour and ¹⁄₈ teaspoon salt. Stir in cherries, flavoring and lemon rind. Pour filling into lined pie plate. Dot with butter
• Roll remaining pastry and cut into strips for lattice crust. Arrange over filling and flute pastry edge to seal.
• Bake at 450 degrees F for 10 minutes; then reduce heat to 350 degrees F and bake 30 to 35 minutes longer or until crust is golden brown and filling is bubbly.

Nutrition Analysis Per Serving: As Originally Published/With Fat-Skimming Options

Calories: 362/296
Protein: 2 g/2 g
Carbohydrate: 58 g/58 g
Fat: 14 g/8 g

Saturated Fat: 6 g/2 g
Cholesterol: 16 mg/4 mg
Sodium: 291 mg/421 mg
Dietary Fiber: 0 g/0 g

Fresh Pumpkin Pie

Yield: 8 servings

1 (12 ounce) can evaporated milk
2 eggs
1 cup firmly packed brown sugar
$^1/_2$ teaspoon salt
1 teaspoon ground cinnamon
$^1/_2$ teaspoon ground ginger
$^1/_4$ teaspoon ground cloves
$2^1/_4$ cups fresh mashed pumpkin*
1 unbaked 9 inch pie shell
Whipped cream (optional)

2 cups fresh, mashed pumpkin = 1 (16 ounce) can pumpkin

Fat-skimming options: Use evaporated skim milk. Use $^1/_2$ cup liquid egg substitute for eggs.
With options, exchange diets count: $1^1/_2$ fruit, 1 starch, $^1/_2$ skim milk, 1 fat.

• In blender, combine first 7 ingredients. Mix for a few seconds.
• Drop in pumpkin and blend until smooth.
• Pour into unbaked pie shell.
• Bake at 375 degrees F for about 1 hour or until center is set and crust is golden.
• Serve with whipped cream, if desired.

Nutrition Analysis Per Serving: As Originally Published/With Fat-Skimming Options

Calories: 280/249
Protein: 6 g/6 g
Carbohydrate: 43 g/43 g
Fat: 10 g/6 g

Saturated Fat: 4 g/2 g
Cholesterol: 67 mg/1 mg
Sodium: 312 mg/330 mg
Dietary Fiber: 0 g/0 g

Pumpkin Pie Squares

Yield: 24 squares

1 cup sifted flour
½ cup quick-cooking oats
½ cup firmly packed brown sugar
½ cup butter
1 (1 pound) can pumpkin (2 cups)
1 (13½ ounce) can evaporated milk
2 eggs
¾ cup sugar
½ teaspoon salt
1 teaspoon ground cinnamon
½ teaspoon ground ginger
¼ teaspoon ground cloves
½ cup chopped pecans
½ cup firmly packed brown sugar
2 tablespoons butter

> *Fat-skimming options: Substitute low-fat margarine for butter, evaporated skim milk for evaporated milk, and ½ cup liquid egg substitute for eggs. Reduced pecans to ¼ cup. With options, exchange diets count: 1 fruit, 1 starch.*

• Combine flour, oats, ½ cup brown sugar and ½ cup butter in mixing bowl. Mix until crumbly, using electric mixer on low speed. Press into ungreased 13x9x2 inch pan. Bake at 350 degrees F for 15 minutes.
• Combine pumpkin, evaporated milk, eggs, sugar, salt and spices in mixing bowl; beat well. Pour into crust. Bake at 350 degrees F 20 minutes.

• Combine pecans, ½ cup brown sugar and 2 tablespoons butter; sprinkle over pumpkin filling. Return to oven and bake 15 to 20 minutes or until filling is set. Cool in pan and cut in 2-inch squares.

Nutrition Analysis Per Serving: As Originally Published/With Fat-Skimming Options	
Calories: 195/142	Saturated Fat: 4 g/1 g
Protein: 3 g/4 g	Cholesterol: 36 mg/18 mg
Carbohydrate: 25 g/24 g	Sodium: 122 mg/105 mg
Fat: 10 g/4 g	Dietary Fiber: 1 g/1 g

Rhubarb Surprise Pie

Yield: 8 servings

1 cup sifted flour
1 teaspoon baking powder
¹/₂ teaspoon salt
2 tablespoons butter
1 egg, beaten
2 tablespoons milk
3 cups diced raw rhubarb
1 (3 ounce) package strawberry-flavored gelatin
¹/₂ cup unsifted flour
1 cup sugar
¹/₂ teaspoon cinnamon
¹/₄ cup melted butter

*Fat-skimming options: Replace butter with 1 tablespoon soft margarine.
Substitute sugar-free strawberry gelatin. With options, exchange diets count: 2 starch, 1 fruit.*

• Sift together 1 cup flour, baking powder and salt. Cut in butter. Add egg and milk; mix. Press into a greased 9 inch pie plate.

• Arrange rhubarb in pie shell. Sprinkle with gelatin. Combine remaining ingredients; sprinkle on top of pie. Bake at 350 degrees F for 50 minutes or until rhubarb is tender.

Nutrition Analysis Per Serving: As Originally Published/With Fat-Skimming Options

Calories: 299/210
Protein: 5 g/4 g
Carbohydrate: 55 g/45 g
Fat: 7 g/2 g

Saturated Fat: 4 g/1 g
Cholesterol: 44 mg/29 mg
Sodium: 237 mg/154 mg
Dietary Fiber: 1 g/1 g

Glazed Strawberry Cream Pie

Yield: 6 to 8 servings

1¼ cups sifted flour
¼ cup sugar
½ cup butter, softened
3 cups sliced strawberries
1½ cups sifted confectioners sugar, divided
2 (3 ounce) packages cream cheese, softened
1 teaspoon vanilla
1 cup heavy cream, whipped
2 teaspoons cornstarch
3 drops red food coloring
1 drop yellow food coloring

> *Fat-skimming options: Substitute low-fat margarine and light (50% reduced fat) cream cheese.*
> *Substitute 2 cups nonfat whipped topping for heavy cream.*
> *With options, exchange diets count: 1½ starch, 2 fruit, 1½ fat.*

• Combine flour and sugar. Cut in butter with pastry blender until crumbly. Mix with hands until dough forms. Press into 9 inch pie plate.
• Bake in 325 degree F oven 25 minutes or until golden brown. Cool well.
• Combine berries and ½ cup confectioners sugar; let stand 30 minutes.
• Meanwhile, cream together cream cheese and remaining 1 cup confectioners sugar until fluffy. Blend in vanilla. Fold in whipped cream. Turn into pie shell. Refrigerate.

• Drain strawberries; reserve juice. Add enough water to juice to make ⅓ cup. Combine cornstarch, ⅓ cup juice and food coloring in small saucepan. Cook, stirring constantly, until thick and clear. Cool slightly.
• Combine sauce with strawberries; mix gently. Spoon over filling. Cover; chill at least 2 hours.

Nutrition Analysis Per Serving: As Originally Published/With Fat-Skimming Options

Calories: 482/312
Protein: 5 g/5 g
Carbohydrate: 50 g/53 g
Fat: 30 g/10 g

Saturated Fat: 19 g/3 g
Cholesterol: 96 mg/8 mg
Sodium: 194 mg/232 mg
Dietary Fiber: 2 g/2 g

CHAPTER FOUR

EGGS, CHEESE AND LEGUMES

Those naughty boys!

Living on what might as well have been Old McDonald's Farm just off Whiskey Point in Little Grant Township, Wis., Marie Cull tended chickens, pigs, cows and a big garden. On those afternoons when she got her work done early, she would clean up to go to town and leave strict orders for her three sons to candle the eggs before she returned. They hated the tedious job! As the clock struck three, they would run out to the old limestone building next to the chicken coop and hastily whip the eggs through the light, hardly noticing embryos or spots. Marie's double-check of their work later led to some scolding.

Most of the eggs found their way to the family's breakfast: eggs fried over easy, bacon, fried potatoes, homemade toast and jam, cookies and loads of coffee. Whatever eggs were left over went into rich custards, puddings, macaroni salad and her son John's favorite, deviled eggs. This chapter features an Easter classic, Curried Creamed Eggs, along with dishes for Sunday brunch like Broccoli and Cheese Strata and Crustless Bacon Quiche.

Broccoli and Cheese Strata

Yield: 12 servings

12 slices firm white bread
¼ cup butter
3 cups sharp Cheddar cheese, shredded
1½ cups cooked, chopped broccoli
2 cups diced cooked chicken
6 eggs, slightly beaten
3½ cups milk
2 tablespoons minced onion
½ teaspoon salt
¼ teaspoon dry mustard

Fat-skimming options: Omit butter. Use reduced-fat Cheddar cheese and skim milk.
Use 1½ cups liquid egg substitute for eggs.
With options, exchange diets count: 4 lean meat, 1 starch, 1 vegetable, ½ fat.

• Spread one side of each slice of bread with butter. Using a doughnut cutter, cut bread slices into rings; set aside rings. Use bread scraps to line the bottom of a 13x9x2 inch baking dish.
• Sprinkle 2¾ cups of the cheese on top of the bread. Add the broccoli, then the chicken. Arrange bread rings, buttered side up, on top.

• Combine next 5 ingredients in bowl, and mix well. Pour egg mixture over chicken in baking dish. Cover and refrigerate overnight.
• Bake uncovered in 325 degree F oven for 50 minutes, or until hot and bubbly.
• Sprinkle with remaining ¼ cup cheese. Bake 5 minutes more, or until cheese melts. Let stand 10 minutes.

Nutrition Analysis Per Serving: As Originally Published/With Fat-Skimming Options

Calories: 480/357
Protein: 31 g/35 g
Carbohydrate: 18 g/19 g
Fat: 32 g/16 g

Saturated Fat: 17 g/8 g
Cholesterol: 208 mg/68 mg
Sodium: 709 mg/783 mg
Dietary Fiber: 1 g/1 g

Carrot Quiche

Yield: 6 to 8 servings.

1 portion pastry for single-crust pie
1 cup shredded Swiss cheese
2½ cups sliced carrots, cooked and drained
1 medium onion, chopped
1 tablespoon butter or margarine
¾ cup milk
3 large eggs
¼ teaspoon ground nutmeg
¼ teaspoons salt
⅛ teaspoons pepper

Fat-skimming options: Substitute reduced-fat Swiss cheese and skim milk.
Use ¾ cup liquid egg substitute for eggs.
With options, exchange diets count: 1 vegetable, 1 starch, 1 lean meat, 2 fat.

• Roll out pastry to a 12 inch circle. Fit into a 10 inch quiche pan and trim edge, or fit into a 9 inch pie plate and flute edge. Sprinkle cheese and then carrots in pastry-lined pan. Set aside.
• Sauté onion in butter until tender. Pour into bowl. Add milk and remaining ingredients; beat until blended. Slowly pour milk mixture over carrots and cheese in pan.

• Bake in 425 degree F oven 10 minutes. Reduce temperature to 325 degrees F and bake 30 minutes more or until set. Serve quiche warm.

Nutrition Analysis Per Serving: As Originally Published/With Fat-Skimming Options

Calories: 274/246
Protein: 10 g/10 g
Carbohydrate: 18 g/18 g
Fat: 18 g/13 g

Saturated Fat: 7 g/4 g
Cholesterol: 114 mg/1 mg
Sodium: 347 mg/410 mg
Dietary Fiber: 2 g/2 g

Crustless Bacon Quiche

Yield: 6 servings

8 strips bacon, diced
3 eggs
1½ cups milk
½ cup buttermilk baking mix
½ cup butter, melted
Dash of pepper
1 cup shredded Cheddar cheese

Fat-skimming options: Use ¾ cup liquid egg substitute for eggs. Use skim milk, reduced-fat baking mix and reduced-fat Cheddar cheese. Omit butter and substitute ¼ cup low-fat margarine. With options, exchange diets count: 3 lean meat, 1 starch, 2 fat.

• Fry bacon in 10 inch skillet over medium heat until crisp. Remove bacon; drain on paper towels.
• Combine eggs, milk, baking mix, melted butter and pepper in blender. Cover and blend 15 seconds or until well mixed.

• Pour mixture into greased 9 inch glass pie plate. Sprinkle with bacon and cheese. Gently press bacon and cheese below the surface, using the back of a spoon.
• Bake in 350 degree F oven 30 minutes or until knife inserted halfway between center and edge comes out clean. Let stand 10 minutes before serving.

Nutrition Analysis Per Serving: As Originally Published/With Fat-Skimming Options

Calories: 450/327
Protein: 18 g/22 g
Carbohydrate: 10 g/11 g
Fat: 37 g/19 g

Saturated Fat: 21 g/5 g
Cholesterol: 200 mg/81 mg
Sodium: 714 mg/797 mg
Dietary Fiber: 0 g/0 g

Miniature Quiches

Yield: 24 servings

Pastry for 2-crust 9 inch pie
8 strips bacon, diced
$\frac{1}{2}$ cup chopped onion
$1\frac{1}{2}$ cups shredded Swiss cheese
$\frac{1}{4}$ cup grated Parmesan cheese
4 eggs
$1\frac{3}{4}$ cups milk
1 teaspoon Worcestershire sauce
3 drops Tabasco sauce
Ground nutmeg

Fat-skimming options: Use reduced-fat Swiss cheese and skim milk.
Use 1 cup liquid egg substitute for whole eggs.
With options, exchange diets count: 1 lean meat, $\frac{1}{2}$ starch, $1\frac{1}{2}$ fat.

• Divide pastry in half. Roll out, one half at a time, on floured surface to $\frac{1}{8}$ inch thickness. Cut 12 rounds from each half, using floured $3\frac{1}{2}$ inch cookie cutter with scalloped edge. Reroll pastry as necessary. Line 3 inch muffin-pan cups with rounds. Set aside.
• Sauté bacon and onion in 10 inch skillet until browned. Drain on paper towels.
• Toss together bacon mixture, Swiss cheese and Parmesan cheese. Place 1 rounded tablespoon of cheese mixture in each prepared shell.

• Beat together eggs, milk, Worcestershire sauce and Tabasco sauce until blended. Spoon 2 tablespoons mixture into each shell. Sprinkle with nutmeg.
• Bake in 425 degree F oven 20 minutes or until set. Cool in pans on racks 5 minutes. Remove from pans and serve immediately; or cool completely, wrap in foil and store in refrigerator.
• To reheat, place on baking sheets and bake in 350 degree F oven 10 minutes.

Nutrition Analysis Per Serving: As Originally Published/With Fat-Skimming Options	
Calories: 173/158	Saturated Fat: 5 g/3 g
Protein: 8 g/9 g	Cholesterol: 52 mg/13 mg
Carbohydrate: 9 g/9 g	Sodium: 193 mg/199 mg
Fat: 12 g/9 g	Dietary Fiber: 0 g/0 g

Curried Creamed Eggs

Yield: 6 servings

12 strips bacon
3 tablespoons butter
1/4 cup finely chopped onion
1/4 cup finely chopped celery
1/4 cup finely chopped green pepper
5 tablespoons flour
1 teaspoon curry powder
1/16 teaspoon pepper
1 1/4 cups milk
1 (13 3/4 ounce) can chicken broth
6 hard-cooked eggs, sliced
9 slices bread, toasted and cut in half diagonally

Fat-skimming options: Reduce bacon to 6 strips. Use skim milk. Reduce eggs to 3.
With options, exchange diets count: 1 1/2 lean meat, 2 starch, 1 fat.

• Fry bacon in 12 inch skillet over medium heat until crisp. Remove bacon; drain on paper towels. Pour off all but 3 tablespoons bacon drippings. Add butter to skillet. Heat over medium heat until melted. Add onion, celery and green pepper. Sauté 8 minutes or until tender.

• Stir flour, curry powder and pepper into skillet. Cook, stirring constantly, 1 minute. Gradually stir milk and chicken broth into flour mixture. Cook, stirring constantly, until mixture boils, about 7 minutes. Cook 1 minute more. Stir in hard-cooked eggs. Cook 2 minutes more or until eggs are hot.
• For each serving, arrange 3 toasted bread halves on plate. Place 2 strips bacon on toast. Spoon 2/3 cup egg mixture over all.

Nutrition Analysis Per Serving: As Originally Published/With Fat-Skimming Options

Calories: 360/278
Protein: 16 g/11 g
Carbohydrate: 28 g/27 g
Fat: 20 g/14 g

Saturated Fat: 8 g/6 g
Cholesterol: 243 mg/128 mg
Sodium: 775 mg/644 mg
Dietary Fiber: 1.5 g/1.5 g

Potato-Bacon Omelet

Yield: 4 servings

6 slices bacon
1 cup diced, pared potatoes
2 tablespoons chopped onion
$3/4$ teaspoon salt, divided
2 tablespoons chopped parsley
1 tablespoon chopped pimiento
1 tablespoon oil
8 eggs, well beaten
1 tablespoon water
$1/8$ teaspoon pepper

> *Fat-skimming options: Substitute $1/4$ cup diced lean ham for the bacon. Use nonstick cooking spray instead of bacon fat for browning potatoes. Use 2 cups liquid egg substitute for eggs.*
> *With options, exchange diets count: 2 lean meat, 1 starch.*

• Fry bacon until crisp; drain and crumble. Reserve 2 tablespoons bacon fat. Add potato, onion and $1/4$ teaspoon salt; cook until potatoes are tender and golden. Stir in parsley, bacon and pimiento; set aside.

• Heat oil in 10 inch skillet over medium heat. Beat together eggs, water, $1/2$ teaspoon salt and the pepper. Stir in vegetable mixture; pour into skillet. With fork, lift cooked edges so uncooked portion flows underneath. Slide pan back and forth to avoid sticking. Cook until mixture is set, but top is creamy. Fold in half and slide onto serving platter.

Nutrition Analysis Per Serving: As Originally Published/With Fat-Skimming Options

Calories: 265/177
Protein: 16 g/17 g
Carbohydrate: 8 g/7 g
Fat: 18 g/8 g

Saturated Fat: 5 g/1 g
Cholesterol: 434 mg/5 mg
Sodium: 679 mg/720 mg
Dietary Fiber: 0.5 g/0.5 g

Potato-Ham Frittata

Yield: 6 to 8 servings

2 tablespoons butter or margarine
1 cup cooked, cubed potatoes
1 small onion, chopped
5 beaten eggs or equivalent egg substitute
$^1/_2$ cup half and half or milk
$^1/_4$ teaspoon salt
Dash pepper
1 cup cubed ham
$^1/_4$ cup Parmesan cheese
1 tablespoon minced fresh parsley
Parmesan cheese and minced fresh parsley for garnish

Fat-skimming options: Omit butter and substitute 1 tablespoon corn oil, using $^1/_2$ teaspoon to cook potatoes and $^1/_2$ teaspoon to cook eggs. Use 1$^1/_4$ cup liquid egg substitute for eggs. Use evaporated skim milk for half and half. With options, exchange diets count: 2 lean meat, $^1/_2$ starch.

• In large ovenproof skillet, heat 1 tablespoon butter. Add potatoes and onion and cook until potatoes are lightly browned and onions are translucent. Remove from heat.
• In medium bowl, combine eggs, cream, salt and pepper. Stir in potato mixture, ham, cheese and parsley.

• Heat remaining 1 tablespoon butter in skillet. Pour in egg mixture and cook slowly over low heat. Lift bottom gently to allow egg mixture to run to bottom. Cook until bottom is brown and set. To finish, heat in 400 degree F oven about 2 minutes.
• Loosen with spatula. Invert plate over pan and turn frittata onto plate. Sprinkle with Parmesan cheese and parsley.

Nutrition Analysis Per Serving: As Originally Published/With Fat-Skimming Options

Calories: 163/144
Protein: 13 g/14 g
Carbohydrate: 6 g/7 g
Fat: 10 g/6 g

Saturated Fat: 4 g/2 g
Cholesterol: 157 mg/16 mg
Sodium: 531 mg/543 mg
Dietary Fiber: 0.5 g/0.5 g

Ranch-Style Eggs

Yield: 4 servings

1 (8 ounce) can tomato sauce
¾ teaspoon chili powder
4 drops hot pepper sauce
4 large eggs
1 tablespoon vegetable oil
4 (6 inch) corn tortillas
¼ cup shredded sharp Cheddar cheese
¼ cup dairy sour half and half
4 pickled jalapeños, sliced

> *Fat-skimming options: Use 1 cup liquid egg substitute for eggs.*
> *Use reduced-fat Cheddar cheese and nonfat sour cream.*
> *With options, exchange diets count: 2 lean meat, 1 starch, 1 vegetable.*

• Mix together first 3 ingredients; pour into greased 9 inch pie plate or divide among 4 greased 10 ounce custard cups.
• Carefully break eggs onto tomato sauce, arranging evenly in pie plate, or break one egg into each custard cup.
• Bake in 350 degree F oven about 20 minutes, or until eggs are set.

• While eggs are baking, heat oil in small skillet over medium heat. Cook tortillas, one at a time, in hot oil to soften, 15 seconds on each side. Drain and blot well with paper towels.
• Place tortillas on plates. Top each with an egg and tomato sauce. Sprinkle with cheese. Serve with dairy sour half and half and jalapeños.

Nutrition Analysis Per Serving: As Originally Published/With Fat-Skimming Options

Calories: 258/213
Protein: 12 g/15 g
Carbohydrate: 19 g/20 g
Fat: 16 g/9 g

Saturated Fat: 6 g/2 g
Cholesterol: 234 mg/11 mg
Sodium: 566 mg/650 mg
Dietary Fiber: 2 g/2 g

Salmon-Egg Pie

Yield: 5 servings

1 (1 pound) can salmon
Milk
1/4 cup chopped onion
3 tablespoons butter or margarine
3 tablespoons flour
1/4 teaspoon dry mustard

1/4 teaspoon salt
1/8 teaspoon pepper
1/2 teaspoon Worcestershire sauce
1 cup frozen peas
3 hard-cooked eggs, peeled and sliced
Biscuits

Fat-skimming options: Replace butter with 1 tablespoon soft margarine. Use skim milk. Use whites of eggs only. For biscuits: Replace shortening with 1 tablespoon soft margarine and use skim milk. With options, exchange diets count: 2 starch, 3 lean meat.

• Drain salmon, reserving liquid. Add enough milk to liquid to make 1 1/3 cups; set aside.
• Discard skin and bones from salmon. Break into chunks and place in 1 1/2-quart casserole dish; set aside.
• In 2-quart saucepan, sauté onion in butter until tender. Stir in flour, mustard, salt and pepper until blended. Stir in 1 1/3 cups milk and salmon-liquid mixture and Worcestershire sauce.
• Cook, stirring constantly, until mixture boils and thickens. Stir in peas. Remove from heat. Spoon half of the sauce over salmon. Cover with egg slices and spread with remaining sauce.
• Prepare Biscuits. Place on top of pie.
• Bake in 400 degree F oven 25 minutes, or until biscuits are golden and pie is bubbly around edge.

Biscuits

Yield: 24 biscuits

1 cup flour
1 1/2 teaspoons baking powder
1 teaspoon sugar
1/4 teaspoon salt
3 tablespoons shortening
1/3 cup milk

In bowl, combine flour, baking powder, sugar, and salt. With pastry blender, cut in shortening until coarse crumbs form. Stir in milk. Turn out dough on lightly floured surface; knead 5 times. Roll out to 1/2-inch thickness; cut with 1 1/4-inch biscuit cutter. Reroll and cut scraps.

Nutrition Analysis Per Serving: As Originally Published/With Fat-Skimming Options

Calories: 480/341
Protein: 29 g/27 g
Carbohydrate: 32 g/32 g
Fat: 26 g/9 g

Saturated Fat 10 g/3 g
Cholesterol: 155 mg/4 mg
Sodium: 1,027 mg/988 mg
Dietary Fiber: 2 g/2 g

Blue Cheese Stuffed Cherry Tomatoes
Yield: 30

1 pint cherry tomatoes (about 30)
Blue Cheese Filling
Paprika (optional)

> *Fat-skimming options: Use light (50% reduced fat) cream cheese.*
> *With options, exchange diets count: 1 vegetable.*

• Cut thin slice from top of each tomato and loosen pulp, using a sharp knife. Remove pulp with handle of teaspoon and discard. Place tomatoes upside-down to drain on paper towels.
• Prepare Blue Cheese Filling. Pipe mixture into tomatoes, using pastry bag with medium star tip (No. 32), or use a measuring teaspoon. Sprinkle with paprika if you wish.
• Cover and chill in refrigerator up to 6 hours before serving.

Blue Cheese Filling
2 (3 ounce) packages cream cheese, softened
3 ounces blue cheese, crumbled

• Beat together cream cheese and blue cheese until smooth, using electric mixer.

Nutrition Analysis Per Serving: As Originally Published/With Fat-Skimming Options	
Calories: 37/29	Saturated Fat: 2 g/1 g
Protein: 1 g/1 g	Cholesterol: 8 mg/4 mg
Carbohydrate: 2 g/2 g	Sodium: 59 mg/74 mg
Fat: 3 g/2 g	Dietary Fiber: 1 g/1 g

Herb Cheese Stuffed Cherry Tomatoes
Yield: 30

1 pint cherry tomatoes (about 30)
Herb Cheese Filling
Paprika (optional)

*Fat-skimming options: Use light (50% reduced fat) cream cheese.
With options, exchange diets count: 1 vegetable.*

• Cut thin slice from top of each tomato and loosen pulp, using a sharp knife. Remove pulp with handle of teaspoon and discard. Place tomatoes upside-down to drain on paper towels.
• Prepare Herb Cheese Filling. Pipe mixture into tomatoes, using pastry bag with medium star tip (No. 32), or use a measuring teaspoon. Sprinkle with paprika if you wish.
• Cover and chill in refrigerator up to 6 hours before serving.

Herb Filling
1 (8 ounce) package cream cheese, softened
2 tablespoons minced fresh parsley
1 tablespoon grated onion
1 small clove garlic, minced
⅛ teaspoon dried tarragon leaves

• Beat together cream cheese, parsley, onion, garlic and tarragon until smooth, using electric mixer.

Nutrition Analysis Per Serving: As Originally Published/With Fat-Skimming Options

Calories: 33/23	Saturated Fat: 2 g/1 g
Protein: 1 g/1 g	Cholesterol: 8 mg/3 mg
Carbohydrate: 2 g/2 g	Sodium: 25 mg/46 mg
Fat: 3 g/1 g	Dietary Fiber: 0.5 g/0.5 g

Pressure-Cooker Baked Beans

Yield: 6 (2 cup) servings

1 pound navy beans
$^1\!/_3$ pound bacon, cut in pieces
3 tablespoons brown sugar
3 tablespoons molasses
3 tablespoons ketchup
$^1\!/_2$ cup chopped onion
$1^1\!/_2$ teaspoons salt
$^1\!/_2$ teaspoon prepared mustard
2 cups water

Fat-skimming options: Use $^1\!/_3$ pound chopped lean ham instead of bacon.
With options, exchange diets count: 1 very lean meat, $3^1\!/_2$ starch.

• Wash beans. Soak overnight in water to cover. Rinse and drain.
• Sauté bacon in 4-quart pressure cooker. Add remaining ingredients. Close cover securely. Cook beans at 15 pounds pressure (following manufacturer's directions for your pressure cooker) for 50 minutes. Let pressure drop of own accord.

• **Oven Method:** Prepare beans following step 1 at left. Place drained beans in saucepan with enough water to cover. Bring to a boil; reduce heat. Cook for 20 minutes.
• Put beans and liquid in a 2-quart bean pot or casserole. Add remaining ingredients. Cover. Bake at 300 degrees F for 6 to 8 hours, adding more water as needed to keep beans moist. Uncover for last 30 minutes of baking. Beans should be tender and not mushy.

Nutrition Analysis Per Serving: As Originally Published/With Fat-Skimming Options

Calories: 328/305	Saturated Fat: 1 g/0 g
Protein: 18 g/21 g	Cholesterol: 5 mg/2 mg
Carbohydrate: 57 g/57 g	Sodium: 656 mg/677 mg
Fat: 4 g/1 g	Dietary Fiber: 18 g/18 g

Sweet and Sour Baked Beans

Yield: 8 to 10 servings

1 cup chopped onion
1 clove garlic, minced
$\frac{1}{2}$ cup bacon drippings
1 cup chopped celery
$\frac{1}{4}$ cup dark brown sugar
$\frac{1}{4}$ cup dark molasses
1 (15 ounce) can tomato sauce
$\frac{1}{2}$ cup chili sauce
1 teaspoon salt
$\frac{1}{4}$ teaspoon pepper
2 dashes Tabasco sauce
1 pound navy beans, cooked and drained
1 (13$\frac{1}{2}$ ounce) can pineapple chunks, drained and cut in half
$\frac{1}{2}$ cup chopped sweet pickles
$\frac{1}{4}$ cup sliced stuffed olives

Fat-skimming options: Reduce bacon drippings to 1 tablespoon.
With options, exchange diets count: 2 starch.

• Sauté onion and garlic in bacon drippings. Stir in next 8 ingredients and simmer for 20 minutes.

• Combine with cooked navy beans, pineapple, pickles and olives. Turn into a 3-quart casserole; cover. Bake at 350 degrees F for 1 hour. Uncover; bake 15 minutes.

Nutrition Analysis Per Serving: As Originally Published/With Fat-Skimming Options

Calories: 233/152
Protein: 4 g/4 g
Carbohydrate: 31 g/31 g
Fat: 11 g/2 g

Saturated Fat: 4 g/1 g
Cholesterol: 10 mg/1 mg
Sodium: 639 mg/539 mg
Dietary Fiber: 1 g/1 g

CHAPTER FIVE

FISH AND SHELLFISH

I smelled like a fish on Friday night dates

There might be chicken thawing in the fridge, but when Grandpa Donlon showed up with fresh fish from the Turkey River, supper was set. Farm Journal reader Elizabeth Donlon Goodfellow remembers being called from her bedroom to the pumphouse to "help clean this mess of fish." It didn't matter if she was primping for a date, because Dad would figure the young man might just as well get his hands into the work.

After the fillets were chilled in salt water, one of her four siblings would whip up an egg and milk, another would get out the flour and Mom would start heating lard in the skillet. Raw-fried potatoes always went along with this meal. Liz's four kids prefer crunchy-coated fish to this day.

As nutrition science uncovered the risks of saturated fat, home-rendering of lard became hazardous to one's health. You will find new and wonderful ways to enjoy the fresh and delicate taste of fish in this chapter.

Baked Stuffed Fish
Yield: 4 servings

1 (2½ to 3 pound) whole fish
Salt
2 cups soft bread cubes (½ inch)
1 cup minced celery and leaves
½ cup butter, melted
¼ cup chopped sweet pickles or pickle relish
2 tablespoons finely chopped onion
½ teaspoon dried rubbed sage
½ teaspoon salt
¹⁄₁₆ teaspoon pepper
2 bacon strips, cut in half
Pimiento (optional)

Fat-skimming options: Omit butter and substitute 2 tablespoons soft margarine.
With options, exchange diets count: 2 starch, 1 vegetable, 6 lean meat.

• Rinse fish in cold water. Scale fish, using a sharp knife. Cut slit in belly from head to ventral fin. Remove entrails and trim fins.
• Sprinkle cavity with salt.
• Combine bread cubes, celery, butter, pickles, onion, sage, ½ teaspoon salt and the pepper in bowl. Mix lightly, but well. Fill cavity with stuffing mixture and close opening with skewers. Place fish on rack in shallow roasting pan. Arrange bacon strips over fish.

• Bake in 325 degree F oven 45 to 55 minutes, or until fish flakes easily with fork, but is still moist. Place fish on serving plate and cover eye with a piece of pimiento, if desired.

Nutrition Analysis Per Serving: As Originally Published/With Fat-Skimming Options

Calories: 665/511
Protein: 55 g/55 g
Carbohydrate: 40 g/40 g
Fat: 36 g/19 g

Saturated Fat: 16 g/2 g
Cholesterol: 65 mg/3 mg
Sodium: 1,510 mg/1,328 mg
Dietary Fiber: 2.5 g/2.5 g

Broiled Fish With Magic Potion
Yield: 4 servings

2 tablespoons finely chopped onion
2 tablespoons butter, melted
1 tablespoon ketchup
2 teaspoons lemon juice
1 teaspoon Worcestershire sauce
1½ pounds fish fillets, fresh or frozen and thawed

Fat-skimming options: Omit butter and spray foil with nonstick cooking spray.
With options, exchange diets count: 4 very lean meat.

• Combine onion, butter, ketchup, lemon juice and Worcestershire sauce in bowl; mix well.
• Cover broiler pan rack with aluminum foil and grease with butter.
• Cut fillets into serving-size pieces and arrange on broiler pan. Brush fillets with half of the sauce.

• Place under broiler, 2 inches from source of heat, and broil 3 minutes. Turn fillets; brush with remaining sauce. Broil 2 to 3 minutes more, or until fish flakes easily with fork, but is still moist.

Nutrition Analysis Per Serving: As Originally Published/With Fat-Skimming Options

Calories: 184/133
Protein: 26 g/26 g
Carbohydrate: 2 g/2 g
Fat: 11 g/5 g

Saturated Fat: 4 g/0 g
Cholesterol: 16 mg/0 mg
Sodium: 253 mg/0 mg
Dietary Fiber: 0 g/0 g

Dilled Salmon Steaks

Yield: 4 servings

1 (8 ounce) carton plain nonfat yogurt
2 tablespoons chopped fresh dill weed
2 tablespoons minced onion
$1/2$ teaspoon grated lemon rind
$1/4$ teaspoon sugar
$1/4$ teaspoon salt
$1/8$ teaspoon pepper
1 medium cucumber, peeled, seeded and chopped
4 (1 inch thick) salmon steaks

Fat-skimming options: none. Exchange diets count: 5 lean meat, 1 vegetable.

• In 8-inch square baking dish, stir together first 7 ingredients. Remove half of the mixture to a bowl and stir in three-fourths of the cucumber. Cover and refrigerate until ready to serve.
• Stir remaining cucumber into remaining yogurt mixture. Add salmon; turn to coat. Cover and refrigerate 2 hours.

• Place salmon on broiler pan; spoon any yogurt marinade in dish over salmon.
• Broil 5 inches from source of heat 4 to 5 minutes on each side or until fish flakes easily with fork. Serve with cucumber sauce.

Nutrition Analysis Per Serving: As Originally Published

Calories: 285
Protein: 27 g
Carbohydrate: 7 g
Fat: 11 g

Saturated Fat: 2 g
Cholesterol: 95 mg
Sodium: 257 mg
Dietary Fiber: 0.5 g

Easy Barbecued Fish
Yield: 4 servings

6 fish fillets (1½ pounds)
¼ cup ketchup
3 tablespoons packed brown sugar
3 tablespoons vinegar
2 tablespoons Worcestershire sauce
2 teaspoons dry mustard
1 teaspoon chili powder
1 teaspoon paprika

Fat-skimming options: none. Exchange diets count: 4 very lean meat, 1 fruit.

• Place 16x10 inch oven cooking bag in 13x9x2 inch baking pan. Fold fish fillets in half and place, in single layer, in bag.
• In bowl, stir together remaining ingredients and pour over fish fillets. Close bag with nylon tie. Make 6 (½ inch) slits in top of bag.
• Bake in 350 degree F oven 15 minutes, or until fish flakes easily with fork. Remove from bag. Pour sauce into bowl. Serve fish with sauce.

• **Microwave method:** Prepare as directed, but place bag in 13x9x2 inch microwave-safe baking dish.
• Microwave at high setting (100% power) 6 minutes, or until fish flakes easily with fork, rotating dish one-half turn after 3 minutes.

Nutrition Analysis Per Serving: As Originally Published

Calories: 187
Protein: 26 g
Carbohydrate: 15 g
Fat: 5 g

Saturated Fat: 0 g
Cholesterol: 0 mg
Sodium: 395 mg
Dietary Fiber: 0 g

Lemon Cod and Rice

Yield: 4 servings

$^{1}/_{2}$ cup instant rice
$^{1}/_{2}$ cup water
1 tablespoon fresh lemon juice
$^{1}/_{2}$ teaspoon pepper
$^{1}/_{2}$ teaspoon salt
1 (10 ounce) package, frozen chopped broccoli, thawed and well drained
2 ounces reduced-fat Cheddar cheese, shredded
1 pound cod fillets
Paprika for garnish

Fat-skimming options: none. Exchange diets count: 4 very lean meat, $^{1}/_{2}$ starch, 1 vegetable.

• Preheat oven to 375 degrees F.
• Spray an 8-inch square baking dish with nonstick cooking spray.
• In a small microwave-safe mixing bowl, combine rice, water, lemon juice, pepper, salt, broccoli, and cheese. Cover and microwave on high power for 4 minutes, stopping to stir once. Mixture will thicken and stick together as cheese melts.

• Or make rice mixture on range: Use a small saucepan and cook over medium heat, stirring occasionally for about 8 minutes.
• Spoon rice mixture on top of each cod fillet. Roll up and secure with a toothpick. Transfer to prepared baking dish, placing seam on bottom. Bake for 30 minutes.
• Garnish with paprika before serving.

Nutrition Analysis Per Serving: As Originally Published	
Calories: 204	Saturated Fat: 1 g
Protein: 29 g	Cholesterol: 68 mg
Carbohydrate: 12 g	Sodium: 471 mg
Fat: 3 g	Dietary Fiber: 2 g

Shrimp Creole
Yield: 4 (2 cup) servings

2 strips bacon, diced
1 cup chopped onion
1 clove garlic, minced
$\frac{1}{2}$ cup chopped green pepper
$\frac{2}{3}$ cup finely diced celery
$1\frac{1}{2}$ cups fresh or canned chunky tomatoes
4 ounces tomato paste
$\frac{1}{2}$ teaspoon basil
$\frac{1}{4}$ teaspoon salt
$\frac{1}{4}$ teaspoon cayenne pepper
1 tablespoon brown sugar
1 teaspoon Worcestershire sauce
$\frac{1}{2}$ teaspoon soy sauce
1 bay leaf
$\frac{1}{4}$ teaspoon black pepper
1 pound fresh or thawed frozen shrimp
2 cups quick rice
2 cups water

Fat-skimming options: none. Exchange diets count: 2 starch, 2 lean meat, 1 vegetable.

• Place diced bacon on a microwave broiling tray. Cover with a paper towel and microwave on high power for 2 minutes. Or cook bacon in a skillet until crisp. Drain well.
• Meanwhile, spray a Dutch oven with non-stick cooking spray. Sauté the onion, garlic, pepper and celery for 4 minutes. Stir in tomatoes, tomato paste, basil, salt, cayenne pepper, brown sugar, Worcestershire sauce, soy sauce, bay leaf and pepper.

• Bring to a boil, then reduce heat and simmer for 10 minutes. Bring to a second boil, then stir in bacon and shrimp. Continue boiling for 3 minutes, or until shrimp is no longer opaque. Discard bay leaf.
• Meanwhile, combine quick rice with water in a 1-quart microwave dish; cover and microwave on high for 4 minutes. Or follow package directions for quick rice.
• Spoon cooked rice onto a serving platter or individual plates. Top with shrimp and sauce.

Nutrition Analysis Per Serving: As Originally Published	
Calories: 300	Saturated Fat: 1 g
Protein: 27 g	Cholesterol: 45 mg
Carbohydrate: 35 g	Sodium: 271 mg
Fat: 3 g	Dietary Fiber: 0.5 g

Stuffed Sole

Yield: 4 servings

1 cup sliced mushrooms
1/2 cup sliced green onions
1 tablespoon vegetable oil
3/4 cup quick-cooking oats or bread crumbs
1/4 cup liquid egg substitute
1/4 teaspoon salt (optional)
2 tablespoons lemon juice, divided
1/2 teaspoon marjoram
1 pound sole, flounder, orange roughy or cod fillets
Paprika

Fat-skimming options: none. For exchange diets, count: 3 lean meat, 1 starch.

• Preheat oven to 375 degrees F. Sauté mushrooms and onions in oil for 3 minutes. Add oatmeal or bread crumbs, egg, salt, 1 tablespoon lemon juice and marjoram.
• Divide stuffing mixture among the fillets, spreading to within 1/2 inch of the edge. Roll up and secure with a toothpick; place seam-side down in an 8 inch square baking dish.

• Sprinkle with the other 1 tablespoon of lemon juice, dust with paprika and bake 20 minutes, or microwave on high 8 minutes, just until the fish flakes easily with a fork.

Nutrition Analysis Per Serving: As Originally Published

Calories: 250	Saturated Fat: 4 g
Protein: 26 g	Cholesterol: 50 mg
Carbohydrate: 15 g	Sodium: 263 mg
Fat: 10 g	Dietary Fiber: 0 g

CHAPTER SIX

PASTA, RICE AND GRAINS

There were corn bowls, corn platters and corn dishes everywhere!

Pride Seed Corn Company of Glen Haven, Wis., was the brain-child of Richard Metcalf, who, in 1934, hybridized corn on the unglaciated windblown soil of the Mississippi River Valley. The yield from his first acre was dried in an upstairs bedroom with an electric fan. He survived the drought of 1936, continued breeding and planting corn and eventually expanded operations to plants in Iowa, Minnesota and Canada.

Daughter Julie Metcalf remembers glorious Thanksgiving feasts at the home farm, a family celebration of the precious grain harvested, dried and poured into cloth bags. The traditional turkey and dressing menu was served in corn bowls, corn platters and corn relish dishes, as her Grandmother Grenalda collected novelty dinnerware. Everyone dressed to the nines for the dinner, and manners were everywhere.

The Pride Seed Corn Company was eventually sold to Northrup King, but the Metcalf descendants still gather together in late November. Gone are the ties and fancy dresses, and today even the men help set the table and clean up the dishes; but traditional Apple Raisin Dressing (found in this chapter) is in a pretty bowl on the buffet table.

Harvest Lasagne

Yield: 12 servings

8 ounces bulk sweet or hot Italian sausage
2 cups sliced zucchini
2 cups cubed, peeled eggplant
2 cups chopped red and/or green bell pepper
1/2 cup chopped onion
2 cloves garlic, chopped
1 cup chicken broth, divided
1 (26 to 28 ounce) jar spaghetti sauce
2 cups small-curd cottage cheese, low-fat (2%) or regular
1/4 cup Italian-style bread crumbs
8 ounces uncooked lasagne noodles
1 cup shredded mozzarella cheese
1/3 cup grated Parmesan cheese

Fat-skimming options: Substitute low-fat turkey sausage.
Use 1% cottage cheese and reduced-fat part-skim mozzarella cheese.
With options, exchange diets count: 2 starch, 1 vegetable, 2 lean meat.

• In 3-quart saucepan, cook sausage until no longer pink. Drain. Return sausage to pan. Stir in zucchini, eggplant, peppers, onion, garlic and 1/4 cup chicken broth. Cover and simmer 5 to 10 minutes or until vegetables are slightly tender. Stir in spaghetti sauce and remaining chicken broth. Cover and simmer another 5 to 10 minutes.
• In another bowl, combine cottage cheese and bread crumbs.

• To assemble lasagne: Spray bottom of 13x9 inch pan with nonstick coating. Spread with about 1/2 cup vegetable-meat sauce. Layer with one-third of noodles, one-third of sauce, half of cottage cheese and one-third each of mozzarella and Parmesan cheeses.
• Add remaining noodles in one layer, then sauce and cottage cheese, ending with mozzarella and Parmesan cheeses.
• Cover tightly with aluminum foil. Bake in 350 degree F oven for about 1 hour until mixture is bubbly. Uncover and bake another 5 to 10 minutes to brown top.
• Let lasagne stand 10 minutes at room temperature before cutting.

Nutrition Analysis Per Serving: As Originally Published/With Fat-Skimming Options

Calories: 414/293
Protein: 24 g/19 g
Carbohydrate: 33 g/32 g
Fat: 21 g/10 g

Saturated Fat: 7 g/3 g
Cholesterol: 54 mg/25 mg
Sodium: 1,221 mg/961 mg
Dietary Fiber: 3 g/3 g

Linguine With White Clam Sauce

Yield: 4 servings

¼ cup butter
¼ cup cooking oil
3 cloves garlic, minced
2 (6½ ounce) cans chopped clams
⅓ cup chopped fresh parsley
¼ teaspoon dried oregano leaves
⅛ teaspoon pepper
8 ounces linguine, cooked and drained
Grated Parmesan cheese

> *Fat-skimming options: Omit butter and substitute 1 teaspoon corn oil.*
> *With options, exchange diets count: 1 starch, 3 very lean meat.*

• Heat butter and oil in 2-quart saucepan over medium heat until butter melts. Add garlic; sauté 2 minutes.

• Add clams with liquid, parsley, oregano and pepper. Cook, stirring constantly, until mixture simmers. Serve over hot linguine with Parmesan cheese.

Nutrition Analysis Per Serving: As Originally Published/With Fat-Skimming Options

Calories: 402/186	Saturated Fat: 9 g/1 g
Protein: 23 g/23 g	Cholesterol: 86 mg/55 mg
Carbohydrate: 15 g/15 g	Sodium: 231 mg/114 mg
Fat: 28 g/3 g	Dietary Fiber: 0.5 g/0.5 g

Quick Ham and Macaroni Skillet
Yield: 6 servings

1 cup chopped onion
2 tablespoons cooking oil
3 cups water
8 ounces elbow macaroni
1 (10³/₄ ounce) can condensed cream of mushroom soup
³/₄ cup milk
1 teaspoon dry mustard
1 pound fully cooked ham slice, cut in 2x¹/₄-inch strips
2 cups shredded Cheddar cheese
1 (10 ounce) package frozen peas, thawed
10 cherry tomatoes, halved

Fat-skimming options: Omit oil. Use nonstick cooking spray to sauté onions. Use reduced-fat cream of mushroom soup. Use skim milk and reduced-fat Cheddar cheese. Reduce portion size to yield 12 servings. With options, exchange diets count: 5 very lean meat, 1 vegetable, 1 starch.

• Sauté onion in hot oil in 12 inch skillet for 2 minutes. Add water to onion, cover and bring to a boil. Add macaroni; cover and cook 10 minutes, stirring occasionally or until water is absorbed.

• Combine soup and milk. Blend in mustard. Stir soup mixture into macaroni. Add ham, cheese and peas. Cover and cook 5 minutes, stirring frequently. Garnish with cherry tomatoes.

Nutrition Analysis Per Serving: As Originally Published/With Fat-Skimming Options

Calories: 636/276
Protein: 71 g/35 g
Carbohydrate: 43 g/21 g
Fat: 18 g/4 g

Saturated Fat: 3 g/1 g
Cholesterol: 176 mg/88 mg
Sodium: 957 mg/478 mg
Dietary Fiber: 2 g/1 g

Smoked-Turkey Stuffed Shells
Yield: 6 servings

$^1/_2$ pound jumbo pasta shells (about 24)
2 cups low-fat cottage cheese
1 (10 ounce) package frozen, chopped spinach, thawed and drained
$^1/_2$ cup cubed smoked turkey or ham
2 eggs
$^1/_2$ teaspoon salt
Dash each nutmeg, pepper
1 (14 ounce) jar spaghetti sauce
$1^1/_4$ cups grated, reduced-fat mozzarella cheese

*Fat-skimming options: Use 1% cottage cheese. Use $^1/_2$ cup liquid egg substitute for eggs.
With options, exchange diets count: $4^1/_2$ lean meat, 2 vegetable, 1 starch.*

• Cook pasta shells according to package directions. Separate and drain well.
• In large bowl, combine cottage cheese, spinach, turkey, eggs, salt, and dash of nutmeg and pepper.

• Line 3-quart casserole with thin layer of spaghetti sauce. Fill each shell with heaping tablespoon of spinach filling. Place shells in casserole, adding a thin layer of spaghetti sauce between layers of shells. Top with remaining spaghetti sauce and cheese.
• Bake at 350 degrees F, uncovered, 30 to 40 minutes until bubbly and golden.

Nutrition Analysis Per Serving: As Originally Published/With Fat-Skimming Options	
Calories: 394/374	Saturated Fat: 8 g/7 g
Protein: 33 g/33 g	Cholesterol: 122 mg/48 mg
Carbohydrate: 27 g/26 g	Sodium: 1,316 mg/1,332 mg
Fat: 17 g/15 g	Dietary Fiber: 0 g/0 g

Spaghetti Sauce
Yield: 3 pints or 12 (¹/₂ cup) servings

16 pounds ripe tomatoes
1 cup chopped onion
4 tablespoons olive oil
1 tablespoon canning/pickling salt
¹/₄ teaspoon black pepper
¹/₂ teaspoon ground bay leaves
2 cloves garlic, minced, or 1 teaspoon garlic powder
1 teaspoon basil leaves
1 teaspoon oregano leaves
¹/₂ teaspoon parsley flakes
2 tablespoons brown sugar

Fat-skimming options: Omit oil and use nonstick cooking spray to sauté onions. With options, exchange diets count: 2 vegetable.

• Dip tomatoes into boiling water for ¹/₂ minute to loosen skins. Cool in cold water. Drain. Remove skins and cores; quarter.
• In 12-quart kettle, sauté onions in olive oil until transparent (do not brown). Add tomatoes. Bring to boil; simmer, uncovered, for 20 minutes.
• Put through sieve or food mill. Return juice to kettle, adding remaining ingredients. Simmer, uncovered, 1¹/₂ to 2 hours, or until thick and mixture rounds up on spoon.

• Use sauce within 5 days, freeze, or process as follows.
• Pour into 3 hot pint jars, filling to within ¹/₄ inch of jar top. Wipe jar rim; adjust lids.
• Process in boiling water bath 20 minutes. Start to count processing time when water in canner returns to boiling. Remove jars and complete seals unless closures are self-sealing.

Nutrition Analysis Per Serving: As Originally Published/With Fat-Skimming Options

Calories: 59/49
Protein: 2 g/2 g
Carbohydrate: 11 g/11 g
Fat: 2 g/0 g

Saturated Fat: 0 g/0 g
Cholesterol: 0 mg/0 mg
Sodium: 549 mg/549 mg
Dietary Fiber: 2 g/2 g

Three Times Three Rotini and Cheese
Yield: 4 servings

3 cups uncooked tricolor rotini or regular macaroni
1/3 cup chopped green onions (include tops)
1 tablespoon butter or margarine
2 tablespoons all-purpose flour
1/4 teaspoon dry mustard
Dash pepper
2 cups milk
1 1/2 cups (6 ounces) shredded, reduced-fat sharp Cheddar cheese
1/2 cup grated Parmesan cheese, divided
1/4 cup low-fat cream cheese
3 tablespoons bread crumbs

> *Fat-skimming options: Use skim milk. Reduce Cheddar cheese to 4 ounces.*
> *Reduce Parmesan cheese to 1/4 cup. Reduce portion size to yield 8 servings.*
> *With options, exchange diets count: 2 lean meat, 4 starch.*

• Cook rotini according to package directions. Drain.
• In medium saucepan, cook green onions in hot butter about 1 minute. Stir in flour, dry mustard and pepper.
• Add milk and bring to boiling. Cook over medium heat, stirring constantly, until mixture bubbles and thickens, about 10 to 12 minutes.
• Remove from heat and stir in Cheddar, 1/3 cup Parmesan and cream cheese.
• Stir in cooked rotini and heat through. Spoon mixture into buttered, ovenproof 2- quart dish.
• Mix bread crumbs and remaining Parmesan cheese. Sprinkle over rotini and brown briefly under broiler.

Nutrition Analysis Per Serving: As Originally Published/With Fat-Skimming Options

Calories: 930/425
Protein: 46 g/20 g
Carbohydrate: 142 g/71 g
Fat: 19 g/6 g

Saturated Fat: 10 g/3 g
Cholesterol: 57 mg/48 mg
Sodium: 678 mg/702 mg
Dietary Fiber: 2.5 g/2.5 g

Risotto

Yield: 12 servings

1 cup sliced green onions
1 cup shredded carrots
$^1/_2$ cup chopped fresh parsley
6 tablespoons butter
$2^1/_2$ cups uncooked regular rice
5 chicken bouillon cubes
$^1/_2$ bay leaf
$^1/_2$ teaspoon salt
$^1/_4$ teaspoon dried thyme leaves
$4^1/_2$ cups water

Fat-skimming options: Omit butter and substitute 1 tablespoon soft margarine.
With options, exchange diets count: $1^1/_2$ starch, 2 vegetable.

• **The day before:** Cut and measure green onions, carrots and parsley. Refrigerate in plastic bags.
• **30 minutes before serving:** Melt butter in 4-quart Dutch oven over medium heat. Add green onions and carrots and sauté. Add rice; cook, stirring occasionally, until rice is opaque.

• Add bouillon cubes, bay leaf, salt, thyme and water. Cook over high heat until mixture comes to a boil. Reduce heat and simmer 15 minutes, or until liquid is absorbed. Remove bay leaf. Stir in parsley.

Nutrition Analysis Per Serving: As Originally Published/With Fat-Skimming Options

Calories: 213/171	Saturated Fat: 4 g/0 g
Protein: 3 g/3 g	Cholesterol: 16 mg/0 mg
Carbohydrate: 33 g/33 g	Sodium: 704 mg/658 mg
Fat: 7 g/2 g	Dietary Fiber: 1.5 g/1.5 g

Spinach Risotto

Yield: 6 servings

Water
2 (13¾ ounce) cans chicken broth
2 tablespoons vegetable oil
1 cup coarsely chopped onion
2 cloves garlic, minced
1 cup uncooked rice
⅛ teaspoon pepper
¼ cup grated Parmesan cheese
¼ cup milk
3 cups shredded fresh spinach

> *Fat-skimming options: Decrease oil to 1 teaspoon. Use skim milk.*
> *With options, exchange diets count: 1½ starch, 2 vegetable.*

• Add enough water to chicken broth to measure 5⅓ cups; set aside.
• In 10 inch skillet over medium-high heat, heat oil. Add onion and garlic; cook, stirring frequently, 3 minutes.
• Add rice; cook, stirring constantly, 2 minutes. Stir in pepper and 1⅓ cups broth mixture. Cook, stirring frequently, until liquid is almost absorbed.

• Continue adding remaining broth mixture, 1 cup at a time, stirring frequently, until it is almost absorbed before adding more.
• Stir in cheese and milk. Cook and stir 1 minute. Remove from heat; stir in spinach. Cover and let stand 5 minutes.

Nutrition Analysis Per Serving: As Originally Published/With Fat-Skimming Options	
Calories: 203/167	Saturated Fat: 1 g/0 g
Protein: 6 g/6 g	Cholesterol: 3 mg/0 mg
Carbohydrate: 30 g/30 g	Sodium: 121 mg/121 mg
Fat: 6 g/2 g	Dietary Fiber: 2 g/2 g

Apple Raisin Dressing
Yield: 8 servings

8 slices whole wheat bread, cubed
2 medium apples, peeled, cored and chopped
2 large ribs celery, finely chopped
1 small onion, chopped
¼ cup chopped fresh parsley
1 clove garlic, minced
1 teaspoon salt
¼ teaspoon paprika
1 chicken bouillon cube
¾ cup boiling water
1 cup raisins
⅔ cup butter, melted

Fat-skimming options: Omit butter and replace with 2 tablespoons soft margarine.
With options, exchange diets count: 2 starch, ½ fruit.

• In large bowl, toss together first 8 ingredients; set aside.
• In small bowl, dissolve bouillon cube in boiling water; add raisins and let stand 5 minutes. Pour raisin mixture and melted butter over bread mixture; mix lightly but well. Spoon into ungreased 8x8x2 inch baking dish.

• Bake in 350 degree F oven 40 minutes, or until browned on top and heated through.

Nutrition Analysis Per Serving: As Originally Published/With Fat-Skimming Options

Calories: 282/180	Saturated Fat: 9 g/2 g
Protein: 4 g/3 g	Cholesterol: 39 mg/8 mg
Carbohydrate: 34 g/34 g	Sodium: 721 mg/604 mg
Fat: 16 g/4 g	Dietary Fiber: 3 g/3 g

Range-Top Pecan Dressing
Yield: 6 to 8 servings

8 cups white bread cubes (⅜ inch)
2 cups celery slices (⅛ inch)
1 cup chopped onion
¼ cup chopped fresh parsley
½ cup butter or regular margarine
1 (4 ounce) can sliced mushrooms
1 (13¾ ounce) can chicken broth
2 teaspoons rubbed sage
⅛ teaspoon pepper
1 cup pecan halves

Fat-skimming options: Use margarine and reduce to 2 tablespoons. Reduce pecans to ¼ cup.
Reduce portion size and increase servings to 16.
With options, exchange diets count: 2 starch, 2 vegetable, 1 fat.

• **Advance preparation:** Toast half of bread cubes by spreading in a single layer in a 15½x10½x1 inch jelly roll pan. Bake in 325 degree F oven, stirring frequently, until dry and golden brown, about 15 minutes. Repeat with remaining bread cubes. Toasted bread cubes may be stored in plastic bag or airtight container up to 6 weeks.
• **The day before:** Cut celery, onion and parsley. Place on plate; cover with plastic wrap. Refrigerate overnight.

• **That day:** Melt butter in Dutch oven. Add celery and onion; sauté until tender, about 10 minutes. Add parsley; cook 2 more minutes. Drain mushrooms, reserving liquid. Add enough water to liquid to make ⅔ cup. Add to Dutch oven with mushrooms, chicken broth, sage and pepper. Cover and simmer 5 more minutes.
• Remove from heat. Stir in toasted bread cubes and pecans. Cover and let stand 10 minutes; serve immediately.

Nutrition Analysis Per Serving: As Originally Published/With Fat-Skimming Options

Calories: 738/259	Saturated Fat: 10 g/1 g
Protein: 17 g/8 g	Cholesterol: 31 mg/0 mg
Carbohydrate: 86 g/41 g	Sodium: 1,386 mg/646 mg
Fat: 37 g/7 g	Dietary Fiber: 7 g/3 g

Barley Pilaf

Yield: 8 servings

2 tablespoons vegetable oil
$\frac{1}{2}$ cup thinly sliced celery
1 cup medium pearled barley
$\frac{1}{2}$ cup chopped onion
3 cups water
3 vegetable, chicken or beef bouillon cubes
$\frac{1}{8}$ teaspoon pepper
$\frac{1}{2}$ cup shredded carrots
$\frac{1}{4}$ cup chopped fresh parsley

Fat-skimming options: Reduce oil to 2 teaspoons. With options, exchange diets count: $\frac{1}{2}$ starch.

• In 3-quart saucepan over medium heat, heat 1 tablespoon oil. Add celery; cook 4 minutes. Remove and set aside.
• In same saucepan over medium heat, heat remaining 1 tablespoon oil. Add barley and onion. Cook and stir 2 minutes.

• Stir in water, bouillon cubes and pepper. Bring to a boil. Reduce heat to low. Cover and simmer 40 minutes.
• Stir in carrots and cooked celery. Cover and cook 15 minutes, or until barley is tender and liquid is absorbed.
• Remove from heat. Gently stir in parsley.

Nutrition Analysis Per Serving: As Originally Published/With Fat-Skimming Options

Calories: 68/47
Protein: 1 g/1 g
Carbohydrate: 7 g/7 g
Fat: 4 g/2 g

Saturated Fat: 0 g/0 g
Cholesterol: 0 mg/0 mg
Sodium: 171 mg/171 mg
Dietary Fiber: 0.5 g/0.5 g

CHAPTER SEVEN

POULTRY

What it all boils down to is friendship

When World War II ended and our pilots came home to the farm, guess what they missed? Flying! So, the Minnesota Flying Farmers were organized in 1944 to travel together and share "pilot talk." The group hosted Farm Journal editors in 1970 on the farm of Donald and Lila Eickhoff near Wykoff, Minn.

Farm Journal later featured favorite potluck recipes from the flying farmer wives, including a chicken salad that is prepared and served to this day in the Bank Gift Haus Tearoom in Wykoff. Lila and Don retired from the farm over a decade ago and developed the gift store and tearoom. Three of their granddaughters help serve in the tearoom during vacations from college, and are learning the art of hostessing.

The flying farmers toured the entire U.S., Canada and Mexico, children tucked in the back of the planes. They continue to rendezvous twice a year, although the group's numbers are dwindling. And while they offer farm tours and agricultural presentations at their meetings, Lila suggests what it really all boils down to is friendship. Look in this chapter for Chicken in Honey Sauce, Crisp Oven-Fried Chicken or Chicken With Artichokes for your next fellowship potluck.

Apricot Glaze
Yield: 4 (¹/₄ cup) servings

¹/₂ cup apricot jam
¹/₄ cup ketchup
1 tablespoon cider vinegar
1 tablespoon Worcestershire sauce
3 tablespoons grated onion
¹/₂ teaspoon paprika

Fat-skimming options: Substitute all-fruit spread for jam.
With options, exchange diets count: 2 fruit.

• In small bowl, combine all ingredients.
• Grill 2 pounds turkey or chicken pieces (or
1¹/₄ pounds beef or pork). Add glaze during
last half of grilling or broiling time.

Nutrition Analysis Per Serving: As Originally Published/With Fat-Skimming Options

Calories: 122/116	Saturated Fat: 0 g/0 g
Protein: 0 g/0 g	Cholesterol: 0 mg/0 mg
Carbohydrate: 30 g/28 g	Sodium: 216 mg/231 mg
Fat: 0 g/0 g	Dietary Fiber: 0 g/0 g

Cheesy Chicken Pie

Yield: 6 servings

1 (9 inch) frozen pie shell or 1 (9 inch) refrigerated ready-made pie crust
3 tablespoons butter or regular margarine
3 tablespoons flour
$\frac{1}{2}$ teaspoon dry mustard
$\frac{1}{2}$ teaspoon rubbed sage
2 cups milk
2 chicken bouillon cubes, crumbled
1 cup shredded American cheese
3 cups cut-up, cooked chicken
3 cups drained, cooked mixed vegetables (such as corn, peas, carrots and lima beans)
2 cups peeled, cubed, cooked potatoes

Fat-skimming options: Reduce margarine to 1 tablespoon. Select reduced-fat American Cheese and skim milk. Reduce portion size to yield 10 servings.
With options, exchange diets count: 3 lean meat, 1 starch, 1 vegetable.

• Invert frozen pie shell onto sheet of plastic wrap. Cover with another sheet of plastic wrap and thaw. Or let refrigerated pie crust come to room temperature according to package directions.
• In 3-quart saucepan over medium heat, melt butter. Stir in flour, mustard and sage until smooth. Gradually stir in milk and bouillon cubes. Cook, stirring constantly, until mixture boils and thickens. Add cheese; stir until melted. Remove mixture from heat. Stir in chicken, vegetables and cubed potatoes. Pour into 2-quart round casserole.
• Flatten pie shell or crust; press together any tears to seal. Place over filling. Fold under edge to form rim; flute. Cut slits in top to vent steam.
• Bake in 400 degree F oven 35 minutes, or until crust is browned. (Check after 15 minutes; if edge of crust is browning too quickly, cover with strips of foil.) Let stand 10 minutes before serving.
• **To Make Ahead and Serve Later:** Prepare filling but do not top with pastry. Cover and refrigerate up to 24 hours.
• Place pastry over filling and cut slits as directed. Bake in 400 degree F oven 50 minutes, or until crust is golden brown and pie is heated through. (Check after 15 minutes; if edge of crust is browning too quickly, cover with foil strips.)

Nutrition Analysis Per Serving: As Originally Published/With Fat-Skimming Options	
Calories: 681/280	Saturated Fat: 17 g/2 g
Protein: 50 g/25 g	Cholesterol: 166 mg/55 mg
Carbohydrate: 36 g/18 g	Sodium: 1,339 mg/651 mg
Fat: 37 g/11 g	Dietary Fiber: 1 g/1 g

Chinese Chicken With Vegetables

Yield: 6 servings

2 whole chicken breasts, split, skinned and boned (about 12 ounces each)
3 tablespoons cooking oil
1 pound fresh mushrooms, sliced
2 medium onions, sliced and separated into rings
1 cup bias-cut celery slices (¼ inch)
2 cloves garlic, minced
¾ teaspoon ground ginger
½ cup water
¼ cup soy sauce
2 (6 ounce) packages frozen pea pods, partially thawed
2 tablespoons cornstarch
2 tablespoons water
Hot cooked rice
½ cup chopped walnuts

Fat-skimming options: Omit oil and use nonstick cooking spray to sauté chicken and vegetables.
Reduce walnuts to 2 tablespoons.
With options, exchange diets count: 3 starch, 2 vegetable, 3 very lean meat.

• Freeze chicken 20 minutes to make cutting easier.
• Cut and measure all ingredients before starting to cook.
• Cut chicken breasts crosswise into strips 2x¼ inches long.
• Cook chicken in hot oil in 12 inch skillet over high heat 5 minutes, stirring constantly. Add mushrooms, onion, celery, garlic, ginger, ½ cup water and soy sauce. Cook until mixture comes to a boil. Reduce heat to low. Cover and simmer 5 minutes. Increase heat to medium. Stir in pea pods. Return to a boil. Cover and cook 3 minutes.

• Dissolve cornstarch in 2 tablespoons water; stir into chicken mixture. Cook and stir until mixture thickens and boils, about 2 minutes. Serve over hot, cooked rice. Garnish with chopped walnuts.

Nutrition Analysis Per Serving: As Originally Published/With Fat-Skimming Options

Calories: 558/410
Protein: 30 g/26 g
Carbohydrate: 64 g/62 g
Fat: 21 g/5 g

Saturated Fat: 2 g/1 g
Cholesterol: 49 mg/49 mg
Sodium: 65 mg/65 mg
Dietary Fiber: 2 g/1 g

Chicken Rice Skillet

Yield: 6 servings

1 cup chopped celery
$\frac{1}{2}$ cup chopped onion
$\frac{1}{2}$ cup butter
2 ($10\frac{3}{4}$ ounce) cans condensed chicken broth
$\frac{1}{8}$ teaspoon powdered saffron
1 cup regular rice
$1\frac{1}{2}$ cups diced, pared carrots
1 teaspoon salt
$\frac{1}{8}$ teaspoon pepper
3 cups cubed cooked chicken
$\frac{1}{4}$ cup chopped fresh parsley

Fat-skimming options: Omit butter and use 1 tablespoon corn oil.
With options, exchange diets count: 4 lean meat, 2 vegetable, 1 starch.

• Sauté celery and onion in melted butter in 12 inch skillet until tender (do not brown).
• Add enough water to chicken broth to make $3\frac{1}{2}$ cups. Add to sautéed vegetables with saffron, rice, carrots, salt and pepper. Cover and simmer 15 minutes.

• Add chicken and parsley; cover and simmer 5 more minutes or until rice is tender.

Nutrition Analysis Per Serving: As Originally Published/With Fat-Skimming Options

Calories: 471/356
Protein: 35 g/34 g
Carbohydrate: 28 g/28 g
Fat: 23 g/10 g

Saturated Fat: 12 g/2 g
Cholesterol: 135 mg/94 mg
Sodium: 632 mg/476 mg
Dietary Fiber: 1.5 g/1.5 g

Chicken in Honey Sauce
Yield: 6 servings

3 whole chicken breasts, split
1 teaspoon salt
¼ teaspoon pepper
2 tablespoons cooking oil
1 (20 ounce) can pineapple chunks in juice
2 cups bias-cut pared carrots
⅓ cup chopped onion
1 cup water
½ cup cider vinegar
⅓ cup honey
1 tablespoon soy sauce
2 chicken bouillon cubes
¼ cup cornstarch
½ cup water
1 (6 ounce) package frozen pea pods, thawed
Hot cooked rice

> *Fat-skimming options: Omit oil and use nonstick cooking spray to brown the chicken.*
> *Reduce portion size and increase yield to 12 servings.*
> *With options, exchange diets count: 2 very lean meat, 1½ fruit, 1 vegetable, 1 starch.*

• Season chicken breasts with salt and pepper. Heat oil in 12 inch skillet or electric frypan over medium heat (350 degrees F) for 5 minutes or until hot. Meanwhile, drain pineapple, reserving juice. Brown chicken in hot oil, about 10 minutes.

• Stir in next seven ingredients and reserved juice. Bring to a boil, about 2 minutes. Reduce heat to low (220 degrees F). Cover; simmer 35 minutes or until chicken is tender.
• Remove chicken. Stir together cornstarch and ½ cup water. Stir cornstarch mixture into pan juices. Cook, stirring constantly, until mixture boils, about 2 minutes. Stir in pea pods and pineapple. Cook 1 minute.
• Arrange chicken and vegetables on rice.

Nutrition Analysis Per Serving: As Originally Published/With Fat-Skimming Options

Calories: 593/265	Saturated Fat: 1 g/2 g
Protein: 33 g/16 g	Cholesterol: 73 mg/42 mg
Carbohydrate: 93 g/35 g	Sodium: 884 mg/436 mg
Fat: 9 g/5 g	Dietary Fiber: 2 g/2 g

Chicken With Artichokes

Yield: 4 to 6 servings

½ cup flour
1 teaspoon salt
½ teaspoon pepper
¼ teaspoon garlic powder
3 chicken breasts, skinned, boned and halved
¼ cup cooking oil
¼ cup butter
¾ pound fresh mushrooms, sliced
1 (6 ounce) jar marinated artichoke hearts
½ cup pitted black olives, drained
1 cup chicken broth
Chopped fresh parsley

Fat-skimming options: Reduce oil to 1 tablespoon.
With options, exchange diets count: 4 lean meat, 1 starch.

• Combine first 4 ingredients in paper bag. Add chicken breasts and shake to coat. Cook chicken in hot oil and melted butter in 12 inch skillet over medium heat, until browned on both sides. Remove from skillet; place in 13x9x2 inch (3 quart) baking dish. Sauté mushrooms in same skillet. Arrange mushrooms around chicken.

• Place artichokes with liquid, olives and chicken broth in skillet. Cook 3 minutes, stirring constantly. Spoon over chicken. Cover with foil.
• Bake in 325 degree F oven 30 minutes. To serve, garnish with parsley.

Nutrition Analysis Per Serving: As Originally Published/With Fat-Skimming Options

Calories: 361/299
Protein: 29 g/29 g
Carbohydrate: 12 g/12 g
Fat: 22 g/15 g

Saturated Fat: 6 g/6 g
Cholesterol: 94 mg/94 mg
Sodium: 794 mg/794 mg
Dietary Fiber: 1 g/1 g

Chicken and Double-Corn Dumplings

Yield: 8 to 10 servings

1½ pounds boneless, skinless chicken, white or dark meat
8 to 10 cups water
3 carrots
4 ribs celery with leaves
1 medium onion
4 to 5 chicken bouillon cubes
Double-Corn Dumplings

Fat-skimming options: none. Exchange diets count: 3 very lean meat, 1 starch, 1 vegetable.

• In large soup kettle place chicken, water, 1 carrot and 1 rib celery, cut in several pieces, half the onion, and bouillon cubes. Bring to boiling and simmer for 15 minutes.
• Remove vegetables and discard. Set chicken aside.
• Chop remaining carrots, celery and onion. Place in broth and bring to boiling. Simmer for 15 minutes.
• Return chicken to broth and return to boiling.
• Meanwhile, prepare dumpling batter.
• Drop 8 to 10 dumplings gently onto top of stew without letting them sink. Cover tightly and return to boiling. Lower heat to medium and cook 15 minutes, not removing cover during cooking.

• Spoon broth and chicken into serving bowls. Top with dumplings and serve.

Double-Corn Dumplings

1 cup all-purpose flour
½ cup yellow cornmeal
2 teaspoons baking powder
½ teaspoon salt
½ cup whole kernel corn
1 egg
1 egg white
¼ cup water

• In small bowl, combine flour, cornmeal, baking powder and salt. Stir in corn.
• In another bowl, beat together 1 egg, 1 egg white and water. Stir egg mixture into dry ingredients just until moistened. Don't overstir.

Nutrition Analysis Per Serving: As Originally Published

Calories: 202
Protein: 20 g
Carbohydrate: 20 g
Fat: 4 g

Saturated Fat: 1 g
Cholesterol: 69 mg
Sodium: 639 mg
Dietary Fiber: 1.5 g

Crisp Oven-Fried Chicken
Yield: 8 servings

1 cup crushed saltines
¼ cup Parmesan cheese
1 tablespoon minced fresh parsley
½ teaspoon salt
½ teaspoon oregano
½ teaspoon basil
½ teaspoon celery salt
½ teaspoon onion salt
¼ teaspoon paprika
¼ teaspoon pepper
½ bay leaf, crushed
2 (3 pound) broiler-fryers, cut up
½ cup evaporated milk
⅓ cup cooking oil

Fat-skimming options: Remove all skin from chicken. Substitute evaporated skim milk. Reduce oil to 2 tablespoons. Reduce portion size to yield 12 servings of chicken. With options, exchange diets count: 8 lean meat.

• Combine saltines, Parmesan cheese, parsley, salt, oregano, basil, celery and onion salt, paprika, pepper and bay leaf. Dip chicken pieces in evaporated milk and coat with crumbs.

• Place in shallow roasting pan, skin side up. Bake at 375 degrees F for 30 minutes. Brush with oil; continue baking for 30 minutes or until golden brown and tender.

Nutrition Analysis Per Serving: As Originally Published/With Fat-Skimming Options

Calories: 856/450
Protein: 85 g/62 g
Carbohydrate: 4 g/3 g
Fat: 54 g/19 g

Saturated Fat: 14 g/6 g
Cholesterol: 267 mg/187 mg
Sodium: 526 mg/359 mg
Dietary Fiber: 0 g/0 g

Golden Glazed Oven Chicken Barbecue

Yield: 4 servings

1 (3 pound) broiler-fryer, cut up
¼ cup biscuit baking mix
½ teaspoon salt
¼ teaspoon rubbed sage
¼ teaspoon basil leaves
¼ cup cooking oil
½ cup frozen orange juice concentrate, thawed
⅓ cup pineapple juice
3 tablespoons firmly packed brown sugar
1 teaspoon prepared mustard
¼ teaspoon ground ginger
Pineapple slices, orange wedges, parsley (optional)

Fat-skimming options: Remove all skin from chicken. Use reduced-fat baking mix. Reduce oil to 2 tablespoons for browning. With options, exchange diets count: 8 lean meat, 2 fruit.

• Coat chicken with a mixture of baking mix, salt, sage and basil. Brown chicken on all sides in hot oil in 10 inch skillet over medium heat. As chicken pieces brown, remove and place in foil-lined 13x9x2 inch baking pan.
• Combine orange juice concentrate, pineapple juice, brown sugar, mustard and ginger; brush on chicken.
• Bake in 325 degree F oven 1 hour, or until a fork can be inserted with ease, brushing chicken every 15 minutes during baking. Garnish with pineapple slices, orange wedges and parsley if you wish.

Nutrition Analysis Per Serving: As Originally Published/With Fat-Skimming Options

Calories: 798/549	Saturated Fat: 9 g/4 g
Protein: 64 g/56 g	Cholesterol: 196 mg/162 mg
Carbohydrate: 31 g/31 g	Sodium: 536 mg/513 mg
Fat: 45 g/21 g	Dietary Fiber: 1 g/1 g

"Pop Eye" Pot Pie

Yield: 6 servings

2 cups sifted flour
½ teaspoon salt
2 tablespoons shortening
2 eggs
¼ cup milk
6 cups chicken or turkey broth
1 cup shredded carrots
½ cup finely chopped, cooked chicken or turkey

> *Fat-skimming options: Omit shortening and use 2 tablespoons margarine.*
> *Use ½ cup liquid egg substitute for eggs. Use skim milk.*
> *With options, exchange diets count: 2 starch, 1 vegetable, 2 lean meat.*

• In bowl, stir together flour and salt. Using pastry blender, cut in shortening. Add eggs and milk. With fork, stir until mixture forms a firm dough.

• On lightly floured surface, roll out dough to an 18x16 inch rectangle. Cut into 2-inch squares.

• In 4-quart Dutch oven over high heat, bring broth, carrots and chicken to a boil. Add dough squares, one at a time, stirring with wooden spoon. When all squares are added, reduce heat to medium. Boil 20 minutes, stirring occasionally, until most of the broth is absorbed.

Nutrition Analysis Per Serving: As Originally Published/With Fat-Skimming Options

Calories: 306/289	Saturated Fat: 2 g/1 g
Protein: 15 g/15 g	Cholesterol: 93 mg/22 mg
Carbohydrate: 34 g/34 g	Sodium: 1,549 mg/1,597 mg
Fat: 11 g/9 g	Dietary Fiber: 1.5 g/1.5 g

Sunday Special Chicken

Yield: 6 servings

3 whole chicken breasts, halved
1/3 cup flour
1/2 teaspoon salt
1/2 cup cooking oil
1/2 cup dairy sour cream
3/4 cup bacon-flavored bits
2/3 cup orange marmalade
1/3 cup maple syrup

Fat-skimming options: Remove all skin from chicken. Reduce oil to 2 tablespoons for browning. Substitute nonfat sour cream. With options, exchange diets count: 4 lean meat, 2 fruit, 1/2 starch.

• Coat chicken breasts with a mixture of flour and salt. Brown chicken on all sides in hot oil in 10 inch skillet over medium heat. As chicken browns, remove and place in 13x9x2 inch baking pan.
• Combine sour cream, bacon-flavored bits, marmalade and maple syrup; mix well. Brush mixture over chicken.

• Bake in 350 degree F oven 45 minutes, or until a fork can be inserted with ease.

Nutrition Analysis Per Serving: As Originally Published/With Fat-Skimming Options

Calories: 570/372
Protein: 32 g/30 g
Carbohydrate: 39 g/43 g
Fat: 32 g/9 g

Saturated Fat: 6 g/2 g
Cholesterol: 92 mg/76 mg
Sodium: 324 mg/338 mg
Dietary Fiber: 0 g/0 g

Sweet-Hot Chicken Stir-Fry

Yield: 5 servings

2 tablespoons vegetable oil
1 pound boneless chicken, cut in 1¹/₂x3 inch pieces
1 (16 ounce) package frozen stir-fry vegetables
¹/₃ cup low-sodium teriyaki sauce or low-sodium soy sauce
2 tablespoons orange juice concentrate
¹/₄ to ¹/₂ teaspoon hot pepper flakes
Hot cooked rice and chow mein noodles

> *Fat-skimming options: Reduce oil to 1 teaspoon, using ¹/₂ teaspoon for chicken and ¹/₂ teaspoon for vegetables in a no-stick skillet or wok.*
> *With options, exchange diets count: 5 very lean meat, 3 starch, 2 vegetable.*

• In wok or skillet, heat 1 tablespoon oil over medium heat. Add chicken and cook until meat is no longer pink. Remove from wok and keep warm.
• Heat remaining oil. Add vegetables and stir-fry 1 minute. Stir in teriyaki sauce, orange juice concentrate and hot pepper flakes. Heat to boiling. Cover and cook 4 to 6 minutes.

• Return meat to wok and toss to warm thoroughly. Serve over rice and chow mein noodles.

Nutrition Analysis Per Serving: As Originally Published/With Fat-Skimming Options

Calories: 502/460
Protein: 36 g/36 g
Carbohydrate: 61 g/61 g
Fat: 11 g/6 g

Saturated Fat: 2 g/2 g
Cholesterol: 80 mg/80 mg
Sodium: 111 mg/111 mg
Dietary Fiber: 3 g/3 g

Swiss Chicken Pie

Yield: 6 servings

1 (10¾ ounce) can condensed cream of mushroom soup
⅓ cup milk
2 whole skinless, boneless chicken breasts, cooked and cubed (1 inch)
1 cup sliced carrots, cooked and drained
1 (10 ounce) package frozen cauliflower, thawed and drained
1 (10 ounce) package frozen broccoli spears, thawed, drained and cut up
1 (4 ounce) jar sliced pimiento, drained
1½ cups shredded Swiss cheese
Pastry for single-crust pie

> *Fat-skimming options: Use fat-free cream of mushroom soup, skim milk,*
> *reduced-fat Swiss cheese. Omit the pastry and sprinkle 1 cup seasoned bread crumbs on top.*
> *With options, exchange diets count: 3 lean meat, 1 vegetable, 1½ starch.*

• In bowl, stir together condensed soup and milk. Fold in remaining ingredients except pastry. Spoon into ungreased 2-quart rectangular baking dish.
• Roll out pastry to ⅛ inch thickness; cut into ¾ inch strips. Twist strips about 4 times each and arrange in a crisscross pattern over ingredients in dish.

• Bake in 400 degree F oven 40 minutes, or until pie is bubbly and pastry is golden brown.

Nutrition Analysis Per Serving: As Originally Published/With Fat-Skimming Options	
Calories: 451/323	Saturated Fat: 9 g/3 g
Protein: 32 g/24 g	Cholesterol: 77 mg/71 mg
Carbohydrate: 27 g/27 g	Sodium: 755 mg/1,044 mg
Fat: 24 g/9 g	Dietary Fiber: 3 g/3 g

Tandoori Chicken

Yield: 8 servings

1 (8 ounce) carton plain nonfat yogurt
1 to 2 cloves garlic, minced
1 tablespoon lemon juice
1 teaspoon ground coriander
1 teaspoon ground ginger
$1/2$ teaspoon salt
$1/2$ teaspoon ground cumin
$1/2$ teaspoon ground turmeric
$1/4$ teaspoon ground cloves
$1/4$ teaspoon pepper
8 whole chicken legs, skin removed
$1^1/2$ cups diced pitted plums
1 cup peeled, seeded and diced cucumber
2 tablespoons sliced green onion
1 tablespoon sugar
1 tablespoon vinegar
$1/8$ teaspoon salt

Fat-skimming options: none. Exchange diets count: 2 lean meat, 1 vegetable.

• In 13x9 inch baking dish, stir together first 10 ingredients. Add chicken legs; turn to coat. Cover and refrigerate 6 hours or overnight.
• In bowl, stir together plums and remaining 5 ingredients. Cover and refrigerate until ready to serve.
• Place chicken on broiler pan; spoon any yogurt marinade over chicken.
• Broil 7 inches from source of heat 12 to 15 minutes on each side. Serve with plum and cucumber relish.

Nutrition Analysis Per Serving: As Originally Published

Calories: 132
Protein: 14 g
Carbohydrate: 9 g
Fat: 4 g

Saturated Fat: 1 g
Cholesterol: 43 mg
Sodium: 237 mg
Dietary Fiber: 1 g

Unfried Chicken

Yield: 8 servings

1½ cups soft bread crumbs
1½ teaspoons paprika
1 teaspoon onion powder
½ teaspoon salt
¼ teaspoon pepper
4 chicken breast halves, skinned (2½ pounds)
4 whole chicken legs, skinned (2½ pounds)
¼ cup evaporated milk

Fat-skimming options: Use evaporated skim milk.
With options, exchange diets count: 3 very lean meat, 1 starch.

• In shallow dish, mix together the first 5 ingredients.
• Dip chicken pieces in evaporated milk and coat with crumb mixture. Place in single layer in shallow roasting pan.

• Bake in 400 degree F oven 45 minutes or until golden brown. Serve hot or cold.

Nutrition Analysis Per Serving: As Originally Published/With Fat-Skimming Options

Calories: 199/195
Protein: 23 g/23 g
Carbohydrate: 15 g/15 g
Fat: 4 g/4 g

Saturated Fat: 1 g/1 g
Cholesterol: 59 mg/57 mg
Sodium: 368 mg/368 mg
Dietary Fiber: 1 g/1 g

Sweet and Sour Turkey

Yield: 6 servings

1 (20 ounce) can pineapple chunks
1/2 cup firmly packed brown sugar
1/4 cup cornstarch
1/2 teaspoon ground ginger
1/2 cup cider vinegar
1/4 cup soy sauce
1 1/4 cups green pepper strips
1 cup sliced onion
1 cup sliced carrots
2 cups cubed cooked turkey
6 cups hot fluffy rice

Fat-skimming options: none. Exchange diets count: 2 lean meat, 1 fruit, 4 1/2 starch.

• Drain pineapple; reserve juice. Add water to juice to make 3 cups.
• Combine brown sugar, cornstarch and ginger. Stir in pineapple juice, vinegar and soy sauce. Bring mixture to a boil, stirring constantly. Add green pepper, onion, carrots and turkey. Cover; simmer 10 minutes or until vegetables are tender-crisp. Serve with rice.

Nutrition Analysis Per Serving: As Originally Published

Calories: 519
Protein: 20 g
Carbohydrate: 98 g
Fat: 5 g

Saturated Fat: 1 g
Cholesterol: 0 mg/0 mg
Sodium: 658 mg
Dietary Fiber: 1 g

Turkey Curry With Rice

Yield: 6 servings

1 cup sliced onion
¼ cup sliced carrots
¼ cup sliced celery
1 apple, pared, cored and sliced
1 clove garlic, minced
¼ cup butter
⅓ cup flour
2½ teaspoons curry powder
¼ teaspoon ground ginger
¼ teaspoon ground mace
¼ teaspoon pepper
2 cups chicken broth
1 (4 ounce) can mushrooms
3 cups cubed cooked turkey
2 cups dairy sour cream
6 cups hot fluffy rice
Condiments: Chopped onion, raisins, chopped green pepper, chopped tomato, chopped hard-cooked eggs, chopped peanuts, coconut, chutney

Fat-skimming options: Replace butter with 1 tablespoon soft margarine.
Substitute nonfat sour cream. With options, exchange diets count: 4 lean meat, 4 starch.

• Sauté onion, carrots, celery, apple and garlic in melted butter.
• Slowly blend in flour, curry powder, ginger, mace and pepper. Gradually add chicken broth and undrained mushrooms. Cook over medium heat, stirring constantly, until mixture comes to a boil. Simmer 5 minutes.

• Stir in turkey. Heat well. Stir in sour cream; heat 2 more minutes. Serve with rice. Pass a selection of condiments.

Nutrition Analysis Per Serving: As Originally Published/With Fat-Skimming Options

Calories: 674/543
Protein: 32 g/37 g
Carbohydrate: 71 g/81 g
Fat: 29 g/7 g

Saturated Fat: 17 g/2 g
Cholesterol: 149 mg/81 mg
Sodium: 633 mg/654 mg
Dietary Fiber: 1 g/1 g

Turkey Bow-Tie Casserole
Yield: 4 servings

1 tablespoon regular margarine or butter
¼ pound mushrooms, sliced
⅓ cup chopped onion
1 cup dairy half and half
2 chicken bouillon cubes, crumbled
¼ teaspoon pepper
1 cup water
1½ tablespoons cornstarch
1 (4 ounce) jar sliced pimientos, drained
3 tablespoons chopped fresh parsley
6 tablespoons grated Parmesan cheese, divided
6 ounces bow-shaped egg noodles, cooked and drained
2 cups cubed (½ inch) cooked turkey

> *Fat-skimming options: Use evaporated skim milk for half and half.*
> *With options, exchange diets count: 4 lean meat, 1½ starch, 1 vegetable.*

• In 3-quart saucepan over medium heat, melt margarine. Add mushrooms and onion; cook until tender. Stir in half and half, bouillon cubes and pepper.
• In bowl, stir together water and cornstarch. Stir into mushroom mixture.
• Cook, stirring constantly, until mixture comes to a boil. Boil 1 minute.
• Stir in pimientos, parsley and 4 tablespoons Parmesan cheese. Remove from heat.

• Stir in noodles and turkey. Spoon into greased 1½-quart baking dish. Sprinkle with remaining 2 tablespoons Parmesan cheese. Cover loosely with foil.
• Bake in 350 degree F oven 25 minutes or until hot and bubbly. Let stand 10 minutes before serving.
• **To freeze and bake later:** Prepare as directed, but do not bake. Wrap in foil; freeze. When ready to bake, unwrap frozen casserole. Loosely cover with foil. Bake in 400 degree F oven 50 minutes; stir. Cover and bake about 30 minutes more or until hot and bubbly. Let stand 10 minutes before serving.

Nutrition Analysis Per Serving: As Originally Published/With Fat-Skimming Options

Calories: 395/365	Saturated Fat: 10 g/5 g
Protein: 29 g/32 g	Cholesterol: 51 mg/29 mg
Carbohydrate: 20 g/25 g	Sodium: 1,824 mg/1,874 mg
Fat: 21 g/14 g	Dietary Fiber: 1 g/1 g

CHAPTER EIGHT

PRESERVED FOODS

Mom, I learned all this from you!

Esther Vermeer has easily managed canning and freezing as well as large-group cooking for years on her farm in northwest Iowa. But she was shocked to visit her grown daughter recently and see home-canned tomato juice on the kitchen counter. All those years on the farm, it felt like she had to twist the kids' arms for help in the kitchen. She never would have predicted the art of food preservation to be carried on in her family.

Her daughter now cans peaches, apricots and applesauce, freezes corn and cooks for large groups at her church, assuring Esther: "Mom, I learned all this from you."

Esther has selected Farm Journal recipe ideas over the years for their reliance on common ingredients and proven results. You will find classic recipes for Rhubarb-Raspberry Jam, Sweet Corn Relish and V-4 Tomato Juice Cocktail in this chapter.

Cherry Jam

Yield: 6 cups jam or 96 (1 tablespoon) servings

5 cups chopped cherries, fresh or frozen
1/4 cup water
4 teaspoons lemon juice
3 cups granulated sugar
1 box (1.75 ounce) reduced-sugar pectin

Fat-skimming options: none. Exchange diets count: 1/2 fruit.

• In large saucepan, stir together cherries, water and lemon juice. Set aside.
• In a bowl, measure sugar. Remove 1/4 cup sugar to mix with pectin in another bowl. Stir pectin-sugar mixture into cherries, reserving remaining sugar.

• Bring mixture to full rolling boil that can't be stirred down over high heat, stirring constantly.
• Stir in remaining sugar and return to full, rolling boil and boil for 1 minute, stirring constantly. Remove from heat.
• Pour into sterilized jars and process in water bath canner, or freeze.

Nutrition Analysis Per Serving: As Originally Published

Calories: 29	Saturated Fat: 0 g
Protein: 0 g	Cholesterol: 0 mg
Carbohydrate: 7 g	Sodium: 0 mg
Fat: 0 g	Dietary Fiber: 0 g

Cranberry Honey

Yield: Makes 5 (6 ounce) glasses or 60 (2 tablespoon) servings

2 cups cranberry cocktail
3 cups sugar
1 teaspoon grated orange rind
1 cup honey
½ bottle or 1 pouch of fruit pectin

Fat-skimming options: Use reduced-sugar pectin. Reduce sugar to 2 cups.
With options, exchange diets count: 1 fruit.

• Bring first 3 ingredients to a boil; simmer 10 minutes. Add honey. Bring to a rapid boil; boil 1 minute. Remove from heat.

• Add pectin; skim. Pour into sterilized jelly glasses. Seal.

Nutrition Analysis Per Serving: As Originally Published/With Fat-Skimming Options

Calories: 64/50	Saturated Fat: 0 g/0 g
Protein: 0 g/0 g	Cholesterol: 0 mg/0 mg
Carbohydrate: 17 g/13 g	Sodium: 1 mg/2 mg
Fat: 0 g/0 g	Dietary Fiber: 0 g/0 g

Rhubarb-Raspberry Jam

Yield: 7¹/₂ cups or 120 (1 tablespoon) servings

6 cups chopped rhubarb
4 cups granulated sugar
1 (21 ounce) can raspberry pie filling
1 (3 ounce) box raspberry-flavored gelatin

Fat-skimming options: none. Exchange diets count: ¹/₂ fruit.

• In large saucepan, combine rhubarb and sugar. Let stand about 1 hour.
• Bring to boiling, and cook over medium heat about 10 minutes, stirring often. Stir in raspberry pie filling and gelatin. Cook for about 10 minutes longer. Remove from heat.

• Pour into sterilized jars and process in water bath canner, or freeze.

Nutrition Analysis Per Serving: As Originally Published

Calories: 33
Protein: 0 g
Carbohydrate: 9 g
Fat: 0 g

Saturated Fat: 0 g
Cholesterol: 0 mg
Sodium: 2 mg
Dietary Fiber: 0 g

Cucumber Refrigerator Pickles

Yield: 1 gallon or 32 (2 tablespoon) servings

4 pounds cucumbers, sliced (1 gallon)
1 quart 5%-acid strength white vinegar
3 cups sugar
1 cup chopped fresh dill
1 tablespoon pickling spice
1 tablespoon whole black peppercorns
8 cloves garlic, sliced

Fat-skimming options: none. Exchange diets count: free.

• Place cucumber slices in 1-gallon glass jar with tight-fitting lid.
• Stir together remaining ingredients in large bowl until well mixed. (Sugar need not dissolve.) Pour over cucumbers. Cover.

• Refrigerate 3 days, carefully inverting jar or stirring once each day. Store in refrigerator up to 3 months.

Nutrition Analysis Per Serving: As Originally Published

Calories: 18	Saturated Fat: 0 g
Protein: 0 g	Cholesterol: 0 mg
Carbohydrate: 5 g	Sodium: 1 mg
Fat: 0 g	Dietary Fiber: 0 g

Dilled Green Beans

Yield: 7 quarts or 112 (¹/₄ cup) servings

9 pounds green beans
Fresh garlic cloves
Fresh dill weed
2 quarts water
1 quart cider vinegar
³/₄ teaspoon salt

Fat-skimming options: none. Exchange diets count: free.

• Wash beans and cut off ends. Cook beans in boiling water for 10 minutes. Cool in cold water. Drain. Pack beans, garlic and dill weed in hot jars.

• Combine water, vinegar and salt in a saucepan. Bring to a boil. Pour over beans in jars. Seal; store in refrigerator. Should keep for a few months. (Do not store at room temperature.)

Nutrition Analysis Per Serving: As Originally Published

Calories: 7
Protein: 0 g
Carbohydrate: 2 g
Fat: 0 g

Saturated Fat: 0 g
Cholesterol: 0 mg
Sodium: 15 mg
Dietary Fiber: 0 g

Homemade Sauerkraut

Yield: 50 pounds of cabbage makes about 15 quarts or 120 (¹/₂) cup servings

You will need roughly 5 pounds cabbage for every gallon of your crock. For instance, a 10 gallon crock would need about 50 pounds of cabbage.

Fat-skimming options: none. Exchange diets count: 1 vegetable.

• Quarter cabbage and shred finely. Place 5 pounds shredded cabbage and 3¹/₂ tablespoons pickling salt in large pan. Mix well with hands. Pack gently in large crock, using a potato masher to press it down. Repeat above procedure until crock is filled to within 5 inches from the top.
• Press cabbage down firmly with potato masher to extract enough juice to cover. Cover with clean cloth. Place a plate on top and weight it with a jar filled with water.

• Keep crock at 65 degrees F to ferment. Check kraut daily. Remove scum as it forms. Wash and scald cloth often to keep it free from scum and mold. Fermentation will be complete in 10 to 12 days. (If no bubbles rise, fermentation has ended.)
• Pack in hot, sterilized jars to within 1 inch from top. Add enough juice to cover. If you need more juice, make a weak brine by combining 2 tablespoon salt and 1 quart water. Cover jars; screw bands tight. Process in boiling water bath 15 minutes.

Nutrition Analysis Per Serving: As Originally Published

Calories: 15
Protein: 1 g
Carbohydrate: 3 g
Fat: 0 g

Saturated Fat: 0 g
Cholesterol: 0 mg
Sodium: 943 mg
Dietary Fiber: 1 g

Potpourri Relish

Yield: 6 cups or 18 (¹/₃ cup) servings

³/₄ cup red wine vinegar
¹/₂ cup olive oil
¹/₄ cup water
2 tablespoons sugar
1¹/₂ teaspoons salt
1 teaspoon oregano
¹/₄ teaspoon pepper
¹/₂ medium cauliflower, cut in flowerets
2 carrots, cut in 2 inch strips
2 stalks celery, cut in 1 inch slices
1 green pepper, cut in 2 inch strips
1 (4 ounce) jar pimiento, drained and cut in strips
¹/₂ cup sliced pimiento-stuffed olives
2 medium onions, sliced
1 clove garlic
1 bay leaf

Fat-skimming options: Omit olive oil. With options, exchange diets count: 1 vegetable.

• Combine first 7 ingredients in a large skillet or Dutch oven. Add cauliflower, carrots, celery and green pepper. Bring to a boil, stirring occasionally. Reduce heat; simmer, covered, for 5 minutes. Cool.
• Combine cooled vegetables with pimiento, olives and onions.

• Place garlic clove and bay leaf in mixture and refrigerate at least 24 hours so vegetables can marinate. Remove bay leaf and garlic clove. Store in refrigerator or process using hot water bath method.

Nutrition Analysis Per Serving: As Originally Published/With Fat-Skimming Options

Calories: 77/24
Protein: 1 g/1 g
Carbohydrate: 5 g/5 g
Fat: 7 g/1 g

Saturated Fat: 1 g/0 g
Cholesterol: 0 mg/0 mg
Sodium: 223 mg/223 mg
Dietary Fiber: 1 g/1 g

Sweet Corn Relish

Yield: 8 pints or 64 (¹/₄ cup) servings

10 cups fresh, frozen or canned whole kernel corn
7 cups shredded cabbage
2 cups chopped onion
³/₄ cup chopped green pepper
³/₄ cup chopped sweet red pepper
2 tablespoons dry mustard
1¹/₂ teaspoons flour
¹/₂ teaspoon turmeric
1 quart cider vinegar
2 cups sugar
2 tablespoons salt

Fat-skimming options: none. Exchange diets count: 1 fruit.

• Combine corn, cabbage, onion, green and red pepper in a large kettle.
• Mix together mustard, flour and turmeric. Add ¹/₄ cup vinegar to mustard mixture, stirring to blend well. Add mustard mixture, remaining vinegar, sugar and salt to corn, mixing well.

• Bring vegetables to a boil; reduce heat and simmer, uncovered, for 15 minutes. Ladle into jars; seal. Process in boiling water bath for 15 minutes.

Nutrition Analysis Per Serving: As Originally Published	
Calories: 52	Saturated Fat: 0 g
Protein: 1 g	Cholesterol: 0 mg
Carbohydrate: 13 g	Sodium: 201 mg
Fat: 0 g	Dietary Fiber: 1 g

V-4 Tomato Juice Cocktail

Yield: 7 quarts or 56 (¹/₂ cup) servings

18 pounds ripe tomatoes (7 quarts juice)
¹/₄ cup chopped onions
1 cup chopped carrots
2 cups chopped celery
¹/₃ cup sugar
4 tablespoons canning/pickling salt
1 tablespoon celery seeds
¹/₈ teaspoon cayenne pepper

Fat-skimming options: none. Exchange diets count: 1 vegetable.

• Dip tomatoes into boiling water for ¹/₂ minute to loosen skins. Cool in cold water. Drain. Remove skins and cores; set aside.
• Place 12-quart kettle over heat. Quarter tomatoes directly into kettle a few at a time so that you maintain a boil; this procedure helps minimize separation of juice.
• Gradually add chopped vegetables, always maintaining boil. Add sugar, salt and spices. Simmer 20 minutes, uncovered.

• Put through sieve or food mill. Return juice to pot; bring to a boil.
• Pour into 7 hot quart jars, filling to within ¹/₂ inch of jar tops. Wipe jar rims; adjust lids.
• Process in boiling water bath 35 minutes. Start to count processing time when water in canner returns to boiling. Remove jars and complete seals unless closures are self-sealing.
• **Note:** If you wish to acidify your juice, add 4 teaspoons lemon juice to each quart jar.

Nutrition Analysis Per Serving: As Originally Published

Calories: 35
Protein: 2 g
Carbohydrate: 8 g
Fat: 0 g

Saturated Fat: 0 g
Cholesterol: 0 mg
Sodium: 709 mg
Dietary Fiber: 0 g

CHAPTER NINE

MEATS

I stay away from anything totally fat-free

These are the words of cooking contest winner Rosalie Seebeck of Bethany, Okla. Her winning recipes have been featured in Farm Journal and she has smoked her competition at Good Housekeeping Kitchens in New York City. A natural competitor, Rosalie has won state and regional beef contests and enjoys the challenge and creative thrill of cooking in front of judges.

Beef contests currently restrict contestants to 30 minutes or less preparation time and the use of five or fewer ingredients. Today's consumers want tasty, quick and healthy food, in that order. The days of touting 12 ounce marbled steaks are gone.

Rosalie aims to protect the flavor and goodness of the beef while whittling away at calories and fats. And that's our aim, too. You will find both the traditional and new meats in this chapter, with a range of recipes for beef, pork, lamb and veal. Contest winners such as Ham-Pineapple Rings are side by side with family favorites like Round Steak with Mushroom Gravy.

Bacon-Wrapped Beef Patties

Yield: 6 servings

2 pounds ground beef
1 cup shredded Cheddar cheese
²/₃ cup chopped onion
¹/₄ cup ketchup
2 tablespoons Parmesan cheese
2 tablespoons Worcestershire sauce
1 teaspoon salt
¹/₄ teaspoon pepper
2 eggs
12 strips bacon

Fat-skimming options: Choose extra-lean ground beef. Substitute reduced-fat Cheddar cheese. Increase servings to 12. With options, exchange diets count: 4 lean meat, 2 fat.

• Combine ground beef, cheese, onion, ketchup, Parmesan cheese, Worcestershire sauce, salt, pepper and eggs. Mix well. Divide mixture in half. Shape each half into an 11 inch roll.
• Place 6 strips bacon on a piece of waxed paper. Place beef roll on one end of bacon strips. Roll up, using waxed paper as an aid, so that roll is wrapped with bacon. Cut into 6 patties. Secure bacon ends with toothpicks. Place on broiler rack. Repeat with other roll.

• Broil 7 inches from source of heat for 6 minutes. Turn patties over and broil 3 minutes.
• **Note:** Whole beef rolls can be baked, if you wish. Bake at 375 degrees F for 40 minutes.

Nutrition Analysis Per Serving: As Originally Published/With Fat-Skimming Options

Calories: 695/312
Protein: 54 g/30 g
Carbohydrate: 3 g/2 g
Fat: 51 g/20 g

Saturated Fat: 23 g/10 g
Cholesterol: 253 mg/122 mg
Sodium: 1,014 mg/440 mg
Dietary Fiber: 0 g/0 g

Barbecued Beef Buns

Yield: 8 servings

4 cups cooked roast beef, cut into strips (2x$\frac{1}{2}$x$\frac{1}{4}$ inch)
1 cup ketchup
$\frac{1}{2}$ cup cider vinegar
$\frac{1}{2}$ cup butter
$\frac{1}{4}$ cup sugar
2 medium onions, thinly sliced
2 lemon slices
2 tablespoons Worcestershire sauce
4 teaspoons prepared mustard
1 teaspoon salt
$\frac{1}{4}$ teaspoon chili powder
$\frac{1}{4}$ teaspoon pepper
$\frac{1}{2}$ cup water
8 hamburger buns

Fat-skimming options: Omit butter.
With options, exchange diets count: 5 lean meat, 1 fat, 1 fruit, 1 starch.

• Combine all ingredients except buns in 4-quart Dutch oven. Simmer, uncovered, 25 minutes or until mixture thickens. Remove lemon slices.

• Serve on hamburger buns.

Nutrition Analysis Per Serving: As Originally Published/With Fat-Skimming Options	
Calories: 468/366	Saturated Fat: 10 g/3 g
Protein: 38 g/38 g	Cholesterol: 126 mg/95 mg
Carbohydrate: 33 g/33 g	Sodium: 1,064 mg/946 mg
Fat: 21 g/9 g	Dietary Fiber: 5 g/5 g

Dill Mustard

Yield: 1 cup or 16 (1 tablespoon) servings

6 tablespoons sugar
6 tablespoons vegetable oil
⅓ cup dry mustard
¼ cup prepared yellow mustard
2 tablespoons hot water
1 tablespoon dried dill weed

Fat-skimming options: Reduce oil to 2 tablespoons. With options, exchange diets count: ½ fruit.

• In medium bowl, using wire whisk, beat all ingredients until well blended and smooth.
• Cover. Refrigerate at least 12 hours before serving, to blend flavors. Keeps up to 1 month in refrigerator.
• Dill Mustard may also be mixed in equal parts with reduced-fat mayonnaise as a sauce for beef, ham or pork chops.

Nutrition Analysis Per Serving: As Originally Published/With Fat-Skimming Options

Calories: 66/35
Protein: 0 g/0 g
Carbohydrate: 5 g/5 g
Fat: 5 g/222 g

Saturated Fat: 0 g/0 g
Cholesterol: 0 mg/0 mg
Sodium: 47 mg/47 mg
Dietary Fiber: 0 g/0 g

Marinated Beef Kabobs

Yield: 6 to 8 servings

2¹/₂ pounds round steak, 1 inch thick
³/₄ cup cooking oil
¹/₃ cup soy sauce
2 tablespoons Worcestershire sauce
¹/₄ cup minced onion
3 tablespoons minced fresh parsley
1 clove garlic, minced
¹/₃ cup lemon juice
¹/₄ teaspoon pepper
1 large green pepper, cut in 1¹/₂-inch chunks
12 small onions
3 small zucchini squash, cut in 1 inch slices
16 cherry tomatoes
1 (13¹/₂ ounce) can pineapple chunks, drained

Fat-skimming options: Reduce oil to 2 tablespoons.
With options, exchange diets count: 5 lean meat, 1 fruit, 1 vegetable.

• Cut beef in 32 (1 inch) pieces. Combine next 8 ingredients; mix well. Pour over beef in bowl. Cover and marinate in refrigerator 24 to 48 hours.
• Cook green pepper, onions and squash until tender-crisp. Drain.

• Thread 8 (12 inch) skewers with alternate pieces of beef, vegetables and pineapple, using 4 pieces of meat on each. Broil 4 skewers at a time, 3 inches from the source of heat, 5 minutes. Turn as needed. Baste with marinade frequently. (Meat will be medium done.) Repeat with remaining skewers.

Nutrition Analysis Per Serving: As Originally Published/With Fat-Skimming Options	
Calories: 535/380	Saturated Fat: 5 g/4 g
Protein: 42 g/42 g	Cholesterol: 107 mg/107 mg
Carbohydrate: 18 g/18 g	Sodium: 137 mg/137 mg
Fat: 33 g/15 g	Dietary Fiber: 2 g/2 g

Meatball Stew

Yield: 6 to 8 servings

1$\frac{1}{2}$ pounds ground beef
1 cup soft bread crumbs
$\frac{1}{4}$ cup finely chopped onions
1 egg, beaten
1 teaspoon salt
$\frac{1}{2}$ teaspoon marjoram
$\frac{1}{4}$ teaspoon thyme
2 tablespoons cooking oil
1 (10$\frac{1}{2}$ ounce) can condensed tomato soup
1 (10$\frac{1}{2}$ ounce) can condensed beef broth
4 medium potatoes, pared and quartered
4 carrots, scraped and cut in 1 inch chunks
8 small white onions, peeled
2 tablespoons chopped parsley

Fat-skimming options: Omit oil and use nonstick spray shortening to brown meatballs.
Use $\frac{1}{4}$ cup liquid egg substitute for egg.
With options, exchange diets count: 4 lean meat, 2 starch, 1 vegetable.

• Combine first 7 ingredients. Shape into 24 meatballs.
• Brown meatballs in oil in a 4-quart Dutch oven. Remove as they brown. Combine soup and broth in Dutch oven. Add meatballs and vegetables. Bring to a boil; cover and simmer for 30 minutes or until vegetables are tender. Add parsley.

Nutrition Analysis Per Serving: As Originally Published/With Fat-Skimming Options

Calories: 436/396
Protein: 27 g/27 g
Carbohydrate: 38 g/38 g
Fat: 20 g/15 g

Saturated Fat: 6 g/5 g
Cholesterol: 98 mg/75 mg
Sodium: 892 mg/892 mg
Dietary Fiber: 3 g/3 g

Old-Fashioned Beef and Biscuits

Yield: 6 servings

3 cups cubed cooked beef
2 cups beef broth
1 cup homemade or canned beef gravy
1 cup frozen peas
1 cup sliced, cooked carrots
1 (4 ounce) can mushroom stems and pieces, drained
$^1/_3$ cup finely chopped onion
$^1/_2$ teaspoon Worcestershire sauce
$^1/_{16}$ teaspoon pepper
3 tablespoons cornstarch
3 tablespoons water
Hot biscuits

Fat-skimming options: none. Exchange diets count: 6 very lean meat, 1 vegetable, $^1/_2$ starch.

• Combine first 9 ingredients in 3-quart saucepan. Simmer, uncovered, 5 minutes, stirring occasionally.
• Blend together cornstarch and water. Stir into beef mixture and cook until mixture thickens.

• Serve over hot biscuits. Also good served over mashed potatoes or buttered noodles.

Nutrition Analysis Per Serving: As Originally Published	
Calories: 281	Saturated Fat: 2 g
Protein: 40 g	Cholesterol: 96 mg
Carbohydrate: 13 g	Sodium: 759 mg
Fat: 7 g	Dietary Fiber: 0 g

Pot Roast With Vegetable Gravy

Yield: 6 to 8 servings

1 (3 pound) boned rump roast
$^1/_2$ teaspoon salt
$^1/_8$ teaspoon pepper
1 tablespoon cooking oil
1 cup chopped celery
$^1/_2$ cup chopped onion
$^1/_2$ cup diced carrot
1 clove garlic, minced
1 beef bouillon cube
1 cup water
1 (8 ounce) can tomato sauce
$^1/_2$ teaspoon oregano
2 tablespoons cornstarch
$^1/_2$ cup water

Fat-skimming options: Omit oil and use nonstick cooking spray to brown meat. Increase servings to 12. With options, exchange diets count: 6 very lean meat.

• Season meat with salt and pepper. Brown well in hot oil in Dutch oven. Remove meat. Add celery, onion, carrots and garlic to hot oil; sauté until tender (do not brown). Add bouillon cube, 1 cup water, tomato sauce and oregano. Bring to a boil. Return meat to Dutch oven. Cover.
• Bake in 325 degree F oven for 2$^1/_2$ hours or until tender.
• Remove meat and keep warm. Skim off excess fat. Slowly stir combined cornstarch and $^1/_2$ cup water into pan juices. Bring to a boil; boil 1 minute.

Nutrition Analysis Per Serving: As Originally Published/With Fat-Skimming Options

Calories: 326/207
Protein: 50 g/33 g
Carbohydrate: 7 g/5 g
Fat: 10 g/5 g

Saturated Fat: 4 g/3 g
Cholesterol: 120 mg/80 mg
Sodium: 570 mg/380 mg
Dietary Fiber: 1 g/1 g

Grilled Southwestern Steak

Yield: 6 servings

¼ cup fresh lime juice
¼ cup bottled steak sauce
¼ cup salsa (mild, medium or hot)
1 tablespoon vegetable oil
1 clove garlic, crushed
½ teaspoon coarse-grind black pepper
1 (1½ pound) beef top round steak, cut 1 inch thick
Salt, as desired

Fat-skimming options: none. Exchange diets count: 4 lean meat, 1 vegetable.

• Combine lime juice, steak sauce, salsa, oil, garlic and black pepper in small saucepan. Bring to a boil; reduce heat. Simmer, uncovered, 5 minutes; cool.
• Place steak in plastic bag; add cooled marinade, turning to coat. Close bag securely and marinate in refrigerator 8 hours (or overnight, if desired), turning occasionally. Remove steak from marinade; discard marinade.

• Place steak on grill over medium coals. Grill 22 to 26 minutes for rare (140 degrees F on meat thermometer) to medium (160 degrees F), or to desired doneness, turning once. Season with salt, as desired.
• Carve steak into thin slices.

Nutrition Analysis Per Serving: As Originally Published

Calories: 242
Protein: 36 g
Carbohydrate: 4 g
Fat: 8 g

Saturated Fat: 2 g
Cholesterol: 95 mg
Sodium: 374 mg
Dietary Fiber: 0 g

Round Steak With Mushroom Gravy

Yield: 8 to 10 servings

3 pounds round steak, ½ inch thick
½ cup flour
1 tablespoon paprika
2 teaspoons salt
½ cup cooking oil, divided
1 cup sliced onion
8 ounces fresh mushrooms, sliced
1 clove garlic, minced
1½ cups water
1 cup dairy sour cream
2 tablespoons chopped fresh parsley
Mashed potatoes

> *Fat-skimming options: Omit oil and use nonstick cooking spray to brown the steak. Substitute nonfat sour cream. With options, exchange diets count: 6 very lean meat, 2 starch.*

• Pound round steak with meat mallet to about ¼-inch thickness. Cut into serving pieces. Dredge meat with combined flour, paprika and salt.
• Heat ¼ cup of the oil in 12 inch skillet. Brown meat on both sides, removing as it browns. Add remaining ¼ cup oil as needed. Add onion, mushrooms and garlic; sauté until tender. Stir in flour mixture if any is left. Slowly stir in water.

• Return meat to skillet. Bring to a boil. Cover and simmer 1½ hours or until meat is tender.
• Remove meat from skillet; keep warm. Stir some of hot gravy into sour cream; blend well. Place skillet over low heat. Gradually stir sour cream mixture back into skillet; heat thoroughly. Do not boil. Spoon some of gravy over meat; garnish with parsley. Pour remaining gravy into serving bowl. Serve meat with gravy and mashed potatoes.

Nutrition Analysis Per Serving: As Originally Published/With Fat-Skimming Options

Calories: 477/360	Saturated Fat: 7 g/3 g
Protein: 43 g/44 g	Cholesterol: 106 mg/98 mg
Carbohydrate: 26 g/30 g	Sodium: 822 mg/844 mg
Fat: 22 g/7 g	Dietary Fiber: 1 g/1 g

Sweet and Sour Beef Ribs
Yield: 6 to 8 servings

5 pounds beef short ribs, trimmed
$^1/_2$ teaspoon salt
$^1/_8$ teaspoon pepper
1 cup ketchup
$^1/_2$ cup cider vinegar
$^1/_3$ cup firmly packed brown sugar
1 teaspoon dry mustard
1 teaspoon salt
$^1/_2$ cup water
1 medium onion, sliced
1 medium green pepper, cut in 1 inch chunks
1 (13$^1/_2$ ounce) can pineapple chunks
2 tablespoons cornstarch
$^1/_3$ cup pineapple juice

Fat-skimming options: Increase servings to 16.
With options, exchange diets count: 6 lean meat, 1 fruit, 2 fat.

• Season ribs with salt and pepper. Brown on all sides in skillet. As meat browns, remove and place in 4-quart casserole. Cover and bake in 325 degree F oven 1$^1/_2$ hours.
• Mix together ketchup, vinegar, brown sugar, mustard, 1 teaspoon salt, and water. Add onion and green pepper.

• Pour off pan drippings from casserole; discard. Add sauce mixture. Cover; bake 1$^1/_2$ hours or until meat is tender.
• Remove meat; keep warm. Combine cooking liquid and undrained pineapple in skillet. Combine cornstarch and $^1/_3$ cup pineapple juice. Stir into hot liquid. Cook, stirring constantly, until mixture boils 2 minutes. Pour sauce into small serving bowl and serve on the side of ribs.

Nutrition Analysis Per Serving: As Originally Published/With Fat-Skimming Options

Calories: 970/485
Protein: 89 g/45 g
Carbohydrate: 32 g/16 g
Fat: 52 g/26 g

Saturated Fat: 22 g/11 g
Cholesterol: 267 mg/133 mg
Sodium: 930 mg/465 mg
Dietary Fiber: 0 g/0 g

Reuben Casserole

Yield: 8 to 10 servings

2 (10¾ ounce) cans condensed cream of chicken or mushroom soup
1⅓ cups milk
½ cup chopped onion
3 tablespoons prepared mustard
2 (16 ounce) cans sauerkraut, drained
1 (8 ounce) package uncooked, medium egg noodles
1 (12 ounce) can corned beef, crumbled
2 cups shredded Swiss cheese (8 ounces)
¾ cup rye bread crumbs, toasted
2 tablespoons butter or regular margarine, melted

> *Fat-skimming options: Use reduced-fat creamed soup, skim milk and reduced-fat Swiss cheese.*
> *With options, exchange diets count: 1½ starch, 2 vegetable, 3 lean meat, 2 fat.*

• In bowl, mix condensed soup, milk, onion and mustard until blended.
• In greased 13x9x2 inch baking dish, spread drained sauerkraut; top with uncooked noodles. Spoon soup mixture evenly over noodles. Sprinkle with corned beef, then cheese.

• In bowl, stir together rye bread crumbs and melted butter until well blended; sprinkle over top of cheese. Cover tightly with foil.
• Bake in 350 degree F oven 1 hour or until noodles are tender.

Nutrition Analysis Per Serving: As Originally Published/With Fat-Skimming Options

Calories: 495/418
Protein: 26 g/28 g
Carbohydrate: 34 g/32 g
Fat: 28 g/19 g

Saturated Fat: 13 g/9 g
Cholesterol: 84 mg/72 mg
Sodium: 2,068 mg/1,818 mg
Dietary Fiber: 0.5 g/0.5 g

Savory Beef Casserole

Yield: 6 to 8 servings

2 pounds stewing beef, cut in 1 inch cubes
¼ cup cooking oil
1½ cups chopped onion
1 (1 pound) can tomatoes
3 tablespoons quick-cooking tapioca
1 (10½ ounce) can condensed beef broth
1 clove garlic, minced
1 tablespoon parsley flakes
2½ teaspoons salt
¼ teaspoon pepper
1 bay leaf
6 medium carrots, pared and cut in strips
3 medium potatoes, pared and cut in quarters
½ cup sliced celery

Fat-skimming options: Omit oil and use nonstick spray shortening to brown beef cubes. With options, exchange diets count: 4 lean meat, 2 vegetable, 1 starch.

• Brown beef cubes on all sides in hot oil in large skillet. Add onion, tomatoes, tapioca, beef broth, garlic, parsley, salt, pepper and bay leaf. Bring mixture to a boil. Turn into 3-quart casserole. Cover.

• Bake at 350 degrees F for 1 hour 30 minutes or until meat is tender.
• Add carrots, potatoes and celery. Continue baking, covered, for 1 hour or until vegetables are tender. Remove bay leaf.

Nutrition Analysis Per Serving: As Originally Published/With Fat-Skimming Options

Calories: 414/352
Protein: 40 g/40 g
Carbohydrate: 25 g/25 g
Fat: 17 g/10 g

Saturated Fat: 4 g/3 g
Cholesterol: 113 mg/113 mg
Sodium: 1,014 mg/1,014 mg
Dietary Fiber: 3 g/3 g

Spinach-Filled Steak Rolls

Yield: 8 servings

2 (1½ pound) flank steaks, ¾ inch thick
¼ teaspoon salt
1 (4 ounce) can chopped mushrooms
1 cup cooked regular rice
1 (10 ounce) package frozen chopped spinach, cooked and drained
½ cup grated carrots
¼ cup chopped onion
¼ teaspoon thyme leaves
3 tablespoons cooking oil
Water
1 (10½ ounce) can condensed beef broth
3 tablespoons flour
¼ cup water
½ teaspoon browning sauce for gravy, such as Kitchen Bouquet

> *Fat-skimming options: Omit oil and brown meat rolls in nonstick skillet using nonstick cooking spray.*
> *With options, exchange diets count: 3 lean meat, 1 vegetable, ½ starch.*

• Score meat in 1 inch diamonds, cutting ⅛ inch deep. Season with salt. Cut each steak in half.
• Drain mushrooms; reserve liquid. Combine mushrooms, rice, spinach, carrots, onion and thyme. Spread scant 1 cup filling on each steak. Roll up like jelly roll. Tie with string. Brown rolls on all sides, two at a time, in hot oil in Dutch oven.
• Add enough water to beef broth and reserved mushroom liquid to make 2 cups. Pour over meat rolls. Cover; simmer 1½ hours or until tender.
• Remove meat rolls and keep warm. Skim off excess fat. Combine flour, ¼ cup water and browning sauce. Stir into hot liquid. Boil 2 minutes, stirring constantly. Strain. Cut meat rolls in slices and serve with gravy.

Nutrition Analysis Per Serving: As Originally Published/With Fat-Skimming Options

Calories: 282/235
Protein: 25 g/25 g
Carbohydrate: 12 g/12 g
Fat: 14 g/9 g

Saturated Fat: 4 g/4 g
Cholesterol: 57 mg/57 mg
Sodium: 327 mg/327 mg
Dietary Fiber: 1 g/1 g

Super Supper Pizza

Yield: 6 servings

2 (8 ounce) tubes refrigerator crescent dinner rolls
1½ pounds ground chuck
1 cup coarsely chopped green pepper
¾ cup sliced onion
1 (14 ounce) jar pizza sauce
1½ cups shredded mozzarella cheese
3 tablespoons grated Parmesan cheese
1 teaspoon dried oregano leaves

> *Fat-skimming options: Use reduced-fat crescent rolls. Use fat-free mozzarella cheese.*
> *Reduce portion size to yield 12 servings.*
> *With options, exchange diets count: 3 lean meat, 1½ starch, 1 vegetable, 2 fat.*

• Without separating triangles, unroll crescent roll dough and press into bottom and up sides of greased 15½x10½x1 inch jelly roll pan.

• Brown ground chuck, green pepper and onion in skillet.
• Spread pizza sauce over dough. Sprinkle with meat mixture, mozzarella, Parmesan and oregano.
• Bake in 375 degree F oven 20 to 25 minutes or until crust is browned.

Nutrition Analysis Per Serving: As Originally Published/With Fat-Skimming Options

Calories: 901/409
Protein: 49 g/25 g
Carbohydrate: 76 g/24 g
Fat: 44 g/23 g

Saturated Fat: 18 g/7 g
Cholesterol: 145 mg/76 mg
Sodium: 1,564 mg/689 mg
Dietary Fiber: 1 g/0.5 g

Zucchini Beef Skillet

Yield: 6 servings

1 pound ground beef
1 cup chopped onion
³/₄ cup chopped green pepper
1 clove garlic, minced
1¹/₂ teaspoons salt
¹/₄ teaspoon pepper
1 teaspoon chili powder
5 cups sliced zucchini or summer squash
2 large tomatoes, peeled and chopped
1¹/₄ cups fresh whole kernel corn (about 3 medium ears)
2 tablespoons chopped pimientos
¹/₄ cup chopped fresh parsley

Fat-skimming options: Use extra lean ground beef.
With options, exchange diets count: 3 lean meat, 1 vegetable, 1 starch.

• Sauté beef, onion, green pepper and garlic
in 12 inch skillet until well browned.
• Add remaining ingredients. Cover and
simmer 10 to 15 minutes, or until vegetables
are tender.

Nutrition Analysis Per Serving: As Originally Published/With Fat-Skimming Options

Calories: 272/262
Protein: 23 g/23 g
Carbohydrate: 17 g/17 g
Fat: 13 g/12 g

Saturated Fat: 5 g/5 g
Cholesterol: 68 mg/66 mg
Sodium: 609 mg/605 mg
Dietary Fiber: 2 g/2 g

Sweet-Soy Marinade

Yield: 4 to 5 servings

¼ cup soy sauce
2 tablespoons honey
2 tablespoons red wine vinegar
1 tablespoon vegetable oil
4 green onions, chopped
1 clove garlic, minced

Fat-skimming options: none. Exchange diets count: 1 fruit.

• In plastic bag or nonporous bowl, mix together all ingredients.
• To use: Combine marinade with 1¼ pounds beef or pork strips, or 2 pounds chicken pieces. Marinate beef or pork up to 24 hours; chicken 2 to 4 hours.
• Thread beef or pork strips on bamboo skewers that have been soaked in water. Grill or broil.

Nutrition Analysis Per Serving: As Originally Published

Calories: 73	Saturated Fat: 0 g
Protein: 2 g	Cholesterol: 0 mg
Carbohydrate: 11 g	Sodium: 825 mg
Fat: 3 g	Dietary Fiber: 1 g

Barbecued Country-Style Ribs and Krau

Yield: 8 servings

4 pounds country-style spareribs
1 teaspoon salt
Spicy Barbecue Sauce
6 cups sauerkraut
2 apples, cored and sliced
1 cup chopped onion
3 tablespoons chopped pimientos
1 clove garlic, minced

Fat-skimming options: Omit butter and reduce brown sugar to ⅓ cup in Spicy Barbecue Sauce.
Reduce portion size to yield 16 servings.
With options, exchange diets count: 4 lean meat, 1 fruit, 5 fat.

• Cut ribs into 1-rib pieces. Place ribs and salt in Dutch oven. Add water to cover. Bring to a boil. Reduce heat; cover and simmer 30 minutes or until meat is tender. Drain.
• Prepare Spicy Barbecue Sauce.
• Combine sauerkraut, apples, onion, pimientos and garlic; mix well. Spread in bottom of 15x10½x2 inch roasting pan. Arrange ribs in a single layer on top. Brush with Spicy Barbecue Sauce.
• Bake in 400 degree F oven 1 hour, basting ribs frequently with sauce. Turn ribs over; brush with sauce. Bake 1 hour longer, brushing frequently with sauce.

Spicy Barbecue Sauce

1 cup chopped celery
½ cup chopped onion
2 cloves garlic, minced
6 tablespoons melted butter or regular margarine
1½ cups ketchup
1 cup cider vinegar
2 cups water
⅔ cup firmly packed brown sugar
2 tablespoons Worcestershire sauce
⅛ teaspoon pepper

• Sauté celery, onion and garlic in butter until tender (do not brown).
• Add ketchup, vinegar, water, brown sugar, Worcestershire sauce and pepper; stir well. Bring to a boil. Reduce heat and simmer 30 minutes, stirring occasionally.

Nutrition Analysis Per Serving: As Originally Published/With Fat-Skimming Options

Calories: 1,107/499
Protein: 67 g/33 g
Carbohydrate: 36 g/13 g
Fat: 77 g/34 g

Saturated Fat: 32 g/13 g
Cholesterol: 294 mg/135 mg
Sodium: 1,795 mg/852 mg
Dietary Fiber: 1 g/1 g

Bratwurst and Onions

Yield: 8 sandwiches

4 cups sliced onion
3 tablespoons cooking oil
2 tablespoons water
4½ teaspoons paprika
¼ teaspoon ground cumin (optional)
8 strips bacon
8 bratwurst (2 pounds)
8 (6 inch) submarine rolls, split

*Fat-skimming options: Omit oil. Substitute reduced-fat turkey brats.
With options, exchange diets count: 1 starch, 1 vegetble, 4 lean meat, ½ fat.*

• Combine onion, oil, water, paprika and cumin; mix well. Place on 20 inch length of heavy-duty aluminum foil. Seal with tight double fold and roll up ends.
• Wrap one bacon strip around each bratwurst, securing bacon with wooden picks.
• Grill onion packet and bratwurst 4 inches from gray coals, turning bratwurst often. Cook 20 minutes, or until onions are tender and bratwurst is cooked through.

• Serve in rolls and top with onions.
• **Broiler Method:** Prepare onion packet and bratwurst as for grill. Broil onion packet 6 inches from source of heat 10 minutes. Turn over packet. Add bratwurst to broiler and continue broiling 15 minutes, turning bratwurst often. Broil until onions are tender and bratwurst is cooked through.

Nutrition Analysis Per Serving: As Originally Published/With Fat-Skimming Options

Calories: 454/345
Protein: 18 g/28 g
Carbohydrate: 24 g/22 g
Fat: 32 g/16 g

Saturated Fat: 10 g/4 g
Cholesterol: 57 mg/90 mg
Sodium: 764 mg/378 mg
Dietary Fiber: 2 g/2 g

Danish Pork Roast

Yield: 6 servings

$^1/_2$ teaspoon salt
$^1/_2$ teaspoon cinnamon
$^1/_2$ teaspoon allspice
$^1/_2$ teaspoon ground pepper
$^1/_4$ teaspoon ground cloves
$^1/_4$ teaspoon mace
3 to 3$^1/_2$ pounds boned pork loin
12 pitted prunes
2 medium apples, pared, cored and cut into sixths
2 tablespoons raisins
$^1/_4$ teaspoon cinnamon
$^1/_4$ cup brandy or apple juice
1$^1/_2$ tablespoons current jelly, melted
1 cup fresh bread crumbs
$^1/_4$ cup melted butter

Fat-skimming options: Omit butter basting. Reduce serving size and increase yield to 12 servings. With options, exchange diets count: 3 lean meat, $^1/_2$ starch, 1 fruit, 5 fat.

• Mix salt, spices; rub in surface of roast. Refrigerate overnight.
• Combine the fruits, cinnamon and brandy. Refrigerate overnight.
• Cut a long, deep pocket the length of the roast. Stuff with fruit. Sew closed with large needle; tie with kitchen twine. Brush roast with liquid left from fruit.

• Roast on rack in 325 degree F oven, 1 hour. Remove from oven; brush with jelly. Roll in bread crumbs. Baste with butter; roast 1$^1/_2$ hours more. Let stand 15 minutes before carving.

Nutrition Analysis Per Serving: As Originally Published/With Fat-Skimming Options

Calories: 1,051/492
Protein: 50 g/25 g
Carbohydrate: 35 g/18 g
Fat: 78 g/35 g

Saturated Fat: 30 g/13 g
Cholesterol: 223 mg/101 mg
Sodium: 552 mg/237 mg
Dietary Fiber: 3 g/1.5 g

Marinated Pork Kabobs

Yield: 6 sandwiches

2 pounds boneless lean pork, cut into 1 inch cubes
½ cup cooking oil
3 tablespoons lemon juice
¼ cup finely chopped onion
1 tablespoon minced fresh parsley
1 clove garlic, minced
¾ teaspoon salt
⅛ teaspoon pepper
½ teaspoon dried marjoram leaves
Cucumber-Yogurt Sauce
6 large pita breads, cut in half

> *Fat-skimming options: Omit oil from marinade. Reduce portions to yield 12 sandwiches.*
> *With options, exchange diets count: 3 lean meat, 1 starch, 1 vegetable.*

• Combine pork, oil, lemon juice, onion, parsley, garlic, salt, pepper and marjoram in glass bowl. Cover and refrigerate 8 hours or overnight.
• Thread pork cubes on 6 skewers.
• Grill kabobs 4 inches from gray coals, turning and basting with marinade often. Cook 15 minutes, or until no longer pink in center.
• Prepare Cucumber-Yogurt Sauce.
• To serve, stuff pita bread with pork and top with Cucumber-Yogurt Sauce.
• **Broiler Method:** Prepare pork as for grill. Broil kabobs 6 inches from source of heat, turning and basting with marinade often. Cook 15 minutes, or until no longer pink in center.

Cucumber-Yogurt Sauce

1 (8 ounce) container plain yogurt
½ cup chopped cucumber
1 tablespoon minced onion
1 tablespoon minced fresh parsley
1 teaspoon lemon juice
⅛ teaspoon garlic salt

• Combine yogurt, cucumber, onion, parsley, lemon juice and garlic salt in bowl; mix well.

Nutrition Analysis Per Serving: As Originally Published/With Fat-Skimming Options

Calories: 741/288
Protein: 51 g /25 g
Carbohydrate: 37 g/18 g
Fat: 42 g/12 g

Saturated Fat: 10 g/4 g
Cholesterol: 128 mg/64 mg
Sodium: 678 mg/338 mg
Dietary Fiber: 1 g/0.5 g

Pork Chop Skillet Dinner

Yield: 6 servings

6 lean pork chops
½ teaspoon salt
¼ teaspoon pepper
1 tablespoon cooking oil
½ teaspoon savory
½ bay leaf
2 cups tomato juice
½ cup water
1 small cabbage, cut in 6 wedges
6 carrots, cut in 1 inch pieces (2 cups)
1½ cups coarsely chopped onion
3 medium potatoes, pared and quartered
¼ teaspoon salt

Fat-skimming options: Trim all visible fat from chops.
Omit oil and use nonstick cooking spray to brown chops.
With options, exchange diets count: 6 very lean meat.

• Season pork chops with ½ teaspoon salt and the pepper. Brown chops in hot oil in a large skillet. Add savory, bay leaf, tomato juice and water. Simmer, covered, for 30 minutes.

• Add cabbage, carrots, onion, potatoes and ¼ teaspoon salt. Cover. Cook for 35 minutes or until vegetables are tender. Remove bay leaf before serving.

Nutrition Analysis Per Serving: As Originally Published/With Fat-Skimming Options

Calories: 326/207
Protein: 50 g/33 g
Carbohydrate: 7 g/5 g
Fat: 10 g/5 g

Saturated Fat: 10 g/5 g
Cholesterol: 120 mg/80 mg
Sodium: 570 mg/380 mg
Dietary Fiber: 1 g/1 g

Pork Chops en Casserole
Yield: 6 servings

6 loin pork chops, ¾ inch thick
Salt
2 tablespoons butter or margarine
6 large potatoes, pared and sliced
3 large onions, peeled and sliced
3 tablespoons cornstarch
¾ cup cooking sherry
1½ cups tomato juice
¼ teaspoon dried rosemary leaves, crumbled
¼ teaspoon salt
¼ teaspoon pepper
½ cup grated Parmesan cheese

Fat-skimming options: Omit butter and brown chops in skillet sprayed with nonstick cooking spray. With options, exchange diets count: 4 lean meat, 2 starch, 2 vegetable.

• Season pork chops with salt. Brown pork chops in melted butter on both sides in large skillet. Remove from skillet as they brown.
• Place potato slices in 4-quart casserole or baking dish. Top with onion slices, then pork chops.
• Combine cornstarch, sherry, tomato juice, rosemary, ¼ teaspoon salt and pepper; stir until smooth. Pour over casserole mixture. Cover with casserole cover or aluminum foil.

• Bake at 400 degrees F for 45 minutes. Remove from oven. Sprinkle with Parmesan cheese. Continue baking, uncovered, 30 minutes or until pork chops and vegetables are tender.

Nutrition Analysis Per Serving: As Originally Published/With Fat-Skimming Options

Calories: 450/416
Protein: 28 g/28 g
Carbohydrate: 44 g/44 g
Fat: 16 g/12 g

Saturated Fat: 7 g/5 g
Cholesterol: 84 mg/73 mg
Sodium: 536 mg/497 mg
Dietary Fiber: 3 g/3 g

Pork Steaks With Mushroom Cream Gravy

Yield: 6 servings

6 lean pork steaks or chops, about ¾ inch thick (2½ pounds)
½ teaspoon salt
¼ teaspoon pepper
2 tablespoons cooking oil
½ cup chopped onion
1 (8 ounce) can mushrooms, stems and pieces
1 (10½ ounce) can condensed beef broth
1 teaspoon Worcestershire sauce
1 cup evaporated milk
1 tablespoon flour

Fat-skimming options: Omit oil and brown meat using nonstick cooking spray.
Substitute evaporated skim milk. With options, exchange diets count: 6 very lean meat.

• Season pork steaks with salt and pepper. Brown well in hot oil in a large skillet. Remove. Add onion; sauté until tender (do not brown).
• Drain mushrooms, reserving liquid. Add reserved mushroom liquid, beef broth, Worcestershire sauce and meat to skillet. Simmer, covered, 1 hour or until meat is tender.

• Remove meat and keep warm. Add mushrooms to pan juices in skillet. Bring mixture to a boil. Combine evaporated milk and flour. Slowly stir into hot liquid. Cook, stirring, until thickened. (Do not boil.)

Nutrition Analysis Per Serving: As Originally Published/With Fat-Skimming Options

Calories: 261/197
Protein: 27 g/27 g
Carbohydrate: 9 g/10 g
Fat: 12 g/4 g

Saturated Fat: 3 g/1 g
Cholesterol: 77 mg/66 mg
Sodium: 503 mg/508 mg
Dietary Fiber: 0 g/0 g

Sausage-Apple-Sauerkraut Supper
Yield: 4 servings

1 pound bulk pork sausage
2 tablespoons chopped onion
1 apple, cored and sliced
1 (1 pound) can sauerkraut
½ teaspoon caraway seeds
4 servings prepared instant seasoned mashed potatoes (2 cups)
⅓ cup shredded Cheddar cheese
Paprika

> *Fat-skimming options: Use reduced-fat turkey sausage and reduced-fat cheddar cheese.*
> *With options, exchange diets count: 3 lean meat, 1 starch, 2 vegetable, 2 fat.*

• Brown sausage in skillet. Drain; turn into a 1½-quart casserole. Sauté onion in 2 tablespoons of drippings.
• Place onion and apple on sausage. Cover with sauerkraut and caraway seeds. Spread potatoes on top; sprinkle with shredded cheese and paprika.

• Bake at 350 degrees F for 35 minutes or until top is golden.

Nutrition Analysis Per Serving: As Originally Published/With Fat-Skimming Options

Calories: 381/386
Protein: 16 g/27 g
Carbohydrate: 28 g/30 g
Fat: 24 g/18 g

Saturated Fat: 10 g/6 g
Cholesterol: 58 mg/58 mg
Sodium: 1,725 mg/1,929 mg
Dietary Fiber: 1 g/1 g

Sausage and Peppers With Noodles
Yield: 4 servings

8 ounces uncooked noodles
1 small onion, thinly sliced
2 tablespoons olive or vegetable oil
1 small red pepper, thinly sliced
1 small green pepper, thinly sliced
1 clove garlic, finely minced, or ⅛ teaspoon garlic powder
2 cups cooked, sliced Italian sausage or cooked, cubed beef, chicken or ham
¼ cup halved black or green olives
¼ cup chopped fresh parsley
⅓ cup grated Parmesan cheese
Lemon wedges (optional)
Red pepper flakes, (optional)

> *Fat-skimming options: Substitute lean ham for sausage. Reduce Parmesan to 2 tablespoons.*
> *With options, exchange diets count: 2½ starch, 2 vegetable, 4 lean meat.*

• Cook pasta according to package directions. Drain.
• In medium skillet, cook onion in hot oil until golden, 5 to 7 minutes. Stir in peppers and garlic; cook until peppers are crisp-tender, about 4 minutes.

• Stir in sausage, olives and parsley and cook until hot, about 2 minutes.
• Toss mixture with hot noodles and Parmesan cheese.
• Serve with lemon wedges and red pepper flakes, if desired.

Nutrition Analysis Per Serving: As Originally Published/With Fat-Skimming Options

Calories: 536/480
Protein: 25 g/32 g
Carbohydrate: 44 g/44 g
Fat: 29 g/19 g

Saturated Fat: 8 g/4 g
Cholesterol: 57 mg/45 mg
Sodium: 776 mg/1,223 mg
Dietary Fiber: 8 g/8 g

Buelah's Ham

Yield: 6 servings

1 (3 pound) ham slice with bone, sliced 2½ inchs thick
1 cup firmly packed brown sugar
¼ cup pineapple juice
¼ cup Mogen David grape wine
1½ tablespoons cinnamon
¾ teaspoon ground cloves
½ teaspoon nutmeg

> *Fat-skimming options: Substitute 2 pounds of 97% fat-free ham. Reduce sugar to ⅔ cup.*
> *Reduce baking time to 30 minutes, as ham will only need to be warmed through.*
> *With options, exchange diets count: 2 fruit, 6 lean meat.*

• Place ham in 9x13 inch baking dish.
• Combine remaining ingredients and pour evenly over ham. Cover and bake at 300 degrees F for 2½ to 3 hours. Turn once at 1½ hours.

• Serve with pan juices, if desired.

Nutrition Analysis Per Serving: As Originally Published/With Fat-Skimming Options

Calories: 839/439
Protein: 55 g/44 g
Carbohydrate: 37 g/25 g
Fat: 50 g/16 g

Saturated Fat: 18 g/6 g
Cholesterol: 208 mg/143 mg
Sodium: 148 mg/109 mg
Dietary Fiber: 0 g/0 g

Country Crusted Ham

Yield: 16 to 20 servings

1 (12 to 15 pound) uncooked bone-in whole ham
Whole cloves
Honey
1 cup firmly packed brown sugar
¼ cup fresh bread crumbs

Fat-skimming options: none. Exchange diets count: 3 lean meat, 1 fruit

---

• Place ham with fat side up on rack in shallow roasting pan. Insert a meat thermometer into center of thickest part of ham; don't let it touch the bone. Bake at 325 degrees F for 4 hours or until meat thermometer registers 155 degrees F. Remove ham from oven.
• Remove excess rind. Score ham by making diagonal cuts, ⅛ inch deep and ¾ inch apart, across fat surface of ham. Repeat, at an angle, to make diamonds. Stud ham with whole cloves. Drizzle with honey.

• Combine brown sugar and bread crumbs. Pat over scored surface. Return to oven. Bake at 325 degrees F for 30 minutes or until meat thermometer registers 160 degrees F. Remove from oven. Let stand 20 minutes before carving.

Nutrition Analysis Per Serving: As Originally Published/With Fat-Skimming Options

Calories: 232	Saturated Fat: 3 g
Protein: 24 g	Cholesterol: 78 mg
Carbohydrate: 13 g	Sodium: 70 mg
Fat: 9 g	Dietary Fiber: 0 g

Ham-Pineapple Rings

Yield: 8 servings

1 pound ground cooked ham
1 pound ground pork
1½ cups fresh bread crumbs
2 eggs, beaten
1 cup milk
2 (8¼ ounce) cans pineapple slices
¾ cup firmly packed brown sugar
¼ cup vinegar
½ teaspoon dry mustard
½ cup shredded Cheddar cheese

Fat-skimming options: Use ½ cup liquid egg substitute for eggs. Reduce brown sugar to ¼ cup. Use reduced-fat cheese. With options, exchange diets count: 5 lean meat, 1 fruit, 1 starch, 2 fat.

• Combine ham, pork, bread crumbs, eggs and milk; mix lightly. Drain pineapple; reserve ¼ cup juice.
• Divide mixture into 8 equal portions. Shape each portion into 2 (4 inch) patties. Place 1 pineapple slice between 2 patties, sealing edges to cover pineapple. Make hole in center with finger. Place on broiler pan.

• Combine brown sugar, vinegar, ¼ cup reserved juice and mustard; blend well. Baste ham rings with sauce. Broil 9 inches from source of heat. Broil 15 minutes, basting twice. Turn patties. Broil 15 more minutes, basting twice. Turn patties again. Top with cheese. Broil until cheese is melted.
• To grill: Grill on foil, over low heat, 6 inches from coals, about 1 to 1¼ hours, turning frequently and basting with sauce. Top with cheese and cook until melted.

Nutrition Analysis Per Serving: As Originally Published/With Fat-Skimming Options

Calories: 596/522
Protein: 31 g/32 g
Carbohydrate: 45 g/32 g
Fat: 32 g/29 g

Saturated Fat: 12 g/11 g
Cholesterol: 151 mg/92 mg
Sodium: 1,115 mg/1,144 mg
Dietary Fiber: 1 g/1 g

Savory Ham Loaf
Yield: 10 to 12 servings

3 cups soft whole wheat bread cubes
1 cup milk or water
2 eggs, lightly beaten
1 teaspoon poultry seasoning or sage
$^1/_2$ teaspoon thyme
$^1/_4$ cup finely chopped celery
$^1/_4$ cup finely chopped onion
1 pound ground boiled ham
$^1/_2$ pound ground pork
$^1/_2$ pound ground turkey
Lemon-Apple Sauce (recipe follows)

> *Fat-skimming options: Use skim milk and $^1/_2$ cup liquid egg substitute for eggs.*
> *With options, exchange diets count: 3 lean meat, 2 fruit.*

• In large bowl, combine all ingredients except meats.
• Gently, but thoroughly, mix in meat.
• Shape into a 9x5$^1/_2$x2 inch loaf in a 9 inch square glass baking dish.
• Bake at 350 degrees F about 1 hour or until meat thermometer registers 145 degrees F. Let stand 10 minutes.
• Serve with Lemon-Apple Sauce.

Lemon-Apple Sauce
1$^1/_2$ cups applesauce
2 to 3 tablespoons lemon juice
3 tablespoons firmly packed brown sugar
$^1/_4$ teaspoon ground cloves
$^1/_4$ teaspoon crushed thyme

• In small saucepan, combine applesauce, lemon juice, brown sugar, cloves and thyme.
• Heat over low heat.

Nutrition Analysis Per Serving: As Originally Published/With Fat-Skimming Options

Calories: 327/321
Protein: 26 g/26 g
Carbohydrate: 28 g/28 g
Fat: 12 g/11 g

Saturated Fat: 4 g/3 g
Cholesterol: 99 mg/63 mg
Sodium: 681 mg/690 mg
Dietary Fiber: 1 g/1 g

Simmered Lamb With Cabbage

Yield: 8 servings

2 pounds lamb, cut into 2- to 3-inch squares
3 pounds cabbage
6 tablespoons all-purpose flour
2 teaspoons salt
4 teaspoons whole black peppercorns
1¹/₂ cups boiling water
Boiled potatoes

Fat-skimming options: none. Exchange diets count: 3 lean meat, 1 vegetable, ¹/₂ starch, 1 fat.

• Trim fat from meat.
• Remove outer leaves of cabbage. Halve cabbage and rinse. Cut into small wedges.
• In small bowl, mix flour and salt.
• In 3-quart soup pot, layer lamb and cabbage: Start with one-fourth of the lamb, using fattiest pieces first. Add one-fourth of the cabbage. Sprinkle with one-third of flour-salt mixture. Repeat until you have four layers of lamb and cabbage, ending with cabbage. Place peppercorns in cheesecloth or teaball and put in center of layers.

• Pour boiling water in at edge of pot. Bring to boiling again and cook over low heat on range top until meat is tender, 1¹/₂ to 3 hours.
• Gently turn top layer of cabbage from time to time to evenly cook, but don't stir entire mixture. Turn pot and move from side to side periodically so mixture doesn't stick to bottom.
• Serve hot on warm plates with boiled potatoes.

Nutrition Analysis Per Serving: As Originally Published

Calories: 262	Saturated Fat: 1 g
Protein: 4 g	Cholesterol: 91 mg
Carbohydrate: 44 g	Sodium: 46 mg
Fat: 8 g	Dietary Fiber: 1.5 g

Honey-Citrus Glazed Veal Chops

Yield: 4 servings

3 tablespoons fresh lime juice
2 tablespoons honey
2 teaspoons grated fresh ginger
$1/2$ teaspoon grated lime peel
4 veal rib chops, cut 1 inch thick (about 8 ounces each)

Fat-skimming options: none. Exchange diets count: 1 fruit, 7 lean meat.

• Stir together lime juice, honey, ginger and peel. Place veal rib chops in utility dish just large enough to hold chops. Brush lime mixture liberally over both sides of chops. Refrigerate, covered, 30 minutes while preparing coals.

• Remove chops from dish, reserving any lime mixture. Place chops on grill over medium coals*, and grill 12 to 14 minutes, turning once, for medium (160 degrees F on meat thermometer), or to desired doneness; brush with reserved lime mixture before turning. Or broil 4 inches to 5 inches from heat 5 to 6 minutes per side, turning once, for medium, or to desired doneness.

*To check temperature of coals, cautiously hold the palm of your hand about 4 inches above the coals. Count the number of seconds you can hold it in that position before the heat forces you to pull it away: 4 seconds for medium coals.

Nutrition Analysis Per Serving: As Originally Published

Calories: 450	Saturated Fat: 5 g
Protein: 60 g	Cholesterol: 267 mg
Carbohydrate: 10 g	Sodium: 226 mg
Fat: 17 g	Dietary Fiber: 0 g

Veal Paprikash
Yield: 6 to 8 servings

3 tablespoons flour
4 teaspoons paprika
1 teaspoon salt
$^1/_4$ teaspoon pepper
2 pounds well-trimmed boneless veal shoulder, cut into 1 inch cubes
4 tablespoons vegetable oil, divided
2 cups water, divided
3 beef bouillon cubes
1 teaspoon Worcestershire sauce
1 pound fresh, peeled, or frozen small white onions
1 pound small mushrooms
3 tablespoons flour
1 (8 ounce) container dairy sour cream
Hot cooked egg noodles
Chopped fresh dill or parsley

Fat-skimming options: Reduce oil to 1 tablespoon. Use nonfat sour cream.
Reduce portion size to yield 16 servings.
With options, exchange diets count: $^1/_2$ skim milk, 2 lean meat, 1 starch, 1 vegetable.

• In plastic bag mix first 4 ingredients. Add veal cubes; shake until coated.
• In 4-quart Dutch oven over medium heat, heat 1 tablespoon oil. Add a fourth of the veal cubes; cook until browned on all sides. Remove and set aside. Repeat with remaining oil and veal cubes.
• Return all of the veal to Dutch oven. Add 1$^1/_2$ cups water, bouillon cubes and Worcestershire sauce. Bring to a boil. Reduce heat; cover. Simmer 30 minutes.
• Add onions and mushrooms; cover. Simmer just until veal is tender, about 30 minutes. (Do not overcook—veal will become stringy.)
• In jar with lid, shake together 3 tablespoons flour and remaining $^1/_2$ cup water. Stir into stew. Cook, stirring constantly, until mixture thickens and boils.
• Stir 1 cup hot gravy from stew into sour cream. Stir sour cream mixture back into stew; stir until blended. Do not boil. Serve over noodles; sprinkle with dill.

Nutrition Analysis Per Serving: As Originally Published/With Fat-Skimming Options

Calories: 575/253
Protein: 41 g/21 g
Carbohydrate: 50 g/27 g
Fat: 22 g/6 g
Saturated Fat: 7 g/1 g
Cholesterol: 196 mg/93 mg
Sodium: 891 mg/458 mg
Dietary Fiber: 4.5 g/2 g

CHAPTER TEN

SALADS

I'm always on the lookout for new recipes

With three grown sons still working on the family farm near Ledyard, Iowa, Georgia Engelby's dining room table has never been made smaller. They still come to her kitchen at noon during planting and harvest season for dinner. And while she insists her meals are just "meat, potatoes, gravy and a salad and dessert thrown in here or there," she is always looking for new recipes.

Georgia's recipe for Golden Autumn Salad is in this chapter and can be prepared with skim milk and nonfat whipped topping—instead of heavy cream—to reduce calories and fat. She says no one has ever known the difference! She likes to take it to potlucks because it travels so well and looks pretty in a bowl or a glass baking dish.

While Georgia hunts for more recipes in Farm Journal, her husband grabs it to keep up on corn and soybean news. She knows neither one of them will ever "really fully retire" from the farm.

Fresh Fruit Slush

Yield: 8 (1 cup) servings

4 large oranges
2 cups sliced fresh strawberries (1 pint)
1 cup seedless green grapes
3 medium bananas, sliced
1 (6 ounce) can frozen lemonade, slightly thawed

Fat-skimming options: none. Exchange diets count: 2 fruit.

• Peel oranges with sharp knife, removing the white part of peel. Remove segments.
• Add remaining ingredients; toss lightly to mix. Spoon into plastic cups. Cover with aluminum foil. Freeze until slightly icy, about 1¼ hours.

• **To make ahead:** Fruit salad can be made the day before and refrigerated. Freeze 1¼ hours before serving.

Nutrition Analysis Per Serving: As Originally Published

Calories: 110	Saturated Fat: 0 g
Protein: 1 g	Cholesterol: 0 mg
Carbohydrate: 28 g	Sodium: 4 mg
Fat: 0 g	Dietary Fiber: 2 g

Fresh Fruit Bowl

Yield: 1¹/₂ gallons or 24 (1 cup) servings

2 (3 ounce) packages lemon-flavored gelatin
1 cup boiling water
1 (12 ounce) can frozen lemonade concentrate, thawed
1 (12 ounce) can ginger ale (1¹/₂ cups)
1¹/₂ gallons mixed fresh fruit (Choose from strawberries, pitted cherries, seedless grapes; cantaloupe or watermelon balls; sliced plums, bananas, peaches, nectarines or kiwi fruit.)

Fat-skimming options: Use sugar-free gelatin. With options, exchange diets count: 1 fruit.

• In large bowl stir gelatin into boiling water until dissolved. Stir in lemonade concentrate and ginger ale.

• Add mixed fresh fruit; toss gently until well coated. Cover; refrigerate at least 4 hours until chilled. If desired, serve in a watermelon shell.

Nutrition Analysis Per Serving: As Originally Published/With Fat-Skimming Options

Calories: 80/53
Protein: 1 g/0 g
Carbohydrate: 19 g/13 g
Fat: 0 g/0 g

Saturated Fat: 0 g/0 g
Cholesterol: 0 mg/0 mg
Sodium: 22 mg/4 mg
Dietary Fiber: 2 g/2 g

Fruit Soup

Yield: 16 (1 cup) servings

1 cup coarsely cut-up dried apricots
1 cup coarsely cut-up dried pitted prunes
1 cup golden or dark raisins
3 quarts water
2 (3 inch) cinnamon sticks
½ cup sugar
1 medium tart apple, peeled, cored and sliced
½ cup quick-cooking tapioca
1 (16 ounce) can pitted sweet cherries
1 cup white or purple grape juice
½ cup orange juice
2 tablespoons lemon juice

Fat-skimming options: none. Exchange diets count: 2 fruit.

• In 6-quart Dutch oven soak apricots, prunes and raisins in water 3 hours.
• Add cinnamon sticks and sugar. Over high heat, bring to a boil. Reduce heat to low. Cover and simmer 1 hour.

• Stir in apple and tapioca; cover. Cook, stirring occasionally 10 to 15 minutes more, or until tapioca is clear. Remove from heat.
• Stir in undrained cherries and grape, orange and lemon juices until well blended. Remove cinnamon sticks. Serve hot or cold.

Nutrition Analysis Per Serving: As Originally Published

Calories: 136
Protein: 1 g
Carbohydrate: 35 g
Fat: 0 g

Saturated Fat: 0 g
Cholesterol: 0 mg
Sodium: 4 mg
Dietary Fiber: 1 g

Golden Autumn Salad

Yield: 16 servings

2 (3 ounce) packages orange-flavored gelatin
2 cups boiling water
1 (6 ounce) can frozen orange juice concentrate
1 (20 ounce) can crushed pineapple, drained
1 (16 ounce) can mandarin orange segments, drained
1 (3.4 ounce) French vanilla instant pudding mix
1½ cups cold skim milk
½ cup heavy cream, whipped, or 1 cup frozen whipped topping, thawed
1 cup shredded yellow Cheddar cheese

> *Fat-skimming options: Use sugar-free gelatin. Use 1 cup nonfat whipped topping for heavy cream.*
> *Use reduced-fat Cheddar cheese.*
> *With options, exchange diets count: 1 fruit, ½ skim milk, ½ fat.*

• Stir gelatin into boiling water until dissolved. Add frozen orange juice concentrate; stir until melted.
• Stir in drained pineapple and oranges. Pour into serving bowl or 13x9x2 inch glass baking dish. Cover; chill until set.

• Prepare pudding mix according to package directions but using only 1½ cups skim milk. Let stand 5 minutes. Fold in whipped cream; spread over top of set gelatin. Sprinkle with cheese.
• Cover; refrigerate 2 hours or until ready to serve.

Nutrition Analysis Per Serving: As Originally Published/With Fat-Skimming Options	
Calories: 183/125	Saturated Fat: 4 g/2 g
Protein: 6 g/6 g	Cholesterol: 19 mg/12 mg
Carbohydrate: 27 g/19 g	Sodium: 222 mg/213 mg
Fat: 6 g/3 g	Dietary Fiber: 0.5 g/0.5 g

Rosy Spring Salad
Yield: 8 servings

4 cups diced raw rhubarb
1½ cups water
½ cup sugar
2 (3 ounce) packages strawberry-flavored gelatin
1 cup orange juice
1 teaspoon grated orange rind
1 cup sliced fresh strawberries

Fat-skimming options: Substitute sugar-free gelatin. With options, count: 1½ fruit.

• Combine rhubarb, water and sugar in saucepan. Cook until tender, about 4 to 5 minutes. Pour over gelatin, stirring until dissolved. Add orange juice and rind.
• Chill until thick and syrupy. Add strawberries. Pour into a lightly oiled 6-cup mold; chill until set.

Nutrition Analysis Per Serving: As Originally Published/With Fat-Skimming Options

Calories: 161/80	Saturated Fat: 0 g/0 g
Protein: 2 g/1 g	Cholesterol: 0 mg/0 mg
Carbohydrate: 38 g/20 g	Sodium: 58 mg/4 mg
Fat: 0 g/0 g	Dietary Fiber: 1 g/1 g

Waldorf Variation Salad

Yield: 8 servings

4 oranges, peeled and cut into sections
4 red apples, cut into wedges
1 cup sliced celery
1 (13$^1/_2$ ounce) can pineapple chunks
1 (6 ounce) can frozen lemonade, slightly thawed

Fat-skimming options: none. Exchange diets count: 2$^1/_2$ fruit.

• Toss all ingredients. Chill well.

Nutrition Analysis Per Serving: As Originally Published

Calories: 138	Saturated Fat: 0 g
Protein: 1 g	Cholesterol: 0 mg
Carbohydrate: 36 g	Sodium: 7 mg
Fat: 0 g	Dietary Fiber: 3 g

Cabbage-Orange Slaw

Yield: 6 servings

3 oranges
2 cups finely shredded cabbage
2 tablespoons finely chopped onion
$1/3$ cup chopped watercress or 2 tablespoons chopped parsley
$1/3$ cup mayonnaise
$1/4$ teaspoon salt
$1/8$ teaspoon sugar
Dash of celery salt
$1^1/2$ teaspoons vinegar
Pepper to taste

*Fat-skimming options: Use nonfat mayonnaise.
With options, exchange diets count: 2 vegetable.*

• Cut oranges in halves; remove pulp, leaving good firm shells. Remove all membrane; cut up orange sections to make 1 cup. Drain.
• Mix cabbage, onion and watercress with orange sections.

• Combine mayonnaise with remaining ingredients; toss with cabbage mixture. Fill orange shells and refrigerate. Serve cold and crisp, garnished with watercress.

Nutrition Analysis Per Serving: As Originally Published/With Fat-Skimming Options

Calories: 122/48
Protein: 1 g/1 g
Carbohydrate: 9 g/12 g
Fat: 10 g/0 g

Saturated Fat: 1.5 g/0 g
Cholesterol: 4 mg/0 mg
Sodium: 153 mg/253 mg
Dietary Fiber: 2.2 g/2.2 g

Freezer Coleslaw

Yield: 3 pints or 12 ($^{1}/_{2}$ cup) servings

1 cup sugar
1 cup vinegar
1 cup water
$^{1}/_{2}$ teaspoon celery seed
5$^{1}/_{3}$ cups shredded cabbage
1 medium onion, finely chopped
1 large carrot, shredded
$^{1}/_{2}$ cup chopped green pepper
$^{1}/_{2}$ cup chopped red pepper
1 teaspoon salt

Fat-skimming options: Omit sugar and add Equal Measure sugar substitute at the end of the cooking time. With options, exchange diets count: free.

• In 2-quart saucepan over high heat, bring first 4 ingredients to a boil, stirring occasionally. Boil 1 minute. Set aside to cool to room temperature.
• Meanwhile, in large bowl, toss together cabbage and remaining ingredients; let set about 30 minutes.
• Drain cabbage mixture. Stir cooled vinegar mixture into cabbage mixture. Mix well.
• Pack coleslaw in 3 (1 pint) freezer-safe containers, leaving $^{1}/_{2}$ inch space at top. Cover and freeze. May be stored in freezer up to 6 months.
• Thaw coleslaw about 3 hours at room temperature before serving.

Nutrition Analysis Per Serving: As Originally Published/With Fat-Skimming Options

Calories: 82/17	Saturated Fat: 0 g/0 g
Protein: 0 g/0 g	Cholesterol: 0 mg/0 mg
Carbohydrate: 21 g/4 g	Sodium: 185 mg/185 mg
Fat: 0 g/0 g	Dietary Fiber: 1 g/1 g

Catalina Tossed Salad

Yield: 8 to 10 servings

2 quarts mixed greens (leaf or romaine lettuce, spinach leaves or tender beet greens)
3 tomatoes, cut in wedges
1 cup raw cauliflowerets
$\frac{1}{2}$ cup crumbled blue cheese
$\frac{1}{2}$ cup crumbled cooked bacon
$\frac{1}{2}$ teaspoon salt
$\frac{1}{4}$ teaspoon pepper
$\frac{1}{2}$ cup Honey French Dressing

> *Fat-skimming options: Reduce blue cheese and bacon to $\frac{1}{4}$ cup each.*
> *Substitute bottled fat-free French dressing for Honey French Dressing.*
> *With options, exchange diets count: 1 vegetable, 1 fat.*

• Wash and drain greens well; shake dry in a dish towel. Break into bite-size pieces before measuring.
• Add tomato wedges, cauliflowerets, blue cheese and bacon to greens. Refrigerate until serving time.
• Prepare Honey French Dressing.
• When ready to serve salad, add seasonings and $\frac{1}{2}$ cup dressing; toss to coat the greens.

Honey French Dressing

Yield: $1\frac{1}{2}$ cups

1 teaspoon salt
$\frac{1}{4}$ teaspoon pepper
1 teaspoon dry mustard
$\frac{1}{3}$ cup cider vinegar
2 tablespoons honey
1 cup salad oil

• In a small bowl, mix salt, pepper and dry mustard; stir in vinegar and honey. Slowly add the salad oil while beating with a rotary beater or electric mixer.

Nutrition Analysis Per Serving: As Originally Published/With Fat-Skimming Options	
Calories: 175/61	Saturated Fat: 3 g/1 g
Protein: 5 g/3 g	Cholesterol: 10 mg/6 mg
Carbohydrate: 6 g/6 g	Sodium: 428 mg/329 mg
Fat: 16 g/3 g	Dietary Fiber: 2 g/2 g

Dilled Beans and Carrots

Yield: 5 to 6 servings

2 cups fresh green beans ($\frac{1}{2}$ pound)
$\frac{3}{4}$ cup boiling water
1 teaspoon sugar
$\frac{1}{2}$ teaspoon salt
$\frac{1}{2}$ teaspoon dill seeds
4 small to medium carrots, peeled and cut in 3 inch strips
$\frac{1}{2}$ cup low-calorie Italian salad dressing

Fat-skimming options: none. Exchange diets count: 2 vegetable.

• Wash and trim beans; leave whole. In a saucepan combine $\frac{3}{4}$ cup boiling water, sugar, salt and dill seeds; bring to a boil and add beans. Cook 5 to 10 minutes, until tender-crisp.

• Add carrots and cook about 10 minutes longer, until vegetables are tender but not soft. With pan still over heat, remove cover and allow liquid to evaporate. Add salad dressing and toss to mix well.
Serve hot or cold.

Nutrition Analysis Per Serving: As Originally Published

Calories: 56	Saturated Fat: 0.3 g
Protein: 1 g	Cholesterol: 1 mg
Carbohydrate: 9 g	Sodium: 354 mg
Fat: 2 g	Dietary Fiber: 2 g

Double Dairy Salad

Yield: 6 to 8 servings

2 cups large-curd cottage cheese
2 cups dairy sour cream
1 cup diced pared cucumber
$^1/_2$ cup sliced radishes
$^1/_4$ cup sliced green onions
$^3/_4$ teaspoon salt
$^1/_4$ teaspoon pepper
Lettuce wedges or tomato slices

*Fat-skimming options: Substitute 1% cottage cheese and nonfat sour cream.
With options, exchange diets count: 1 skim milk, 1 vegetable.*

• Mix together cottage cheese, sour cream, cucumber, radishes, onions, salt and pepper. Chill well.

• Serve over wedges of lettuce or tomato slices.

Nutrition Analysis Per Serving: As Originally Published/With Fat-Skimming Options

Calories: 175/105
Protein: 8 g/11 g
Carbohydrate: 7 g/14 g
Fat: 13 g/1 g

Saturated Fat: 9 g/0 g
Cholesterol: 45 mg/3 mg
Sodium: 450 mg/510 mg
Dietary Fiber: 0 g/0 g

Easy Blue Cheese Dressing

Yield: 32 (1 tablespoon) servings

1 cup mayonnaise (not salad dressing)
1 cup buttermilk
1 ounce blue cheese, crumbled
1 teaspoon Worcestershire sauce

Fat-skimming options: Use nonfat mayonnaise. With options, exchange diets count: free.

• In small bowl, combine mayonnaise, buttermilk, cheese and Worcestershire sauce. Drizzle over tossed salad. Keeps about a week in the refrigerator. Recipe can be halved.

Nutrition Analysis Per Serving: As Originally Published/With Fat-Skimming Options

Calories: 56/12	Saturated Fat: 1 g/0 g
Protein: 0 g/0 g	Cholesterol: 3 mg/0 mg
Carbohydrate: 0 g/2 g	Sodium: 47 mg/117 mg
Fat: 6 g/0 g	Dietary Fiber: 0 g/0 g

Frosty Tomato Cups

Yield: 8 servings

3 (1 pound 12 ounce) cans tomatoes, drained,
or 5 medium fresh tomatoes, chopped
1½ cups green pepper strips
1 medium onion, cut into rings
⅓ cup oil
2 tablespoons vinegar
1 teaspoon salt
¾ teaspoon oregano
¾ teaspoon basil
¼ teaspoon pepper

Fat-skimming options: Reduce oil to 2 tablespoons. With options, exchange diets count: 2 vegetable.

• Combine all ingredients. Chill.

Nutrition Analysis Per Serving: As Originally Published/With Fat-Skimming Options

Calories: 104/55	Saturated Fat: 1 g/0 g
Protein: 1 g/1 g	Cholesterol: 0 mg/0 mg
Carbohydrate: 6 g/6 g	Sodium: 274 mg/274 mg
Fat: 9 g/4 g	Dietary Fiber: 1 g/1 g

Garden Fresh Vegetable Salad

Yield: 8 servings

2 (3 ounce) packages lemon-flavored gelatin
1 teaspoon salt
2 cups boiling water
1½ cups cold water
2 tablespoons vinegar
1½ cups peeled, diced and seeded tomato
1½ cups grated carrot
⅓ cup minced green onions
¼ cup finely chopped green pepper

Fat-skimming options: Use sugar-free gelatin. With options, exchange diets count: free.

• Dissolve gelatin and salt in boiling water. Stir in cold water and vinegar. Chill until thick and syrupy.

• Fold in tomato, carrot, green onions and green pepper. Pour into lightly oiled 7-cup mold. Chill until set.

Nutrition Analysis Per Serving: As Originally Published/With Fat-Skimming Options

Calories: 92/11
Protein: 2 g/0 g
Carbohydrate: 21 g/3 g
Fat: 0 g/0 g

Saturated Fat: 0 g/0 g
Cholesterol: 0 mg/0 mg
Sodium: 325 mg/271 mg
Dietary Fiber: 1 g/1 g

Kidney Bean Salad

Yield: 16 (1/2 cup) servings

5 (15 ounce) cans red kidney beans, drained
1 cup chopped onion
1/2 cup chopped celery
1/3 cup sweet pickle relish
1/2 cup cider vinegar
1/2 cup sugar
1 egg, slightly beaten
2 teaspoons dry mustard

Fat-skimming options: Use 1/4 cup liquid egg substitute for egg.
Omit sugar and stir in 1/2 cup Equal Measure sugar subsitute at end of cooking time.
With options, exchange diets count: 2 starch.

• Combine kidney beans, onion, celery and pickle relish in bowl.
• Combine vinegar, sugar, egg and mustard in small saucepan. Cook over low heat stirring constantly, 7 minutes or until mixture thickens.

• Pour vinegar mixture over vegetables, tossing gently to coat. Cover and chill in refrigerator at least 6 hours.

Nutrition Analysis Per Serving: As Originally Published/With Fat-Skimming Options

Calories: 180/155
Protein: 10 g/10 g
Carbohydrate: 34 g/28 g
Fat: 1 g/1 g

Saturated Fat: 0 g/0 g
Cholesterol: 13 mg/0 mg
Sodium: 45 mg/48 mg
Dietary Fiber: 0 g/0 g

Marinated Corn Salad

Yield: 6 main-dish servings

3 cups whole kernel corn
1 to 1½ pounds Romaine or iceberg lettuce, cut in ¾ inch strips
1 pound smoked turkey or ham, cubed
½ cup sliced black or green olives
½ cup Italian dressing
½ red onion, thinly sliced

> *Fat-skimming options: Use nonfat Italian dressing.*
> *With options, exchange diets count: 1½ starch, 2 lean meat.*

• In large bowl combine corn, lettuce, turkey, olives and Italian dressing. Top with red onion rings. Chill about 30 minutes.

Nutrition Analysis Per Serving: As Originally Published/With Fat-Skimming Options

Calories: 294/224	Saturated Fat: 3 g/2 g
Protein: 18 g/17 g	Cholesterol: 0 mg/1 mg
Carbohydrate: 25 g/24 g	Sodium: 839 mg/842 mg
Fat: 15 g/8 g	Dietary Fiber: 4 g/4 g

Mixed Vegetable Marinade

Yield: 10 servings

1 medium cauliflower, cut up
4 medium carrots, pared and cut in 2-inch strips
1 (1 pound) can wax beans, drained
1 (1 pound) can whole green beans, drained
1 cup sliced celery
1 medium onion, sliced
1 (8 ounce) bottle regular Italian salad dressing
12 medium pitted ripe olives

Fat-skimming options: Use reduced-fat Italian Dressing.
With options, exchange diets count: 3 vegetable, ¹/₂ fat.

• Cook cauliflower and carrots in boiling salted water in Dutch oven 5 minutes or until tender-crisp. Drain. Plunge into ice water; drain well.

• Combine cooled vegetables with remaining ingredients in bowl. Toss gently to mix. Cover; refrigerate overnight. Can be stored up to 5 days.

Nutrition Analysis Per Serving: As Originally Published/With Fat-Skimming Options

Calories: 192/107
Protein: 5 g/5 g
Carbohydrate: 18 g/16 g
Fat: 12 g/3 g

Saturated Fat: 2 g/0 g
Cholesterol: 0 mg/0 mg
Sodium: 313 mg/316 mg
Dietary Fiber: 2 g/2 g

Orange-Pecan Salad

Yield: 8 servings

1 recipe Vinaigrette
2 medium oranges, peeled and sliced
8 cups torn romaine leaves
½ small red onion, thinly sliced and separated into rings
¼ cup coarsely chopped or broken, toasted pecans

> *Fat-skimming options: Reduce oil in vinaigrette to 2 tablespoons.*
> *Reduce pecans to 1 tablespoon. With options, exchange diets count: 1 vegetable, 1 fat.*

• Prepare Vinaigrette in advance.
• Cut orange slices in half crosswise.
• In bowl, toss oranges, romaine, onion and pecans with enough Vinaigrette to coat leaves.

Vinaigrette

Yield: ½ cup

⅓ cup vegetable oil
2 tablespoons red wine vinegar
2 tablespoons lemon juice
1 teaspoon sugar
½ teaspoon Worcestershire sauce
¼ teaspoon dry mustard
⅛ teaspoon pepper

• In jar with lid, shake together the oil, vinegar, lemon juice, sugar, Worcestershire sauce, dry mustard and pepper. Refrigerate 2 hours. Shake well before using.

Nutrition Analysis Per Serving: As Originally Published/With Fat-Skimming Options

Calories: 154/61
Protein: 2 g/1 g
Carbohydrate: 8 g/7 g
Fat: 14 g/4 g

Saturated Fat: 1 g/0 g
Cholesterol: 0 mg/0 mg
Sodium: 7 mg/7 mg
Dietary Fiber: 2 g/2 g

Overnight Tossed Green Salad

Yield: 8 servings

1 medium iceberg lettuce
1 (10 ounce) package fresh spinach
$^1/_2$ cup sliced green onions
1 pint cherry tomatoes, halved
1 (10 ounce) package frozen peas, thawed
1 pound bacon, diced, cooked and drained
$1^1/_2$ cups mayonnaise
1 cup dairy sour cream
2 tablespoons lemon juice
$^1/_2$ teaspoon oregano leaves
$^1/_4$ teaspoon basil leaves
$^1/_4$ teaspoon salt
$^1/_8$ teaspoon pepper

> *Fat-skimming options: Reduce bacon to $^1/_4$ pound. Substitute nonfat mayonnaise and nonfat sour cream. With options, exchange diets count: 4 vegetable.*

• Tear lettuce and spinach into bite-size pieces in a very large salad bowl. Add onion, tomatoes, peas and bacon; toss gently.
• Combine mayonnaise, sour cream, lemon juice, oregano, basil, salt and pepper; mix well. Spread dressing over greens; be sure to "frost" entire surface. (Do not mix in.) Cover with plastic wrap. Refrigerate salad mixture overnight.
• To serve, toss dressing with greens.

Nutrition Analysis Per Serving: As Originally Published/With Fat-Skimming Options

Calories: 435/108
Protein: 5 g/4 g
Carbohydrate: 7 g/21 g
Fat: 46 g/1 g

Saturated Fat: 11 g/0 g
Cholesterol: 33 mg/2 mg
Sodium: 466 mg/741 mg
Dietary Fiber: 1 g/1 g

Refrigerator Vegetable Salad
Yield: 8 servings

5 tablespoons salad oil
2 tablespoons wine vinegar
$1/2$ teaspoon salt
$1/4$ teaspoon pepper
$1/8$ teaspoon dried oregano leaves, crushed
1 clove garlic, cut in half
4 cups shredded cabbage
1 (1 pound) can French-style green beans, drained
$1^1/2$ cups shredded peeled carrots
$2/3$ cup chopped green pepper
$1/4$ cup finely chopped onion

Fat-skimming options: Reduce oil to 2 tablespoons.
With options, exchange diets count: 1 vegetable, $1/2$ fat.

• Combine salad oil, vinegar, salt, pepper, oregano and garlic; let stand 15 minutes for flavors to blend. Discard garlic.

• Meanwhile, combine vegetables in salad bowl. Stir dressing and pour over vegetables. Toss gently. Cover and chill at least 1 hour to mellow flavors.

Nutrition Analysis Per Serving: As Originally Published/With Fat-Skimming Options

Calories: 101/55
Protein: 1 g/1 g
Carbohydrate: 6 g/6 g
Fat: 9 g/4 g

Saturated Fat: 0 g/0 g
Cholesterol: 0 mg/0 mg
Sodium: 228 mg/228 mg
Dietary Fiber: 2 g/2 g

Sauerkraut Slaw

Yield: 6 to 8 servings

3 tablespoons vegetable oil
3 tablespoons sugar
2 tablespoons vinegar
1 teaspoon prepared mustard
$^1/_2$ teaspoon celery seed
2 pounds sauerkraut, drained well
1 (4 ounce) jar sliced pimientos, drained
$^1/_4$ cup chopped onion

Fat-skimming options: Reduce oil to 1 tablespoon.
With options, exchange diets count: 1 vegetable, $^1/_2$ fat.

• In large bowl, mix first 5 ingredients until blended.

• Add sauerkraut, pimientos and onion; toss well. Cover and refrigerate 1 to 3 days before serving.

Nutrition Analysis Per Serving: As Originally Published/With Fat-Skimming Options

Calories: 85/54
Protein: 0 g/0 g
Carbohydrate: 10 g/10 g
Fat: 5 g/2 g

Saturated Fat: 0 g/0 g
Cholesterol: 0 mg/0 mg
Sodium: 1,130 mg/1,130 mg
Dietary Fiber: 0 g/0 g

Sliced Tomatoes With Sweet and Sour Dressing

Yield: 8 servings

4 beefsteak tomatoes, sliced
2 tablespoons chopped scallions or green onions
¼ cup sugar
2 tablespoons cider vinegar

> *Fat-skimming options: Use ¼ cup Equal Measure sugar substitute for sugar.*
> *With options, exchange diets count: 1 vegetable.*

• Arrange tomatoes on a platter. Sprinkle with chopped scallions.

• Combine sugar and vinegar; mix well. Drizzle over sliced tomatoes.

Nutrition Analysis Per Serving: As Originally Published/With Fat-Skimming Options

Calories: 38/14	Saturated Fat: 0 g/0 g
Protein: 0 g/0 g	Cholesterol: 0 mg/0 mg
Carbohydrate: 9 g/3 g	Sodium: 5 mg/5 mg
Fat: 0 g/0 g	Dietary Fiber: 1 g/1 g

Spinach-Mushroom Vinaigrette

Yield: 8 servings

2 pounds fresh spinach
$1/2$ pound fresh mushrooms, sliced
$1/4$ cup minced fresh parsley
$3/4$ cup salad oil
$1/4$ cup lemon juice
1 clove garlic, minced
$3/4$ teaspoon salt
$1/4$ teaspoon sugar
Dash of pepper

Fat-skimming options: Reduce oil to $1/4$ cup. With options, exchange diets count: 1 fat, 1 vegetable.

• Wash spinach and drain well. Stem spinach. Tear into bite-size pieces and place in salad bowl. Add mushrooms and parsley. Toss lightly.

• Combine oil, lemon juice, garlic, salt, sugar and pepper in jar. Cover and shake well.
• Pour dressing over spinach mixture. Toss gently and serve immediately.

Nutrition Analysis Per Serving: As Originally Published/With Fat-Skimming Options

Calories: 197/73
Protein: 1 g/1 g
Carbohydrate: 2 g/2 g
Fat: 21 g/7 g

Saturated Fat: 1 g/0 g
Cholesterol: 0 mg/0 mg
Sodium: 222 mg/222 mg
Dietary Fiber: 1 g/1 g

Sour Cream Potato Salad

Yield: 16 (¹/₂ cup) servings

2¹/₂ pounds new potatoes
¹/₂ teaspoon salt
¹/₂ cup bottled Italian salad dressing
4 hard-cooked eggs
³/₄ cup thinly sliced celery
²/₃ cup sliced green onions
1¹/₂ cups mayonnaise
¹/₂ cup dairy sour cream
1¹/₂ teaspoons prepared mustard
³/₄ teaspoon salt
¹/₂ teaspoon prepared horseradish
¹/₄ teaspoon celery seeds
¹/₈ teaspoon pepper
²/₃ cup chopped pared cucumber
1 tablespoon sliced green onion tops

> *Fat-skimming options: Use fat-free Italian dressing, nonfat mayonnaise and nonfat sour cream.*
> *With options, exchange diets count: 1 starch, 1 fat.*

• Cook potatoes in 1 inch boiling water with ¹/₂ teaspoon salt in Dutch oven 30 minutes or until tender. Drain; cool 10 minutes.
• Peel potatoes and slice into bowl. Pour Italian dressing over potatoes. Cover and refrigerate 2 hours.
• Remove egg yolks from egg whites; set aside. Chop egg whites. Toss egg whites, celery and green onions with potatoes.

• Press egg yolks through sieve. Reserve 2 tablespoons sieved yolk. Mix together remaining sieved yolk, mayonnaise, sour cream, mustard, salt, horseradish, celery seeds and pepper in bowl. Pour mayonnaise mixture over potatoes. Toss lightly. Cover and refrigerate at least 2 hours.
• Before serving, toss cucumbers with potato salad. Garnish with remaining sieved egg yolk and green onion tops.

Nutrition Analysis Per Serving: As Originally Published/With Fat-Skimming Options

Calories: 278/106
Protein: 3 g/3 g
Carbohydrate: 15 g/16 g
Fat: 24 g/6 g

Saturated Fat: 5 g/4 g
Cholesterol: 63 mg/61 mg
Sodium: 360 mg/368 mg
Dietary Fiber: 1 g/1 g

BLT Salad

Yield: 16 cups or 12 (1¹/₃ cup) servings

Creamy Garlic Dressing
3 medium tomatoes, each cut into 6 wedges
1 pound bacon, cut into 2 inch pieces, cooked and drained
1 medium head leaf lettuce, torn into bite-size pieces (8 cups)
1 small head iceberg lettuce, shredded (4 cups)
2 cups croutons

Fat-skimming options: Use nonfat mayonniase in the dressing.
With options, exchange diets count: 2 vegetable, 1 fat.

• Prepare Creamy Garlic Dressing
• In bowl toss together tomatoes, bacon, lettuce and croutons. Pour dressing over salad; toss until well coated.

Creamy Garlic Dressing
1 cup mayonnaise or salad dressing
3 tablespoons milk
2 tablespoons red wine vinegar
¹/₂ teaspoon sugar
¹/₄ teaspoon salt
¹/₄ teaspoon onion powder
¹/₈ teaspoon black pepper
1 small clove garlic, minced

• In small bowl using wire whisk, beat together mayonnaise, milk, red wine vinegar, sugar, salt, onion powder, pepper and garlic. Cover and refrigerate at least 12 hours to blend flavors. Keeps up to 1 month in refrigerator.

Nutrition Analysis Per Serving: As Originally Published/With Fat-Skimming Options

Calories: 206/88	Saturated Fat: 4 g/1 g
Protein: 3 g/3 g	Cholesterol: 12 mg/5 mg
Carbohydrate: 7 g/11 g	Sodium: 282 mg/442 mg
Fat: 20 g/4 g	Dietary Fiber: 1 g/1 g

Tortellini Salad

Yield: 4 servings

1 pound fresh or frozen cheese-filled tortellini or ravioli
2 medium carrots, sliced
3 tablespoons lemon juice
1½ teaspoons dried basil leaves
5 tablespoons vegetable oil, divided
2 cloves garlic, minced
2 small zucchini, halved lengthwise and sliced
2 green onions, sliced
12 cherry tomatoes, quartered
¼ cup sliced ripe olives
¾ cup shredded Parmesan cheese

Fat-skimming options: Reduce oil to 1 tablespoon, using 1 teaspoon to toss with lemon juice and tortellini and 2 teaspoons to sauté vegetables. Reduce Parmesan cheese to ¼ cup. Reduce portion size and increase yield to 8 servings. With options, exchange diets count: 1 starch, ½ skim milk, 1 fat.

• Cook tortellini in boiling water according to package directions, adding carrots to tortellini during last 2 minutes of cooking time. Drain well.
• Pour into large bowl; toss with lemon juice, basil and 3 tablespoons oil.

• In 10 inch skillet over medium-high heat, heat remaining 2 tablespoons oil. Add garlic; cook until golden brown. Add zucchini and green onions; stir-fry 2 minutes. Remove from heat.
• Toss zucchini mixture, tomatoes and olives with tortellini mixture. Cover; refrigerate at least 3 hours. Serve with Parmesan cheese.

Nutrition Analysis Per Serving: As Originally Published/With Fat-Skimming Options

Calories: 536/183	Saturated Fat: 8 g/3 g
Protein: 21 g/8 g	Cholesterol: 80 mg/36 mg
Carbohydrate: 47 g/23 g	Sodium: 550 mg/182 mg
Fat: 31 g/7 g	Dietary Fiber: 4 g/2 g

Warm Chicken Salad
Yield: 4 servings

¼ cup soy sauce
2 tablespoons sugar
1½ teaspoons grated fresh ginger
2 cloves garlic, minced
4 skinless, boneless chicken breast halves, cut into ½-inch-thick strips
4 tablespoons vegetable oil, divided
2 tablespoons lemon juice
2 teaspoons sugar
1½ teaspoons soy sauce
⅛ teaspoon hot pepper sauce
4 teaspoons sesame seed
1 (10 ounce) package frozen cut green beans, cooked and drained
1 (5 ounce) can sliced water chestnuts, drained
¾ cup sliced scallions (6 medium)
½ cup sliced celery
½ cup diced peeled cucumber
½ cup slivered or sliced radishes
8 cups bite-size pieces of romaine and/or Boston lettuce

Fat-skimming options: Reduce oil to 1 tablespoon using it for browning the chicken and omitting it from the dressing. With options, exchange diets count: 3 lean meat, 4 vegetable.

• Stir together first 4 ingredients. Stir in chicken strips to coat. Cover, and refrigerate 2 hours.
• In jar with lid, shake together 3 tablespoons oil and next 4 ingredients; set aside.
• In 10 inch skillet over medium-high heat, heat remaining 1 tablespoon oil. Drain chicken; add to skillet and sprinkle with sesame seed. Stir-fry until chicken is done (no pink remains in center of strips when cut). Remove from heat; stir in green beans and next 5 ingredients.

• Divide lettuce among four plates. Top each with a fourth of the chicken and vegetables. Shake dressing and drizzle over each salad.

Nutrition Analysis Per Serving: As Originally Published/With Fat-Skimming Options	
Calories: 367/274	Saturated Fat: 2 g/1 g
Protein: 32 g/32 g	Cholesterol: 73 mg/73 mg
Carbohydrate: 20 g/20 g	Sodium: 1,244 mg/1,244 mg
Fat: 19 g/8 g	Dietary Fiber: 3 g/3 g

CHAPTER ELEVEN

Soups, Stews and Sandwiches

Our kind of food

Jennifer Sechler Bennett still remembers tasting Quick Baked Stew (in this chapter) as a member of the Family Test Group for Farm Journal. She was 9 years old growing up on a farm near Pleasant Hope, Mo. During the 1970s, the magazine's food editor would select recipes and ask readers to test them in their own home kitchens.

Jennifer's mother, Emogene, prepared this practical one-dish meal using farm-ready ingredients like minute steaks, potatoes, carrots, onions and green beans, then flavored it with beef bouillon, lemon juice, thyme and bay leaf. Texas toast and a green salad completed the menu. When the recipe was tested in 1970, Emogene described it as "our kind of food" and "a great way to sell the family on vitamins from vegetables!"

For Jennifer, it was a dish that stayed on the family's table long after the test was done. For farm daughters who married and moved to the city, cooking would naturally change. She still buys farm beef, a half at a time, but no longer has to help milk the cows. She doesn't have time for a garden, but trips to the farmers market rekindle her memories of snipping green beans and digging potatoes for supper.

Beefy Barley Soup

Yield: 8 (1½ cup) servings

1 tablespoon vegetable oil
1 pound boneless beef chuck, cut into ½ inch cubes
8 cups water
1 small rutabaga, peeled and cut into ½ inch cubes (about ¾ pound)
1½ cups shredded cabbage
1 cup sliced carrots
1 cup sliced celery
1 cup coarsely chopped onions
½ cup medium pearled barley
¼ cup chopped fresh parsley
6 beef bouillon cubes
2 bay leaves
1 clove garlic, minced
¾ teaspoon dried thyme leaves
¼ teaspoon pepper
1 cup frozen peas

Fat-skimming options: none. Exchange diets count: 2 vegetable, 3 lean meat.

• In 6-quart Dutch oven over high heat, heat oil. Add beef and brown well.

• Stir in remaining ingredients except peas. Bring to a boil. Reduce heat to medium-low. Cover and simmer 1 hour.
• Add peas; cook 5 minutes. Remove bay leaves.

Nutrition Analysis Per Serving: As Originally Published

Calories: 198	Saturated Fat: 2 g
Protein: 21 g	Cholesterol: 54 mg
Carbohydrate: 11 g	Sodium: 1026 mg
Fat: 7 g	Dietary Fiber: 1 g

Old-Fashioned Hamburger Soup
Yield: 8 (1½ cup) servings

1 pound lean ground beef
1½ cups chopped onions
2 cloves garlic, minced
1 (28 ounce) can tomatoes, undrained and cut up
1 cup chopped celery
1 cup diced, pared carrots
8 cups beef broth
1 cup water
2 teaspoons dried basil leaves, crushed
¼ teaspoon pepper
1½ cups finely shredded cabbage
1 (9 ounce) package frozen cut green beans
1 cup tiny pasta (such as tripolini, tiny shells, tubetti, alphabets or stars)

Fat-skimming options: Choose 95% lean ground meat.
With options, exchange diets count: 1 vegetable, ½ starch, 1 lean meat, 1 fat.

• In 6-quart Dutch oven over high heat, cook first 3 ingredients until meat is browned. Spoon off excess fat.

• Add undrained, cut-up tomatoes and next 6 ingredients. Cover; bring to a boil. Reduce heat; simmer 10 minutes.
• Stir in cabbage, green beans and pasta. Cover; return to a boil. Simmer 10 minutes more.

Nutrition Analysis Per Serving: As Originally Published/With Fat-Skimming Options

Calories: 169/165	Saturated Fat: 3 g/2 g
Protein: 13 g/13 g	Cholesterol: 34 mg/33 mg
Carbohydrate: 14 g/14 g	Sodium: 1,072 mg/1,070 mg
Fat: 7 g/6 g	Dietary Fiber: 1 g/1 g

Quick Baked Stew

Yield: 6 servings

4 minute cube steaks (about 1$\frac{1}{2}$ pounds)
$\frac{1}{2}$ cup flour
2 tablespoons shortening
2 cups diced potatoes
2 cups sliced carrots
1 cup chopped onions
1 cup sliced celery
1 cup frozen loose-pack green beans
1 beef bouillon cube or 1 envelope beef broth mix
1 cup hot water
2 tablespoons lemon juice
1$\frac{1}{2}$ teaspoons salt
$\frac{1}{4}$ teaspoon pepper
$\frac{1}{4}$ teaspoon thyme leaves (optional)
1 bay leaf

Fat-skimming options: Omit shortening and brown steaks in a nonstick skillet sprayed with nonstick cooking spray. With options, exchange diets count: 5 lean meat, 2 starch, 2 fat.

• Cut steaks in strips $\frac{1}{2}$ inch wide. Shake in bag with flour. Brown in hot fat. Combine with remaining ingredients (mix bouillon cube with hot water before adding).

• Turn into 2$\frac{1}{2}$-quart casserole. Cover and bake at 350 degrees F about 1 hour and 15 minutes. Stir once or twice during cooking.

Nutrition Analysis Per Serving: As Originally Published/With Fat-Skimming Options

Calories: 551/513
Protein: 35 g/35 g
Carbohydrate: 34 g/34 g
Fat: 32 g/27 g

Saturated Fat: 12 g/11 g
Cholesterol: 113 mg/113 mg
Sodium: 835 mg/835 mg
Dietary Fiber: 2 g/2 g

Stefado

Yield: 6 to 8 servings

2 tablespoons vegetable oil
2 pounds well-trimmed beef bottom round, cut into 1 inch cubes
3 cups water, divided
4 medium onions, peeled and quartered
2 cloves garlic, minced
¼ cup red wine vinegar
1 (6 ounce) can tomato paste
1 tablespoon packed brown sugar
1 teaspoon salt
¼ teaspoon pepper
1 (1½ inch) cinnamon stick
1 bay leaf
10 whole cloves
½ teaspoon ground allspice
4 medium potatoes (1½ pounds), peeled and cut into 1 inch cubes
2 medium green sweet peppers, seeded and cut into strips
8 ounces small mushrooms
2 tablespoons flour
½ cup pitted ripe olives

Fat-skimming options: Omit oil and use nonstick spray shortening.
With options, exchange diets count: 1 starch, 2 vegetable, 4 lean meat.

• In 6-quart Dutch oven over medium-high heat, heat 1 tablespoon oil. Add half of the beef cubes; cook until browned on all sides. Remove and set aside. Repeat with remaining oil and beef cubes.
• Return all of the beef to Dutch oven. Add 2½ cups water and next 11 ingredients. Bring to a boil. Reduce heat; cover. Simmer 45 minutes.
• Add potatoes, green peppers and mushrooms; cover. Simmer until beef and potatoes are tender, about 45 minutes.
• In jar with lid, shake together flour and remaining ½ cup water. Stir into stew. Add olives. Cook, stirring constantly, until mixture boils and thickens. Remove cinnamon stick, bay leaf and cloves.

Nutrition Analysis Per Serving: As Originally Published/With Fat-Skimming Options

Calories: 383/352
Protein: 37 g/37 g
Carbohydrate: 28 g/28 g
Fat: 14 g/10 g

Saturated Fat: 4 g/3 g
Cholesterol: 91 mg/91 mg
Sodium: 390 mg/390 mg
Dietary Fiber: 3 g/3 g

Chicken Vegetable Soup

Yield: 2 quarts or 8 (1 cup) servings

1 (3 pound) broiler-fryer, quartered
2 quarts water
4 medium onions, quartered
4 stalks celery, cut in 3 inch chunks
3 medium carrots, cut in 3 inch chunks
10 sprigs fresh parsley
1 tablespoon salt
1 clove garlic
1 bay leaf
$1/2$ teaspoon dried thyme leaves
2 whole cloves
$1/4$ teaspoon pepper
$1/16$ teaspoon powdered saffron
1 cup sliced carrot
1 cup sliced celery
2 eggs, well beaten
1 tablespoon lemon juice
Sliced green onions and tops
Dairy sour cream

> *Fat-skimming options: Remove all skin and fat from chicken.*
> *With options, exchange diets count: 6 very lean meat, 2 vegetable, 1 fat.*

• Place first 13 ingredients in 6-quart Dutch oven. Bring to a boil; reduce heat. Cover; simmer 1 hour 15 minutes. Strain broth. Place broth back into Dutch oven; boil, uncovered, 15 minutes. Add 1 cup sliced carrots and 1cup sliced celery. Cover; simmer 10 minutes or until vegetables are tender. Remove chicken from bones; cut in chunks. Add to broth.

• Remove from heat. Let stand 10 minutes. Gradually add 2 cups hot broth to eggs, stirring vigorously. Slowly add mixture to Dutch oven, stirring constantly. Add lemon juice. Serve in bowls topped with green onions and sour cream.
• To reheat, place over low heat. Do not boil.

Nutrition Analysis Per Serving: As Originally Published/With Fat-Skimming Options

Calories: 437/350	Saturated Fat: 7 g/3.5 g
Protein: 46 g/48 g	Cholesterol: 191 mg/191 mg
Carbohydrate: 9 g/9 g	Sodium: 969 mg/968 mg
Fat: 23 g/13 g	Dietary Fiber: 2 g/2 g

Parsleyed Chicken Chowder

Yield: 1³/₄ quarts or 7 (1 cup) servings

2 tablespoons butter
¹/₄ cup chopped onion
1¹/₂ cups cubed (1 inch) cooked chicken
1¹/₂ cups cubed (¹/₂ inch) pared potatoes
1¹/₂ cups cubed (¹/₄ inch) pared carrots
2 chicken bouillon cubes
1 teaspoon salt
¹/₈ teaspoon pepper
2 cups water
3 tablespoons flour
2¹/₂ cups milk, divided
Chopped fresh parsley

*Fat-skimming options: Omit butter and sauté onions in nonstick cooking spray. Use skim milk.
With options, exchange diets count: 2 lean meat, 1 starch.*

• Melt butter in 3-quart saucepan. Add onion and sauté until tender.
• Add chicken, potatoes, carrots, bouillon cubes, salt, pepper and water. Cover and simmer 20 minutes or until vegetables are tender.

• Combine flour and ¹/₂ cup of the milk in a jar. Cover and shake until blended. Add flour mixture and remaining 2 cups milk to vegetables. Cook over medium heat, stirring constantly, until mixture thickens. Sprinkle with parsley.

Nutrition Analysis Per Serving: As Originally Published/With Fat-Skimming Options	
Calories: 219/178	Saturated Fat: 4 g/1 g
Protein: 19 g/19 g	Cholesterol: 54 mg/40 mg
Carbohydrate: 17 g/17 g	Sodium: 801 mg/769 mg
Fat: 8 g/3 g	Dietary Fiber: 1.5 g/1.5 g

Mulligatawny Soup

Yield: 6 (1 cup) servings

1 medium onion, sliced
1 tablespoon butter or margarine
1 carrot, sliced
1 green pepper, cut in ¹/₂ inch pieces
1 apple, cored and sliced
1 cup chopped tomato or 1 (8 ounce) can tomato sauce
2 cups water
2 cubes chicken bouillon
2 whole cloves
1 to 1¹/₂ teaspoons curry powder
1 cup cooked chicken
¹/₄ cup all-purpose flour
¹/₂ cup cold water

Fat-skimming options: none. Exchange diets count: 1 lean meat, 2 vegetable.

• In 3-quart soup pot, cook onion in butter.
• Stir in next 8 ingredients. Simmer 20 to 30 minutes. Stir in chicken.

• In small bowl combine flour and water and stir into soup. Bring to boiling, stirring constantly until chicken is cooked and mixture is thickened.
• Remove cloves. Serve hot.

Nutrition Analysis Per Serving: As Originally Published

Calories: 111	Saturated Fat: 1 g
Protein: 8 g	Cholesterol: 23 mg
Carbohydrate: 13 g	Sodium: 329 mg
Fat: 3 g	Dietary Fiber: 2 g

Ham and Cabbage Soup

Yield: 6 to 8 servings

¼ cup chopped onion
¼ cup chopped celery
2 tablespoons butter
¼ cup flour
½ teaspoon salt
⅛ teaspoon pepper
3 cups hot water
2 cups shredded cabbage
1 bay leaf
2 cups diced cooked ham
¾ cup dairy sour cream
2 tablespoons chopped fresh parsley

> *Fat-skimming options: Omit butter and replace with 1 teaspoon corn oil. Use nonfat sour cream. With options, exchange diets count: 1 lean meat, ½ skim milk, 1 vegetable.*

• Cook onion and celery in melted butter in Dutch oven until onion is tender. Blend in flour, salt and pepper. Stir in water and cook, stirring constantly, until mixture is boiling. Add cabbage and bay leaf; cover. Simmer 8 to 10 minutes or until cabbage is tender. Remove bay leaf.

• Stir in ham and cook 3 to 4 minutes. Gently blend in sour cream. Heat a few more minutes. Do not boil. Garnish with parsley.

Nutrition Analysis Per Serving: As Originally Published/With Fat-Skimming Options

Calories: 174/132
Protein: 12 g/13 g
Carbohydrate: 5 g/9 g
Fat: 11 g/4 g

Saturated Fat: 6 g/1 g
Cholesterol: 37 mg/21 mg
Sodium: 743 mg/735 mg
Dietary Fiber: 1 g/1 g

Lentil Sausage Soup

Yield: 3 quarts or 12 (1 cup) servings

1 pound fresh pork sausage links
3 tablespoons water
2 cups chopped onion
1 clove garlic, minced
4 carrots, sliced
¾ cup sliced celery
¼ cup chopped fresh parsley
2 cups lentils, rinsed and drained
1 (1 pound) can tomatoes, cut up
2½ quarts water
1½ tablespoons salt
½ teaspoon dried marjoram leaves
¼ teaspoon pepper

Fat-skimming options: Substitute reduced-fat pork or turkey sausage.
With options, exchange diets count: 1 starch, 1 vegetable, 1½ lean meat.

• Cook sausage in 3 tablespoons water in covered Dutch oven or kettle for 5 minutes. Remove cover; continue cooking until sausage is brown, turning frequently. Drain sausage on paper towels. Cut in chunks; set aside.

• Pour off all but ¼ cup pan drippings. Sauté onion and garlic in drippings until tender (do not brown). Add carrots, celery, parsley, lentils, tomatoes, 2½ quarts water, salt, marjoram and pepper. Bring mixture to a boil. Reduce heat; cover and simmer 25 to 30 minutes or until vegetables are tender. Add sausage chunks and heat thoroughly.

Nutrition Analysis Per Serving: As Originally Published/With Fat-Skimming Options

Calories: 178/176
Protein: 12 g/16 g
Carbohydrate: 23 g/24 g
Fat: 5 g/3 g

Saturated Fat: 1 g/0 g
Cholesterol: 11 mg/11 mg
Sodium: 958 mg/1015 mg
Dietary Fiber: 1 g/1 g

Louisiana Gumbo

Yield: 8 servings

¼ cup all-purpose flour
1 tablespoon vegetable oil
1 medium onion, chopped
1 rib celery, chopped
4 cloves garlic, minced or ½ teaspoon garlic powder
4 cups chicken broth
1 (16 ounce) can whole tomatoes, undrained and chopped
1 (10 ounce) package frozen okra or 1 cup fresh okra, sliced
2 tablespoons fresh minced parsley or 2 teaspoons dried parsley, crushed
⅛ to ¼ teaspoon cayenne pepper
1 bay leaf
½ cup uncooked long-grain white rice
1 (6 ounce) package small frozen shrimp
¼ pound boneless chicken breast or thigh, cut into ½ inch pieces
2 ounces andouille or kielbasa sausage, thinly sliced
Hot pepper sauce, as desired

Fat-skimming options: none. Exchange diets count: 1 starch, 2 vegetable, 2 lean meat.

• In a heavy cast-iron skillet, heat flour, stirring constantly for 7 to 10 minutes until deep golden brown. If browning too fast, lower heat and keep stirring. Place on plate; set aside to cool.
• In a heavy 3-quart saucepan, heat oil. Add onion, celery and garlic. Cook about 5 minutes or until onions are translucent.
• Stir in toasted flour and slowly stir in chicken broth.

• Add tomatoes, okra, parsley, cayenne pepper and bay leaf. Cover and cook over medium heat for about 10 minutes. Stir in rice and return to boiling. Reduce heat to simmer, cover and cook for 15 minutes.
• Add shrimp, chicken and sausage. Cook over low heat for 5 minutes longer, until shrimp and chicken are firm and cooked through and rice is tender. Discard bay leaf.
• Spoon gumbo into bowls and serve with hot pepper sauce, if desired.

Nutrition Analysis Per Serving: As Originally Published

Calories: 179
Protein: 15 g
Carbohydrate: 26 g
Fat: 9 g
Saturated Fat: 3 g
Cholesterol: 25 mg
Sodium: 791 mg
Dietary Fiber: 2 g

Oyster Stew

Yield: 2 quarts or 8 (1 cup) servings

1 quart milk
1 cup light cream
1 teaspoon salt
1/8 teaspoon pepper
1/2 cup butter
2 pints shucked stewing oysters with their liquor

> *Fat-skimming options: Use skim milk. Use evaporated skim milk for cream.*
> *Omit butter and replace with 2 tablespoons soft margarine.*
> *With options, exchange diets count: 1 skim milk, 1 lean meat, 1 fat.*

• Combine milk, cream, salt and pepper in 4-quart Dutch oven. Heat over medium heat until milk is scalded.

• Meanwhile, melt butter in 2-quart saucepan over low heat. Add oysters with liquor. Cook just until oysters start to curl around edges. Pour oyster mixture into hot milk. Heat and serve immediately.

Nutrition Analysis Per Serving: As Originally Published/With Fat-Skimming Options

Calories: 300/249
Protein: 13 g/15 g
Carbohydrate: 12 g/14 g
Fat: 23 g/7 g

Saturated Fat: 13 g/0 g
Cholesterol: 233 mg/66 mg
Sodium: 123 mg/97 mg
Dietary Fiber: 0 g/0 g

Quick Clam Soup

Yield: 6 (1 cup) servings

1 cup chopped onion
1/3 cup chopped celery
1/3 cup chopped sweet green pepper
2 cloves garlic, minced
2 tablespoons vegetable oil
1 (28 ounce) can tomatoes, undrained and cut up
2 (6 1/2 ounce) cans chopped clams, undrained
1 cup tomato juice
1/2 teaspoon dried oregano leaves, crushed
1/8 teaspoon pepper
1/2 cup chopped fresh parsley
Grated Parmesan cheese

Fat-skimming options: Reduce oil to 1 teaspoon.
With options, exchange diets count: 3 vegetable, 1 lean meat.

• In 3-quart saucepan over medium heat, sauté onion, celery, green pepper and garlic in oil until tender.

• Add undrained, cut-up tomatoes and next 4 ingredients. Bring to a boil; reduce heat. Cover; simmer 10 minutes. Stir in parsley.
• Serve sprinkled with Parmesan cheese.

Nutrition Analysis Per Serving: As Originally Published/With Fat-Skimming Options

Calories: 168/133
Protein: 13 g/13 g
Carbohydrate: 17 g/17 g
Fat: 6 g/3 g

Saturated Fat: 1 g/0 g
Cholesterol: 28 mg/28 mg
Sodium: 557 mg/557 mg
Dietary Fiber: 1 g/1 g

Seafood Chowder

Yield: 2 quarts or 8 (1 cup) servings

¹/₂ cup chopped onion
¹/₂ cup chopped celery
¹/₂ cup chopped green pepper
2 cloves garlic, minced
2 tablespoons vegetable oil
1 (28 ounce) can crushed tomatoes
2 cups tomato juice or chicken broth
¹/₄ teaspoon pepper
¹/₄ teaspoon dried oregano, crushed
¹/₂ pound fresh or frozen fish fillets (thawed), cut into 1 inch pieces
¹/₂ pound fresh or frozen shrimp, shelled
1 (6¹/₂ ounce) can minced clams
¹/₃ cup chopped fresh parsley

Fat-skimming options: Reduce oil to 2 teaspoons to sauté vegetables.
With options, exchange diets count: 1 very lean meat, 2 vegetable.

• In 4-quart Dutch oven over medium-high heat, cook onion, celery, green pepper and garlic in hot oil, 5 minutes.
• Stir in undrained tomatoes, tomato juice, pepper and oregano. Bring to a boil. Reduce heat; cover and simmer 15 minutes.

• Stir in fish, shrimp and undrained clams; return to a boil. Reduce heat; cover and simmer 5 minutes, or until fish flakes easily with fork and shrimp is done. Stir in parsley.

Nutrition Analysis Per Serving: As Originally Published/With Fat-Skimming Options

Calories: 120/99	Saturated Fat: 0 g/0 g
Protein: 10 g/10 g	Cholesterol: 21 mg/211 mg
Carbohydrate: 12 g/12 g	Sodium: 549 mg/549 mg
Fat: 5 g/2 g	Dietary Fiber: 0.5 g/0.5 g

Pasta and Bean Soup

Yield: 3¹/₂ quarts or 12 (1 cup) servings

1 pound dry Great Northern beans
2 quarts water
2¹/₂ teaspoons salt
1 large whole carrot
6 strips bacon
¹/₂ cup chopped onion
¹/₂ cup chopped celery
1 small clove garlic, minced
1 (1 pound) can stewed tomatoes
¹/₂ bay leaf
¹/₂ teaspoon oregano
¹/₂ teaspoon salt
¹/₄ teaspoon pepper
¹/₄ cup water
1 cup ditalini or small elbow macaroni

Fat-skimming options: none. Exchange diets count: 2 very lean meat, 1¹/₂ starch, 1 vegetable.

• Soak beans 8 hours or overnight. Rinse and drain. Combine beans, water, salt and carrot; simmer in a 6-quart pot 2 hours or until beans are tender.
• Fry bacon until crisp. Remove bacon. Reserve ¹/₄ cup bacon drippings in pan. Add onion, celery and garlic. Sauté. Stir in tomatoes and next five ingredients. Bring to a boil; simmer 30 minutes.

• Cook macaroni according to package directions. Drain.
• Purée half of the beans. Cube carrot. Crumble bacon. Combine all ingredients.

Nutrition Analysis Per Serving: As Originally Published

Calories: 209
Protein: 11 g
Carbohydrate: 37 g
Fat: 2 g

Saturated Fat: 1 g
Cholesterol: 3 mg
Sodium: 708 mg
Dietary Fiber: 1 g

Split Pea Soup

Yield: 2 quarts or 8 (1 cup) servings

1 pound green split peas
2 quarts water
2 teaspoons salt
$^1/_4$ teaspoon pepper
$^1/_4$ teaspoon dried marjoram leaves
$1^1/_2$ cups chopped onion
1 pound ham hocks or 1 meaty ham bone
1 cup chopped celery
1 cup cubed, pared potatoes
1 cup sliced carrots

Fat-skimming options: Substitute $^1/_2$ pound chopped lean ham for ham hocks.
With options, exchange diets count: $1^1/_2$ lean meat, 2 starch, 1 vegetable.

• Wash and sort peas. Add water, salt, pepper, marjoram, onion and ham hocks. Bring mixture to a boil. Reduce heat and simmer, covered, $1^1/_2$ hours (stirring occasionally).
• Remove ham. Discard fat and bones. Cut meat in pieces and return to soup mixture. Add celery, potatoes and carrots. Cover. Simmer 30 minutes, stirring occasionally, or until vegetables are tender. If you prefer a thinner soup, add water.

Nutrition Analysis Per Serving: As Originally Published/With Fat-Skimming Options

Calories: 356/265
Protein: 26 g/22 g
Carbohydrate: 36 g/36 g
Fat: 12 g/4 g

Saturated Fat: 4 g/1 g
Cholesterol: 49 mg/30 mg
Sodium: 593 mg/583 mg
Dietary Fiber: 1 g/1 g

Tortellini-Kale Soup

Yield: 5 (1¹/₂ cup) servings

6 cups reduced-sodium chicken broth
1 cup firmly packed, coarsely chopped kale
2 cloves garlic, finely minced or ¹/₄ teaspoon garlic powder
1 (9 ounce) package refrigerated tortellini, any flavor
¹/₄ cup sliced green onions (include tops)
¹/₂ cup grated Parmesan cheese

> *Fat-skimming options: Reduce cheese to ¹/₄ cup.*
> *With options, exchange diets count: 2 lean meat, 1 vegetable, 1 starch.*

• In medium saucepan bring chicken broth, kale and garlic to boiling.
• Add tortellini and cook according to package directions until tortellini is tender, but firm. For last 2 minutes of cooking time, stir in green onions.

• Serve with Parmesan cheese.

Nutrition Analysis Per Serving: As Originally Published/With Fat-Skimming Options

Calories: 220/202	Saturated Fat: 4 g/3 g
Protein: 14 g/12 g	Cholesterol: 42 mg/39 mg
Carbohydrate: 23 g/23 g	Sodium: 373 mg/299 mg
Fat: 8 g/7 g	Dietary Fiber: 1 g/1 g

Dutch Potato Soup

Yield: 6 (1 cup) servings

4 cups cubed (½ inch) peeled potatoes
3 cups water
1½ teaspoons salt
¼ teaspoon dried thyme leaves
⅛ teaspoon pepper
6 slices bacon, diced
1 medium onion, chopped
2 tablespoons flour
1 cup milk

Fat-skimming options: Use skim milk. With options, exchange diets count: 1½ starch, ½ fat.

• In 3-quart saucepan over high heat, bring potatoes, water, salt, thyme and pepper to a boil. Reduce heat to low. Cover and simmer 15 minutes or until potatoes are tender.
• Drain potatoes, reserving broth. Mash half of the potatoes. Set aside broth, cubed potatoes and mashed potatoes. Wipe saucepan dry.

• In same saucepan over medium-high heat, cook bacon until browned. Drain on paper towels. Pour off all but 2 tablespoons bacon drippings. Reduce heat to medium. Add onion; cook until tender. Stir in flour.
• Gradually stir in reserved broth until smooth. Stir in mashed potatoes until smooth. Add bacon and cubed potatoes; cook, stirring constantly, until soup is thickened. Stir in milk; cook until heated through.

Nutrition Analysis Per Serving: As Originally Published/With Fat-Skimming Options

Calories: 148/142
Protein: 5 g/5 g
Carbohydrate: 17 g/23 g
Fat: 4 g/3 g

Saturated Fat: 1 g/1 g
Cholesterol: 8 mg/6 mg
Sodium: 659 mg/660 mg
Dietary Fiber: 1.5 g/1.5 g

Cream of Potato Soup

Yield: 2 quarts or 8 (1 cup) servings

6 cups sliced potatoes (5 large)
$^1/_2$ cup sliced carrots
6 slices bacon
1 cup chopped onion
1 cup sliced celery
$1^1/_2$ teaspoons salt
$^1/_4$ teaspoon pepper
2 cups milk
2 cups light cream
Finely shredded Cheddar cheese (optional)
Parsley sprigs (optional)

*Fat-skimming options: Use skim milk. Substitute evaporated skim milk for light cream.
With options, exchange diets count: 1 skim milk, 1 starch, 1 fat*

• Cook potatoes and carrots in boiling water until tender. Drain.
• Sauté bacon until crisp; drain and crumble. Sauté onion and celery in 2 tablespoons of the bacon fat.

• Combine cooked vegetables, bacon, salt, pepper, milk and cream. Simmer for 30 minutes. (Do not boil.) Garnish with shredded Cheddar cheese and parsley.

Nutrition Analysis Per Serving: As Originally Published/With Fat-Skimming Options

Calories: 287/206
Protein: 9 g/11 g
Carbohydrate: 25 g/29 g
Fat: 18 g/5 g

Saturated Fat: 10 g/2 g
Cholesterol: 56 mg/14 mg
Sodium: 586 mg/628 mg
Dietary Fiber: 2 g/2 g

Creamy Vegetable Soup

Yield: 8 (1 cup) servings

3 cups water
2 cups shredded peeled potatoes
1 cup shredded carrot
$\frac{1}{2}$ cup shredded onions
2 tablespoons chopped fresh parsley
1$\frac{1}{2}$ teaspoons salt
$\frac{1}{8}$ teaspoon white pepper
$\frac{1}{2}$ cup frozen corn
$\frac{1}{2}$ cup frozen peas
3 cups evaporated milk, warmed
1 tablespoon butter or regular margarine
1 tablespoon chopped fresh dill

> *Fat-skimming options: Use evaporated skim milk. Omit butter.*
> *With options, exchange diets count: 1 skim milk, $\frac{1}{2}$ starch.*

• In 3-quart saucepan over high heat, bring first 7 ingredients to a boil. Reduce heat to low.
• Cover and simmer 15 minutes. Add corn and peas. Cover and simmer 5 minutes.

• Remove from heat. Gradually stir in warm evaporated milk and butter until well blended.
• To serve, ladle soup into bowls; garnish with chopped fresh dill.

Nutrition Analysis Per Serving: As Originally Published/With Fat-Skimming Options

Calories: 192/128
Protein: 8 g/9 g
Carbohydrate: 22 g/23 g
Fat: 8 g/0 g

Saturated Fat: 5 g/0 g
Cholesterol: 31 mg/3 mg
Sodium: 528 mg/525 mg
Dietary Fiber: 1 g/1 g

Souper Gazpacho

Yield: 1¾ quarts or 7 (1 cup) servings

1 cup chopped tomato
1 cup chopped green pepper
1 cup chopped, pared cucumber
½ cup chopped onion
1 clove garlic, minced
3 cups tomato juice
1 (10¾ ounce) can condensed tomato soup
1 cup water
¼ cup vinegar
2 tablespoons cooking oil
4 drops Tabasco sauce
2 slices white bread, broken up

Fat-skimming options: Omit oil. With options, exchange diets count: ½ starch, 2 vegetable.

• Combine all ingredients except garnish in large bowl. Place half of mixture in blender jar. Cover and blend until smooth. Turn blended mixture into a clean bowl. Blend remaining ingredients until smooth; turn into bowl. Cover; chill 3 hours.

• Serve with assorted chopped vegetable garnishes.

Nutrition Analysis Per Serving: As Originally Published/With Fat-Skimming Options

Calories: 118/82
Protein: 3 g/3 g
Carbohydrate: 17 g/17 g
Fat: 5 g/1 g

Saturated Fat: 0 g/0 g
Cholesterol: 0 mg/0 mg
Sodium: 722 mg/722 mg
Dietary Fiber: 1 g/1 g

Curried Squash Bisque

Yield: 1¹/₂ quarts or 6 (1 cup) servings

1 cup sliced, pared carrots
¹/₂ cup chopped onion
¹/₄ teaspoon salt
1 chicken bouillon cube
1 cup water
2 medium unpared yellow summer squash, cut in half lengthwise and sliced
¹/₄ cup flour
2 cups milk
1 teaspoon curry powder
1 cup shredded Cheddar cheese
1 (13 ounce) can evaporated milk

*Fat-skimming options: Use skim milk, evaporated skim milk and reduced-fat Cheddar cheese.
With options, exchange diets count: 1 skim milk, 2 vegetable, 2 lean meat.*

• Combine carrots, onion, salt, bouillon cube and water in 3-quart saucepan. Cook over high heat until it comes to a boil. Reduce heat; cover and simmer 5 minutes. Add squash. Cover and simmer 5 minutes more, or until tender.

• Combine flour and milk in jar. Cover and shake until smooth. Stir flour mixture and curry powder into vegetables. Cook over medium heat, stirring, until mixture boils.
• Remove from heat. Slowly stir in cheese and evaporated milk. Return to low heat and heat thoroughly.

Nutrition Analysis Per Serving: As Originally Published/With Fat-Skimming Options

Calories: 336/242
Protein: 19 g/22 g
Carbohydrate: 21 g/23 g
Fat: 20 g/8 g

Saturated Fat: 12 g/5 g
Cholesterol: 66 mg/30 mg
Sodium: 662 mg/730 mg
Dietary Fiber: 2 g/2 g

Chicken Waldorf Pockets

Yield: 4 servings

2 cups diced, cooked chicken
1 medium Red Delicious apple, cored and diced
$\frac{1}{2}$ cup calorie-reduced mayonnaise
$\frac{1}{2}$ cup chopped celery
$\frac{1}{2}$ cup shredded carrot
$\frac{1}{4}$ cup slivered almonds, toasted
3 tablespoons raisins
5 teaspoons lemon juice
4 (5 inch) loaves pita bread

Fat-skimming options: Use nonfat mayonnaise.
With options, exchange diets count: 6 very lean meat, 3 starch, 1 fruit.

• In medium bowl, stir together first 8 ingredients.

• Cut pita loaves in half crosswise and open each half to form a pocket. Fill each pocket with chicken mixture.

Nutrition Analysis Per Serving: As Originally Published/With Fat-Skimming Options

Calories: 588/512
Protein: 43 g/43 g
Carbohydrate: 51 g/55 g
Fat: 23 g/13 g

Saturated Fat: 4 g/2 g
Cholesterol: 95 mg/95 mg
Sodium: 638 mg/798 mg
Dietary Fiber: 2.5 g/2.5 g

Curried Smoked Turkey in a Pocket

Yield: 4 to 5 servings (8 to 9 sandwich halves)

1½ cups smoked turkey, cubed
1 cup fresh or frozen, thawed snow peas, halved
½ cup well-drained pineapple chunks
2 medium carrots, grated
¼ to ⅓ cup low-fat mayonnaise
2 tablespoons orange juice
½ to 1 teaspoon curry powder
¼ teaspoon red pepper flakes
4 to 5 (6 inch) loaves pita bread, halved to form pockets

Fat-skimming options: Use nonfat mayonnaise.
With options, exchange diets count: 2 very lean meat, 3 starch, 1 vegetable.

• In medium bowl, combine turkey, snow peas, pineapple chunks and carrots. Mix gently.

• Combine mayonnaise, orange juice, curry powder and red pepper flakes. Toss with turkey mixture. Chill 1 to 4 hours.
• At serving time, evenly divide mixture among pocket halves.

Nutrition Analysis Per Serving: As Originally Published/With Fat-Skimming Options

Calories: 360/322
Protein: 20 g/20 g
Carbohydrate: 46 g/48 g
Fat: 10 g/5 g

Saturated Fat: 2 g/1 g
Cholesterol: 0 mg/0 mg
Sodium: 1,027 mg/1,107 mg
Dietary Fiber: 2 g/2 g

Garden Club Sandwiches

Yield: 4 servings

12 very thin slices whole wheat bread
6 tablespoons bottled Russian dressing or calorie-reduced mayonnaise
12 radishes, thinly sliced
6 ounces sliced Muenster cheese
Fresh spinach leaves
1/2 large cucumber, thinly sliced
1 large tomato, thinly sliced
8 ounces sliced cooked turkey breast
16 radish slices for garnish
16 pimiento-stuffed green olives for garnish

Fat-skimming options: Use nonfat mayonnaise and reduced-fat cheese.
With options, exchange diets count: 2 1/2 starch, 1 vegetable, 5 lean meat.

• Spread one side of each bread slice with Russian dressing.
• On each of 4 of the bread slices, layer radishes, cheese, spinach, 1 bread slice, cucumber, tomato and turkey. Top with remaining bread slices.

• Cut sandwiches into quarters; insert toothpick into each quarter. Secure a radish slice and an olive on each toothpick for garnish.

Nutrition Analysis Per Serving: As Originally Published/With Fat-Skimming Options

Calories: 585/408	Saturated Fat: 11 g/1 g
Protein: 38 g/38 g	Cholesterol: 95 mg/55 mg
Carbohydrate: 42 g/45 g	Sodium: 1,061 mg/1,389 mg
Fat: 30 g/9 g	Dietary Fiber: 4 g/4 g

Ham and Cheese Caesar

Yield: 4 servings

1½ cups torn lettuce
6 ounces thin-sliced ham, cut in 1¼x¾ inch pieces
2 ounces shredded low-fat Mozzarella cheese
½ cup finely chopped onion
½ cup green pepper, cut in 1½x¼ inch matchsticks
¼ cup prepared Caesar salad dressing
4 (6 inch) whole-wheat pita breads, halved

Fat-skimming options: Substitute reduced-fat Caesar salad dressing or fat-free Italian dressing. With options, exchange diets count: 2 lean meat, 2 starch, 1 vegetable.

• In medium bowl, combine lettuce, ham, cheese, onion and green pepper strips. Toss with salad dressing. Cover and chill from 1 to 4 hours.

• At serving time, evenly divide mixture among pocket halves.

Nutrition Analysis Per Serving: As Originally Published/With Fat-Skimming Options

Calories: 367/305
Protein: 23 g/22 g
Carbohydrate: 39 g/38 g
Fat: 13 g/8 g

Saturated Fat: 2 g/1 g
Cholesterol: 24 mg/25 mg
Sodium: 1,369 mg/1,369 mg
Dietary Fiber: 2 g/2 g

Tuna Salad Subs

Yield: 4 sandwiches

1 (6½ ounce) can chunk-style tuna in oil or water, drained
¼ cup finely chopped celery
¼ cup finely chopped onion
½ cup mayonnaise
¼ cup sweet pickle relish
4 (6 inch) submarine rolls, cut almost in half lengthwise
4 ounce sliced Swiss cheese
8 pimiento-stuffed olives, cut in half lengthwise
Lettuce leaves

Fat-skimming options: Use water-packed tuna, nonfat mayonnaise and reduced-fat Swiss cheese. With options, exchange diets count: 2 starch, 2 vegetable, 3 lean meat.

• Break up tuna in bowl with a fork. Add celery, onion, mayonnaise and pickle relish to tuna. Mix well.
• Place ½ cup of tuna mixture on bottom half of each submarine roll.
• Top each with Swiss cheese slices and 4 olive halves.

• Place sandwiches in 12x8x2 inch glass baking dish. Cover with waxed paper.
• Microwave (high setting) 4½ minutes or until cheese melts. Or, to warm in conventional oven, cover with aluminum foil and bake at 300 degrees F for 15 minutes.
• Top with lettuce.

Nutrition Analysis Per Serving: As Originally Published/With Fat-Skimming Options

Calories: 592/364
Protein: 26 g/26 g
Carbohydrate: 38 g/44 g
Fat: 39 g/9 g

Saturated Fat: 10 g/4 g
Cholesterol: 44 mg/33 mg
Sodium: 978 mg/1,207 mg
Dietary Fiber: 2 g/2 g

CHAPTER TWELVE

VEGETABLES

When you'd planted, plucked and picked,
how could you turn it down?

With four freezers full of vegetables and meat, the Norman Huwe family never went hungry when the winter winds on the border of North Dakota and Minnesota began to howl. Cindy Huwe Appleton, now a family physician, remembers cutting out pictures of cows and tractors from Farm Journal when she wasn't milking cows or working in the garden.

She simply adores all vegetables for their taste and knows it is because as she planted, weeded and picked, she grew hungry for even parsnips and beets! Her parents never seemed to struggle introducing vegetables to the children, because everyone just took some. To this day, during family reunions back on the farm, the cooks will simply go to one of the freezers for the next meal.

As a physician concerned about lifelong eating habits, Cindy won't use the "clean your plate" line with her daughter Holly. Children must be trusted to eat when they are hungry and quit when they are full, as long as nutritious choices surround them. This final chapter dresses up all the garden bounty in fine style, providing recipes from asparagus to zucchini.

Citrus Asparagus

Yield: 6 servings

¼ cup butter or regular margarine
½ cup orange juice
1 teaspoon grated orange rind
¼ teaspoon salt
2 pounds asparagus, trimmed
1 tablespoon flour
2 tablespoons water

> *Fat-skimming options: Omit butter and use 1 tablespoon soft margarine.*
> *With options, exchange diets count: 1 vegetable, ½ fat.*

• In 12 inch skillet over medium heat, melt butter. Stir in orange juice, grated rind and salt until well blended; add asparagus.
• Cover and cook 8 to 10 minutes or until tender-crisp. With slotted spoon remove asparagus to serving platter.

• In small bowl stir flour and water until smooth. Stir into juice mixture. Cook, stirring constantly, until mixture boils and thickens.
• To serve, spoon sauce over asparagus.

Nutrition Analysis Per Serving: As Originally Published/With Fat-Skimming Options

Calories: 90/39
Protein: 2 g/2 g
Carbohydrate: 5 g/5 g
Fat: 8 g/2 g

Saturated Fat: 5 g/0 g
Cholesterol: 21 mg/0 mg
Sodium: 168 mg/107 mg
Dietary Fiber: 0 g/0 g

Herbed Asparagus

Yield: 8 servings

4 pounds fresh asparagus
3 teaspoons salt
$1/4$ cup butter
2 tablespoons lemon juice
$1/2$ teaspoon basil leaves

*Fat-skimming options: Replace butter with 1 tablespoon soft margarine.
With options, exchange diets count: 1 vegetable.*

• Scrub asparagus thoroughly to remove sand. Remove tough ends.
• Spread stalks in a Dutch oven or large skillet. Sprinkle with salt. Add 2 inches boiling water. Boil, uncovered, 5 minutes. Cover and cook 7 to 10 minutes longer, or until stalks are tender-crisp. Drain well.

• Melt butter. Stir in lemon juice and basil. Pour over asparagus.

Nutrition Analysis Per Serving: As Originally Published/With Fat-Skimming Options

Calories: 65/19
Protein: 2 g/2 g
Carbohydrate: 2 g/2 g
Fat: 6 g/1 g

Saturated Fat: 4 g/0 g
Cholesterol: 16 mg/0 mg
Sodium: 859 mg/706 mg
Dietary Fiber: 1 g/1 g

Basil Beans and Tomatoes

Yield: 4 servings

2 tablespoons cooking oil
1 pound fresh green beans, bias-cut into 1½ inch pieces
⅓ cup chopped onion
1 clove garlic, minced
½ cup water
1 teaspoon dried basil leaves
½ teaspoon salt
⅛ teaspoon pepper
2 tomatoes, chopped

Fat-skimming options: Reduce oil to 1 teaspoon. With options, exchange diets count: 2 vegetable.

• Heat oil in 12 inch skillet over high heat. Add green beans, onion and garlic. Stir-fry 4 minutes. Add water, basil, salt and pepper. Reduce heat to low. Cover and steam 20 minutes, or until tender-crisp.

• Stir in tomatoes. Cook over medium heat, stirring constantly, 2 minutes.

Nutrition Analysis Per Serving: As Originally Published/With Fat-Skimming Options

Calories: 101/49
Protein: 2 g/2 g
Fat: 7 g/1 g
Saturated Fat: 0 g/0 g

Cholesterol: 0 mg/0 mg
Sodium: 276 mg/276 mg
Dietary Fiber: 2 g/2 g

Cabbage Frances

Yield: 6 servings

3 tablespoons butter
³/₄ cup finely chopped onion
5 cups shredded cabbage
2 apples, pared and thinly sliced
¹/₄ cup water
3 tablespoons lemon juice
2 tablespoons packed brown sugar
¹/₂ teaspoon salt

> *Fat-skimming options: Substitute 1 teaspoon oil for butter.*
> *With options, exchange diets count: 1 vegetable, ¹/₂ fruit.*

• Melt butter in 12 inch skillet over medium heat. Add onion and sauté until tender.
• Add cabbage, apples and water. Reduce heat and cover. Simmer 20 minutes, stirring occasionally.

• Stir in lemon juice, brown sugar and salt. Simmer 10 minutes, or until cabbage is tender.

Nutrition Analysis Per Serving: As Originally Published/With Fat-Skimming Options

Calories: 117/73
Protein: 1 g/1 g
Carbohydrate: 16 g/16 g
Fat: 6 g/1 g

Saturated Fat: 4 g/0 g
Cholesterol: 16 mg/0 mg
Sodium: 249 mg/190 mg
Dietary Fiber: 2.75 g/2.75 g

Herbed Carrots

Yield: 4 to 6 servings

6 to 8 medium carrots, pared and cut into 3 inch sticks
$1/2$ cup mayonnaise
2 tablespoons horseradish
2 tablespoons grated onion
$1/2$ teaspoon salt
$1/4$ teaspoon pepper
$1/2$ cup fine bread or cracker crumbs
1 tablespoon melted butter
Dash paprika

Fat-skimming options: Use nonfat mayonnaise and substitute 1 teaspoon margarine for the butter. With options, exchange diets count: 1 starch, 1 vegetable.

• Cook carrots in a little water until tender. Reserve $1/4$ cup of the cooking liquid and discard the rest. Arrange carrots in a shallow baking dish.
• Mix together mayonnaise, horseradish, onion, salt, pepper and reserved cooking liquid. Pour over carrots.
• Mix together crumbs, melted butter and paprika; sprinkle over top.
• Bake in 375 degree F oven 15 to 20 minutes.

Nutrition Analysis Per Serving: As Originally Published/With Fat-Skimming Options

Calories: 229/100
Protein: 2 g/2 g
Carbohydrate: 17 g/21 g
Fat: 19 g/1 g

Saturated Fat: 4 g/0 g
Cholesterol: 12 mg/0 mg
Sodium: 406 mg/553 mg
Dietary Fiber: 3.5 g/3.5 g

Orange-Glazed Carrots
Yield: 6 servings

1½ pounds carrots, cut in strips
2 teaspoons flour
¼ cup brown sugar, firmly packed
½ teaspoon salt
1 tablespoon vinegar
1 tablespoon lemon juice
½ cup orange juice
1 tablespoon grated orange peel
2 tablespoons butter

Fat-skimming options: Omit butter. With options, exchange diets count: 1 fruit, 1 vegetable.

• Blanch carrots in boiling water 5 minutes. Drain.
• Blend together flour, sugar and salt. Add vinegar, juices and orange peel. Bring to a boil. Add butter; cook 5 minutes.
• To freeze: Pour sauce over carrots in 1 quart foil-lined pan; freeze. Remove from pan; wrap, label, date and store in freezer. Recommended storage time: 6 weeks.

• To serve: Turn carrots upside down in same pan. Cover. Bake at 350 degrees F about 1 hour, until tender. Uncover for last 20 minutes.

Nutrition Analysis Per Serving: As Originally Published/With Fat-Skimming Options

Calories: 122/88
Protein: 1 g/1 g
Carbohydrate: 22 g/22 g
Fat: 4 g/0 g

Saturated Fat: 2 g/0 g
Cholesterol: 10 mg/0 mg
Sodium: 272 mg/233 mg
Dietary Fiber: 0 g/0 g

Cauliflower With Shrimp Sauce

Yield: 4 to 6 servings

1 head cauliflower
1 can condensed cream of shrimp soup
$^1/_2$ cup dairy sour cream
$^1/_2$ teaspoon salt
$^1/_8$ teaspoon pepper
$^1/_4$ cup slivered, toasted almonds

Fat-skimming options: Substitute nonfat sour cream. Reduce almonds to 1 tablespoon garnish. With options, exchange diets count: 2 vegetable, 1 fat.

• Separate cauliflower into flowerets. Cook in boiling salted water until tender; drain.
• Meanwhile, blend together soup, sour cream, salt and pepper in saucepan. Heat, but do not boil.

• Place cauliflower in serving bowl. Top with shrimp sauce, then toasted almonds.

Nutrition Analysis Per Serving: As Originally Published/With Fat-Skimming Options

Calories: 152/90
Protein: 4 g/4 g
Carbohydrate: 10 g/11 g
Fat: 11 g/4 g

Saturated Fat: 4 g/1 g
Cholesterol: 17 mg/3 mg
Sodium: 534 mg/553 mg
Dietary Fiber: 2 g/2 g

Boston Baked Corn

Yield: 6 to 8 servings

8 ears fresh-picked corn
1/3 cup ketchup
3 tablespoons finely chopped onion
2 tablespoons packed brown sugar
1/4 teaspoon dry mustard
2 slices uncooked bacon, diced

Fat-skimming options: none. Exchange diets count: 1½ starch.

• With sharp knife, cut corn kernels from cobs at two-thirds of kernel depth; then scrape cobs with dull side of knife to remove remaining pulp. Measure 4 cups corn with pulp.
• In 2-quart saucepan over high heat, bring 1 inch water to a boil. Add corn; return to a boil. Reduce heat to medium-low. Cover and cook 5 minutes, or until corn is tender-crisp. Remove from heat; drain well.

• Stir ketchup, onion, brown sugar and dry mustard into corn in saucepan. Pour into greased 1½-quart casserole. Sprinkle with diced uncooked bacon.
• Bake in 350 degree F oven 40 minutes, or until casserole is bubbly around edge and bacon is cooked.

Nutrition Analysis Per Serving: As Originally Published	
Calories: 121	Saturated Fat: 0 g
Protein: 3 g	Cholesterol: 1 mg
Carbohydrate: 27 g	Sodium: 154 mg
Fat: 2 g	Dietary Fiber: 3 g

Corn Casserole

Yield: 12 servings

About 8 ears fresh-picked corn
2 tablespoons regular margarine or butter
1 medium green pepper, seeded and chopped
2 cups cooked rice
2 cups shredded Cheddar cheese
1/2 cup milk
1 (4 ounce) jar sliced pimientos, drained
1/2 teaspoon salt
1/8 teaspoon pepper

Fat-skimming options: Reduce margarine to 1 teaspoon. Use reduced-fat Cheddar cheese. With options, exchange diets count: 1 starch, 1 skim milk, 1 fat.

• With sharp knife, cut corn kernels from cobs at two-thirds of their depth, then scrape cobs with dull side of knife to remove remaining pulp. Measure 4 cups corn with pulp; set aside.
• In 10 inch skillet over medium-high heat, melt margarine. Add green pepper; cook 2 minutes. Stir in corn. Cover and cook, stirring occasionally, 5 minutes, or until corn is tender-crisp. Pour into large bowl.

• Gently stir in remaining ingredients. Spread in greased 12x8x2 inch baking dish.
• Bake in 325 degree F oven 35 minutes, or until casserole is bubbly around edges and hot in center.

Nutrition Analysis Per Serving: As Originally Published/With Fat-Skimming Options

Calories: 276/217
Protein: 13 g/15 g
Carbohydrate: 24 g/25 g
Fat: 15 g/8 g

Saturated Fat: 9 g/4 g
Cholesterol: 41 mg/27 mg
Sodium: 359 mg/403 mg
Dietary Fiber: 2 g/2 g

Colorful Vegetables

Yield: 6 (¹/₂ cup) servings

2 tablespoons margarine or butter
2 medium zucchini, sliced
2 cups sliced mushrooms
¹/₂ green bell pepper, cut into 2x¹/₄-inch strips
1 teaspoon cumin seeds or ¹/₂ teaspoon ground cumin
¹/₂ teaspoon salt
¹/₄ teaspoon coarse-grind black pepper
1 cup finely chopped tomato
¹/₄ cup chopped green onion

Fat-skimming options: Reduce margarine to 1 tablespoon.
With options, exchange diets count: 1 vegetable.

• On grill, over medium coals, melt margarine in large heavy frying pan with heatproof handle. Add zucchini, mushrooms, green bell pepper, cumin seeds, salt and black pepper.

• Cook and stir 4 to 5 minutes or until vegetables are crisp-tender. Add tomato and green onion; continue to cook and stir 1 minute.

Nutrition Analysis Per Serving: As Originally Published/With Fat-Skimming Options

Calories: 54/38
Protein: 1 g/1 g
Carbohydrate: 4 g/4 g
Fat: 4 g/2 g

Saturated Fat: 0 g/0 g
Cholesterol: 0 mg/0 mg
Sodium: 217 mg/199 mg
Dietary Fiber: 1 g/1 g

Butter-Glazed Root Vegetables

Yield: 6 to 8 servings

1 pound turnips, pared
1 pound carrots, pared
1/2 pound parsnips, pared
3 tablespoons butter or margarine
1 tablespoon grated fresh ginger or 1 1/2 teaspoons ground ginger
1 tablespoon sugar
1/2 teaspoon salt
1/2 cup chicken broth

> *Fat-skimming options: Omit butter and use 1 teaspoon soft margarine.*
> *With options, exchange diets count: 2 vegetable.*

• Cut small turnips (2 inches diameter) in half; larger turnips in quarters or eighths.
• Diagonally slice carrots and parsnips 1/2 inch thick. Also cut large slices in half lengthwise.

• In 12 inch skillet over medium-high heat, melt butter. Stir in ginger, sugar, salt, broth and turnips; bring to a boil. Reduce heat to medium; cover and cook 5 minutes.
• Stir in carrots and parsnips; cover. Simmer 12 minutes, or until vegetables are tender and liquid is reduced to a thin sauce. Stir to coat before serving.

Nutrition Analysis Per Serving: As Originally Published/With Fat-Skimming Options

Calories: 90/56	Saturated Fat: 3 g/0 g
Protein: 1 g/1 g	Cholesterol: 12 mg/0 mg
Carbohydrate: 12 g/12 g	Sodium: 317 mg/277 mg
Fat: 5 g/0 g	Dietary Fiber: 1 g/1 g

Farm Garden Eggplant

Yield: 4 servings

1 medium eggplant (about 1½ pounds), pared and cut into ½ inch cubes
2 tomatoes, diced
¼ cup flour
12 strips bacon, diced
¾ cup coarsely chopped onion
¼ cup water
1 teaspoon salt
⅛ teaspoon pepper

Fat-skimming options: Reduce bacon to 4 strips. With options, exchange diets count: 1 starch, ½ fat.

• Shake eggplant and tomato with flour in plastic bag; set aside.
• Fry bacon in 4-quart Dutch oven over medium heat until crisp. Remove bacon and drain on paper towels. Pour off all but ¼ cup bacon drippings.

• Add onion to bacon drippings and sauté 10 minutes, or until tender. Stir in eggplant, tomatoes, bacon, water, salt and pepper. Cover and cook over medium heat 35 minutes, or until eggplant is tender, stirring occasionally.

Nutrition Analysis Per Serving: As Originally Published/With Fat-Skimming Options

Calories: 182/109
Protein: 8 g/4 g
Carbohydrate: 16 g/16 g
Fat: 10 g/3 g

Saturated Fat: 3 g/1 g
Cholesterol: 16 mg/5 mg
Sodium: 845 mg/642 mg
Dietary Fiber: 1.5 g/1.5 g

Oriental Stir-Fried Vegetables

Yield: 6 servings

1½ pounds fresh broccoli
4 tablespoons cooking oil
½ teaspoon salt
1 clove garlic, minced
1 cup chicken broth, divided
1 (16 ounce) can bean sprouts, drained
1 (8 ounce) can water chestnuts, drained and sliced
¼ pound fresh mushrooms, sliced
1 (6 ounce) package frozen pea pods, thawed
2 teaspoons cornstarch
1 teaspoon sugar
⅛ teaspoon ground ginger
1 tablespoon soy sauce
1 tablespoon toasted sesame seeds

Fat-skimming options: Reduce oil to 1 tablespoon.
With options, exchange diets count: 11 vegetable, 1 fat.

• Remove flowerets from broccoli and cut in half. Cut stalks into 2x¼-inch strips. Heat cooking oil in 12 inch skillet or electric frypan over medium heat (325 degrees F) for 5 minutes.
• Add broccoli and stir-fry 1 minute. Add salt, garlic and ½ cup of the chicken broth. Cover and cook 3 minutes.

• Uncover; stir-fry 3 minutes. Add bean sprouts, water chestnuts, mushrooms and pea pods; stir-fry 2 minutes.
• Combine cornstarch, sugar, ginger, soy sauce and remaining ½ cup chicken broth; stir to blend. Stir cornstarch mixture into skillet. Cook until it boils, stirring constantly, about 1 minute. Boil 1 minute more. Sprinkle with sesame seeds.

Nutrition Analysis Per Serving: As Originally Published/With Fat-Skimming Options

Calories: 380/313
Protein: 18 g/18 g
Carbohydrate: 53 g/53 g
Fat: 12 g/5 g

Saturated Fat: 1 g/0 g
Cholesterol: 0 mg/0 mg
Sodium: 589 mg/589 mg
Dietary Fiber: 0 g/0 g

Baked Onions

Yield: 8 servings

8 medium white onions
Salt
½ cup dark corn syrup
¼ cup melted butter
2 teaspoons lemon juice

Fat-skimming options: Omit butter and substitute 2 tablespoons melted soft margarine. With options, exchange diets count: 1 fruit, 1 vegetable, ½ fat.

• Peel onions. Place in buttered 11x7x1½-inch baking dish. Sprinkle with salt. Combine corn syrup, butter and lemon juice in small saucepan. Heat to boiling. Baste onions with syrup mixture.

• Bake in 325 degree F oven 1½ hours, basting often with syrup mixture, until onions are tender.

Nutrition Analysis Per Serving: As Originally Published/With Fat-Skimming Options

Calories: 137/111
Protein: 1 g/1 g
Carbohydrate: 22 g/22 g
Fat: 6 g/3 g

Saturated Fat: 3 g/0 g
Cholesterol: 16 mg/0 mg
Sodium: 225 mg/193 mg
Dietary Fiber: 1 g/1 g

Cheesed Mashed Potatoes

Yield: 8 servings

4 cups hot, seasoned mashed potatoes or prepared instant mashed potatoes
1 cup dairy sour cream
$1/3$ cup chopped green onions
4 ounces sharp Cheddar cheese, cut in $1/4$ inch cubes

Fat-skimming options: Substitute nonfat sour cream and reduced-fat Cheddar cheese.
With options, exchange diets count: $1^{1}/_{2}$ starch, $1/2$ skim milk.

• Combine potatoes, sour cream, green onions and cheese in bowl; mix well. Turn into greased $1^{1}/_{2}$-quart casserole.

• Bake in 350 degree F oven 25 minutes or until heated.

Nutrition Analysis Per Serving: As Originally Published/With Fat-Skimming Options

Calories: 190/151
Protein: 6 g/9 g
Carbohydrate: 20 g/25 g
Fat: 10 g/3 g

Saturated Fat: 6 g/2 g
Cholesterol: 27 mg/12 mg
Sodium: 418 mg/468 mg
Dietary Fiber: 0 g/0 g

Extra-Special Mashed Potatoes

Yield: 6 servings

2 pounds Idaho potatoes (4 large), pared and cut up
1 teaspoon salt
$^1/_2$ teaspoon minced fresh garlic
1 tablespoon butter
$^3/_4$ cup milk
$^1/_3$ cup butter
$^1/_{16}$ teaspoon paprika
$^1/_8$ teaspoon celery seed

Fat-skimming options: Omit butter and replace with equal amount of skim milk.
For exchange diets, count: $1^1/_2$ starch.

• Place potatoes and salt in 1 inch water in 2-quart saucepan. Cover; simmer 20 minutes or until tender. Drain. Shake pan over low heat until all the water is absorbed.

• Meanwhile, sauté garlic in 1 tablespoon melted butter 1 minute. Heat milk and $^1/_3$ cup butter until butter melts.
• Mash potatoes with vegetable masher. Gradually add milk mixture; mix until smooth and fluffy. Stir in sautéed garlic, paprika and celery seed.

Nutrition Analysis Per Serving: As Originally Published/With Fat-Skimming Options

Calories: 194/105
Protein: 3 g/3 g
Carbohydrate: 19 g/19 g
Fat: 12 g/2 g

Saturated Fat: 8 g/1 g
Cholesterol: 33 mg/6 mg
Sodium: 492 mg/395 mg
Dietary Fiber: 1 g/1 g

Golden Parmesan Potatoes

Yield: 6 to 8 servings

6 large potatoes (about 3 pounds)
¼ cup sifted flour
¼ cup grated Parmesan cheese
¾ teaspoon salt
⅛ teaspoon pepper
⅓ cup butter
Chopped parsley

*Fat-skimming options: Replace butter with 2 tablespoons soft margarine.
With options, exchange diets count: 2 starch.*

• Pare potatoes; cut into quarters. Combine flour, cheese, salt and pepper in a bag. Moisten potatoes with water and shake a few at a time in bag, coating potatoes well with cheese mixture.

• Melt butter in a 13x9 inch baking pan. Place potatoes in a layer in pan. Bake at 375 degrees F for about 1 hour, turning once during baking. When golden brown, sprinkle with parsley.

Nutrition Analysis Per Serving: As Originally Published/With Fat-Skimming Options

Calories: 211/160
Protein: 4 g/4 g
Carbohydrate: 28 g/28 g
Fat: 10 g/4 g

Saturated Fat: 6 g/2 g
Cholesterol: 25 mg/10 mg
Sodium: 340 mg/282 mg
Dietary Fiber: 2 g/2 g

Golden Twice-Baked Potatoes

Yield: 8 servings

4 Idaho potatoes, about 4 inches long (approximately 2½ pounds)
¼ cup butter
½ teaspoon salt
¼ teaspoon garlic powder
Milk
1 (3 ounce) package cream cheese, cut in small cubes
2 tablespoons minced onion
2 tablespoons minced fresh parsley
1 cup shredded Cheddar cheese
Paprika

> *Fat-skimming options: Omit Butter. Substitute light (50% reduced fat) cream cheese and reduced-fat Cheddar cheese. With options, exchange diets count: 1 skim milk, 1 starch, 1 fat.*

- Bake potatoes at 400 degrees F for 1 hour or until done.
- Cut potatoes in half lengthwise. Scoop out potatoes with a spoon. Combine potatoes, butter, salt and garlic powder. Mash with potato masher, adding enough milk to make them fluffy. Fold in cream cheese, onion and parsley.

- Spoon potato mixture lightly into potato shells. Place on baking sheet. Sprinkle on Cheddar cheese. Dust with paprika. Cover with plastic wrap. Refrigerate overnight.
- To serve, heat potatoes at 450 degrees F for 25 minutes or until cheese melts.

Nutrition Analysis Per Serving: As Originally Published/With Fat-Skimming Options

Calories: 316/216	Saturated Fat: 12 g/4 g
Protein: 11 g/12 g	Cholesterol: 58 mg/19 mg
Carbohydrate: 26 g/28 g	Sodium: 411 mg/275 mg
Fat: 19 g/7 g	Dietary Fiber: 0 g/0 g

Gourmet Cheese Potatoes

Yield: 6 to 8 servings

6 medium all-purpose potatoes
2 cups shredded Muenster cheese
$1/4$ cup butter
1 cup dairy sour cream
$1/3$ cup finely chopped onion
1 teaspoon salt
$1/4$ teaspoon pepper
Paprika

*Fat-skimming options: Use reduced-fat cheese, omit butter, and use nonfat sour cream.
Instead of heating cheese, fold directly into potatoes.
With options, exchange diets count: 1 starch, 1 skim milk, 1 lean meat.*

• Cook potatoes in 1 inch of boiling water in 3 quart saucepan until tender. Drain. Peel and shred into bowl.
• Combine cheese and butter in 2-quart saucepan over low heat. Stir until almost melted. Remove from heat. Stir in sour cream, onion, salt and pepper. Fold into potatoes.

• Pour into greased 8 inch square baking dish. Sprinkle with paprika.
• Bake at 350 degrees F 30 minutes.

Nutrition Analysis Per Serving: As Originally Published/With Fat-Skimming Options

Calories: 403/222
Protein: 16 g/18 g
Carbohydrate: 23 g/29 g
Fat: 28 g/4 g

Saturated Fat: 18 g/0 g
Cholesterol: 80 mg/0 mg
Sodium: 698 mg/991 mg
Dietary Fiber: 0 g/0 g

Potato Puffs

Yield: 24 puffs

4 pounds boiling potatoes
1 cup milk (amount varies with moisture in potatoes)
¼ cup butter
1½ teaspoons salt
½ cup grated Cheddar cheese
¾ cup cornflake crumbs
3 tablespoons toasted sesame seeds

Fat-skimming options: Use skim milk. Substitute nonfat sour cream for butter. Select reduced-fat Cheddar cheese. With options, exchange diets count: 1 starch.

• Peel potatoes. Boil until soft; drain. Press potatoes through a ricer or mash.
•Heat milk, butter and salt together. Gradually whip into potatoes until the potatoes are smooth and fluffy.
• Mix in cheese. Chill. Form into balls; roll in a mixture of cornflake crumbs and sesame seeds. Freeze on tray until firm. Package, label and return to freezer.

• To serve: Place frozen puffs on baking sheet. Brush lightly with melted butter, if desired. Bake in hot oven (400 degrees F) 30 minutes.
• To serve without freezing: Omit optional brushing with butter and bake puffs only until they brown, 5 to 10 minutes.

Nutrition Analysis Per Serving: As Originally Published/With Fat-Skimming Options

Calories: 109/87	Saturated Fat: 2 g/0 g
Protein: 3 g/3 g	Cholesterol: 11 mg/3 mg
Carbohydrate: 15 g/16 g	Sodium: 199 mg/166 mg
Fat: 4 g/1 g	Dietary Fiber: 1 g/1 g

Holiday Potato Dish
Yield: 12 servings

4 pounds unpared potatoes, cooked and drained
1 cup chopped onion
¼ cup butter
1 (10¾ ounce) can condensed cream of celery soup
1 pint dairy sour cream
1½ cups shredded Cheddar cheese
½ cup crushed cornflakes
3 tablespoons melted butter
Pimiento strips
Chopped fresh parsley

Fat-skimming options: Omit all butter. Sauté onions with fat free nonstick cooking spray. Choose reduced-fat cream of celery soup, nonfat sour cream and reduced-fat Cheddar cheese.
With options, exchange diets count: 1½ starch, 1 skim milk, ½ fat.

• Remove skins from potatoes; shred into bowl. Sauté onion in ¼ cup melted butter until tender. Remove from heat. Stir in soup and sour cream. Pour over potatoes and cheese; mix well. Turn into greased 13x9x2 inch baking dish. Cover, and refrigerate overnight.

• Sprinkle with cornflakes; drizzle with 3 tablespoons butter. Bake in 350 degree F oven 1 hour. Garnish with pimiento and parsley, if desired.

Nutrition Analysis Per Serving: As Originally Published/With Fat-Skimming Options

Calories: 354/237
Protein: 11 g/14 g
Carbohydrate: 28 g/35 g
Fat: 22 g/5 g

Saturated Fat: 14 g/3 g
Cholesterol: 60 mg/20 mg
Sodium: 421 mg/394 mg
Dietary Fiber: 0 g/0 g

Butternut Squash With Peas
Yield: 12 servings

3 (1½ pound) butternut squash
1 teaspoon salt
2 (10 ounce) packages frozen peas
6 tablespoons butter or regular margarine

Fat-skimming options: Reduce margarine to 1 tablespoon.
With options, exchange diets count: 1 starch, 1 vegetable.

• Pare the squash. Cut in half and remove seeds. Cut in 1-inch chunks. In Dutch oven put salt in 1 inch of water and bring to a boil. Add squash and cook, covered, 10 minutes.

• Add peas. Cook, covered, 5 to 7 minutes more or until vegetables are tender. Drain well. Add butter.

Nutrition Analysis Per Serving: As Originally Published/With Fat-Skimming Options

Calories: 139/96
Protein: 3 g/3 g
Carbohydrate: 21 g/21 g
Fat: 6 g/1 g

Saturated Fat: 4 g/0 g
Cholesterol: 16 mg/0 mg
Sodium: 271 mg/222 mg
Dietary Fiber: 0 g/0 g

Yellow Squash Casserole
Yield: 8 servings

5 cups sliced yellow squash (2 to 3 squash)
1/2 cup chopped onions
1/2 cup chopped green bell pepper
1/2 cup chopped red bell pepper
2 tablespoons butter or margarine
3/4 cup mayonnaise
1/2 cup grated medium Cheddar cheese
1 egg, beaten
1 tablespoon sugar
3/4 teaspoon garlic powder
1/2 teaspoon salt
1/4 teaspoon ground red pepper
1 1/2 teaspoons Worcestershire sauce
1/2 cup crushed cracker crumbs

Fat-skimming options: Use nonfat mayonnaise. Use reduced-fat Cheddar cheese.
With options, exchange diets count: 2 vegetable, 1/2 skim milk, 1 fat.

• In large saucepan, cook squash, onion, green and red bell peppers in melted butter over medium heat 7 to 9 minutes or until vegetables are slightly softened.
• Thoroughly mix mayonnaise, cheese, egg, sugar and seasonings into vegetables.
• Spoon into 2 1/2-quart baking dish, sprayed with nonstick coating. Sprinkle with cracker crumbs.
• Bake at 350 degrees F for about 30 minutes or until bubbly and browned.

Nutrition Analysis Per Serving: As Originally Published/With Fat-Skimming Options

Calories: 289/140
Protein: 6 g/7 g
Carbohydrate: 9 g/14 g
Fat: 27 g/7 g

Saturated Fat: 8 g/4 g
Cholesterol: 57 mg/44 mg
Sodium: 405 mg/607 mg
Dietary Fiber: 1 g/1 g

New England-Style Sweet Potatoes
Yield: 6 servings

6 sweet potatoes or yams (about 2½ pounds), peeled and cut lengthwise in quarters
1 cup maple-flavored syrup
3 tablespoons butter
1½ teaspoons salt

Fat-skimming options: Substitute reduced-fat margarine for butter.
With options, exchange diets count: 2 starch, 2 fruit.

• **Range Top: 25 minutes cooking time**
Place sweet potatoes in 10 inch skillet. Combine remaining ingredients; pour over potatoes. Bring to boiling; reduce heat. Cover and simmer 25 minutes or until potatoes are tender. Turn potatoes twice during cooking to glaze evenly.

• **Electric Frypan: 25 minutes cooking time**
Place sweet potatoes in electric frypan. Combine remaining ingredients; pour over potatoes. Cover and cook at 225 degrees F with vent closed, 25 minutes or until potatoes are tender. Turn potatoes twice during cooking to glaze evenly.

• **Microwave: 15-17 minutes cooking time**
Place potatoes in 12x8x2 inch baking dish (2 quart). Combine remaining ingredients. Pour over potatoes. Cover with plastic wrap and microwave on high 15 to 17 minutes, or until potatoes are tender, stirring twice.

• **Pressure Cooker: 9 minutes cooking time**
Place sweet potatoes in 4-quart pressure cooker. Combine remaining ingredients; pour over potatoes. Close cover securely. Place over high heat. Bring to 15 pounds pressure, according to manufacturer's directions for your pressure cooker. When pressure is reached (control will begin to jiggle), reduce heat immediately and cook 6 minutes. Remove from heat. Reduce pressure instantly by placing cooker under cold running water. Follow manufacturer's instructions for opening cooker. Remove sweet potatoes to serving dish; keep warm. Cook liquid in uncovered pressure cooker on high heat about 3 minutes to reduce by one half. Pour over potatoes.

Nutrition Analysis Per Serving: As Originally Published/With Fat-Skimming Options

Calories: 296/275
Protein: 2 g/2 g
Carbohydrate: 67 g/67 g
Fat: 3 g/1 g

Saturated Fat: 2 g/1 g
Cholesterol: 8 mg/0 mg
Sodium: 578 mg/613 mg
Dietary Fiber: 0 g/0 g

Broiled Tomatoes Parmesan
Yield: 4 servings

4 medium tomatoes
½ cup mayonnaise or salad dressing
3 tablespoons grated Parmesan cheese
½ teaspoon prepared mustard
¼ teaspoon Worcestershire sauce
Paprika

Fat-skimming options: Use nonfat mayonnaise. With options, exchange diets count: 3 vegetable.

• Cut tomatoes in half crosswise. Arrange, cut sides up, on broiler pan. Place tomatoes 6 inches from source of heat, and broil 5 minutes.

• Meanwhile, combine mayonnaise, cheese, mustard and Worcestershire sauce in bowl; mix well.
• Spread some of mayonnaise mixture on each tomato half and sprinkle with paprika. Broil 1 minute, or until golden.

Nutrition Analysis Per Serving: As Originally Published/With Fat-Skimming Options

Calories: 244/68
Protein: 3 g/2 g
Carbohydrate: 6 g/12 g
Fat: 26 g/1 g

Saturated Fat: 5 g/0 g
Cholesterol: 13 mg/3 mg
Sodium: 232 mg/471 mg
Dietary Fiber: 1.5 g/1.5 g

Candied Yams With Pecans
Yield: 12 servings

5 pounds yams or sweet potatoes
1 teaspoon salt
1 lemon, cut in half slices
Whole cloves
2 cups firmly packed brown sugar
1 cup dark corn syrup
$1/2$ cup hot water
2 teaspoons grated orange rind
$1/4$ teaspoon ground cinnamon
1 cup coarsely chopped pecans
2 tablespoons butter

> *Fat-skimming options: Reduce pecans to $1/4$ cup. Omit butter. Increase servings to 24.*
> *With options, exchange diets count: $1^1/2$ starch, 1 fruit.*

• Place yams and salt in Dutch oven with water to cover. Bring to a boil. Reduce heat; cover and simmer 30 minutes or until yams are tender. Drain and cool.
• Remove peels. Cut in $1/4$ inch slices. Place yam slices in 4 rows in greased 13x9x2 inch baking dish. Stud lemon slices with cloves. Place 2 or 3 in each row.

• Combine brown sugar, corn syrup, water, orange rind and cinnamon in saucepan. Cook over medium heat until sugar is dissolved, stirring occasionally. Cool slightly.
• Sprinkle pecans over yams. Then pour syrup over all. Dot with butter. Cover with foil; refrigerate several hours or overnight.
• Remove foil. Bake in 400 degree F oven for 30 minutes or until bubbly.

Nutrition Analysis Per Serving: As Originally Published/With Fat-Skimming Options

Calories: 490/190
Protein: 3 g/1 g
Carbohydrate: 92 g/45 g
Fat: 15 g/1 g

Saturated Fat: 2 g/0 g
Cholesterol: 5 mg/0 mg
Sodium: 263 mg/0 mg
Dietary Fiber: 2 g/1 g

Zucchini Skillet Medley

Yield: 6 servings

¼ cup cooking oil
¾ cup sliced celery
½ cup sliced onion
1 clove garlic, minced
1 pound unpared zucchini, sliced ¼ inch thick (about 4 cups)
2 tomatoes, cut into eighths
½ cup green pepper strips
½ cup shredded, pared carrot
1 (8 ounce) can tomato sauce
2 teaspoons prepared yellow mustard
¼ teaspoon dried basil leaves
¾ teaspoon salt
⅛ teaspoon pepper

Fat-skimming options: Reduce oil to 1 tablespoon.
With options, exchange diets count: 2 vegetable, ½ fat.

• Heat oil in 12 inch skillet over medium heat. Add celery, onion and garlic; sauté until tender.
• Add zucchini, tomatoes, green pepper and carrot. Sauté 10 minutes.

• Stir in remaining ingredients. Reduce heat and simmer 5 minutes, or until vegetables are tender, stirring occasionally. Serve hot or cold.

Nutrition Analysis Per Serving: As Originally Published/With Fat-Skimming Options

Calories: 128/66
Protein: 2 g/2 g
Carbohydrate: 10 g/10 g
Fat: 10 g/3 g

Saturated Fat: 0 g/0 g
Cholesterol: 0 mg/0 mg
Sodium: 547 mg/547 mg
Dietary Fiber: 2 g/2 g

INDEX

A

All-Purpose Baking Mix, 44
Almond Pastry for Pie, 99
Amish Oatmeal Cookies, 74
Appetizers and Snacks, 2 - 13,
apple
    Baked Apples in Caramel Cream, 85
    Sausage-Apple-Sauerkraut
      Supper, 193
    Snowy Glazed Apple Squares, 86
Apple Bread Pudding, 84
Apple Crisp
    Orange-Coconut Apple Crisp, 83
apple juice
    Cranberry-Apple Cooler, 17
Apple Pancakes, 37
Apple Pie, 97
    French Apple Pie, 98
Apple-Raisin Dressing, 136
Applesauce Cake, 65
apricot
    Grandmom's Apricot Squares, 87
Apricot Glaze, 140
artichokes
    Chicken With Artichokes, 145
asparagus
    Citrus Asparagus, 260
    Herbed Asparagus, 261
Asparagus Roll-ups, 2

B

BLT Salad, 228
Bacon
    BLT Salad, 228
    Crustless Bacon Quiche, 108
    Curried Creamed Eggs, 110
    Farm Garden Eggplant, 271
    Hot Spinach-Bacon Dip, 6
Bacon-Wrapped Beef Patties, 170
Baked Apples in Caramel Cream, 85
Baked Onions, 273
Baked Stuffed Fish, 120

banana
    Tropical Fruit Shake, 22
Banana Nut Muffins, 30
Banana Walnut Bread, 27
Banana-Lemon Loaf, 26
barbecue
    Easy Barbecued Fish, 123
    Golden Glazed Oven Chicken
      Barbecue, 148
Barbecue Sauce, 186
Barbecued Beef Buns, 171
Barbecued Country-Style Ribs and
    Kraut, 186
barley
    Beefy Barley Soup, 232
Barley Pilaf, 138
Basil Beans and Tomatoes, 262
bean soup
    Pasta and Bean Soup, 245
beans
    Dilled Beans and Carrots, 213
    Kidney Bean Salad, 218
    Pressure-Cooker Baked Beans, 117
    Sweet and Sour Baked Beans, 118
Beef, 170 - 185
Beefy Barley Soup, 232
beef bottom round
    Stefado, 235
berry
    Breakfast Berry Pizza, 78
Beverages, 14 - 24
blue cheese
    Catalina Tossed Salad, 212
    Easy Blue Cheese Dressing, 215
Blue Cheese Stuffed Tomatoes, 115
Boston Baked Corn, 267
bran
    Date Nut Bran Muffins, 33
    Refrigerated Bran Muffins, 31
Bratwurst and Onions, 187
Bread Machine Kulich, 47
Bread Pudding, 84
Breads, 26 - 55
Breakfast Berry Pizza, 78
broccoli
    Ham and Broccoli Loaves, 5

Lemon Cod and Rice, 124
Swiss Chicken Pie, 152
Broccoli and Cheese Strata, 106
Broiled Fish with Magic Potion, 121
Broiled Tomatoes Parmesan, 284
Browned Butter Icing, 52
brownie
    Light Chocolate Brownie
        Cupcakes, 66
Buelah's Ham, 195
buns
    Golden Pecan Cinnamon Buns, 52
    Hot Cross Buns, 53
Butter-Glazed Root Vegetables, 270
Butternut Squash With Peas, 281

C

cabbage
    Cabbage-Orange Slaw, 210
    Freezer Coleslaw, 211
    Pork Chop Skillet Dinner, 190
    Refrigerator Vegetable Salad, 223
    Simmered Lamb with Cabbage, 199
    Sweet Corn Relish, 167
Cabbage Frances, 263
Caesar salad dressing
    Ham and Cheese Caesar, 256
Cakes, 58 - 65
Candied Yams with Pecans, 285
caramel
    Double Chocolate Caramel Bars, 70
Carrot Cake, 58
Carrot Cookies, 72
Carrot Quiche, 107
carrots
    Butter-Glazed Root Vegetables, 270
    Dilled Beans and Carrots, 213
    Herbed Carrots, 264
    Orange-Glazed Carrots, 265
    Potpourri Relish, 166
casserole
    Reuben Casserole, 180
    Savory Beef Casserole, 181
Catalina Tossed Salad, 212

cauliflower
    Potpourri Relish, 166
    Swiss Chicken Pie, 152
Cauliflower With Shrimp Sauce, 266
cheese
    Broccoli and Cheese Strata, 106
    Double Cheese Fondue, 4
    Gourmet Cheese Potatoes, 278
    Ham and Cheese Caesar, 256
    Herb Cheese Stuffed Cherry
        Tomatoes, 116
    Savory Potted Cheese, 10
    Spinach-Cheese Loaves, 11
    Three Times Three Rotini and
        Cheese, 133
cheesecake
    Deluxe Cheesecake, 80
Cheesed Mashed Potatoes, 274
Cheesy Chicken Pie, 141
cherry
    Door County Cherry Pie, 100
Cherry Jam, 160
Chicken, 141 - 154
    "Pop Eye" Pot Pie, 149
    Broccoli and Cheese Strata, 106
    Crisp Oven-Fried Chicken, 147
    Mulligatawny Soup, 238
    Parsleyed Chicken Chowder, 237
    Swiss Chicken Pie, 152
    Warm Chicken Salad, 230
Chicken and Double-Corn
    Dumplings, 146
Chicken in Honey Sauce, 144
Chicken Rice Skillet, 143
Chicken Salsa Dip, 3
Chicken Vegetable Soup, 236
Chicken Waldorf Pockets, 253
Chicken with Artichokes, 145
Chinese Chicken With Vegetables, 142
chocolate
    Double Chocolate Caramel Bars, 70
    Minty Fudge Sauce, 81
Chocolate Chip Cookies, 68
Chocolate Icing, 67
Chocolate-Covered Turtle Cookies, 67
Cinnamon Filling, 52

Citrus Asparagus, 260
Citrus Slush, 16
clam
    Linguine with White Clam
        Sauce, 129
    Quick Clam Soup, 243
Classic Chocolate Chip Cookies, 68
coconut
    Just-N-Trails Coconut-Topped
        Chocolate Orange Muffins, 35
    Orange-Coconut Apple Crisp, 83
Coconut Topping, 61
Coconut-Date Mounds, 69
cod, 124
Coffeecake, 42 - 45
coleslaw
    Freezer Coleslaw, 211
Colorful Vegetables, 269
Cookies and Bars, 67 - 77
corn
    Boston Baked Corn, 267
    Marinated Corn Salad, 219
    Sweet Corn Relish, 167
Corn Casserole, 268
corned beef
    Reuben Casserole, 179
    Reuben Loaves, 6
cottage cheese
    Double Dairy Salad, 214
    Golden Delight Pancakes, 40
    Orange County Rice Pudding, 82
Country Crusted Ham, 196
Country Pancakes, 38
Cow Pumpkin, 57
Cranberry Honey, 161
Cranberry Muffins, 32
Cranberry-Apple Cooler, 17
Cranberry-Raspberry Pie, 99
Cream Cheese Frosting, 58
Cream of Potato Soup, 249
cream puffs
    Lemon Cream Puffs, 91
Creamy Garlic Dressing, 228
Creamy Orange Charlotte, 88
Creamy Vegetable Soup, 250
Crisp Oven-Fried Chicken, 147

Crunchy Ice Cream Squares, 79
Crustless Bacon Quiche, 108
Crusty Brown Rolls, 48
Cucumber Refrigerator Pickles, 163
cupcakes
    Light Chocolate Brownie
        Cupcakes, 66
Curried Creamed Eggs, 110
Curried Smoked Turkey in a
    Pocket, 254
Curried Squash Bisque, 252

D

dates
    Coconut-Date Mounds, 69
    Orange Walnut Bread, 28
Date Nut Bran Muffins, 33
Deluxe Cheesecake, 80
Desserts, 58 - 104
dill
    Cucumber Refrigerator Pickles, 163
    Dilled Beans and Carrots, 213
Dill Mustard, 172
Dilled Green Beans, 164
Dilled Salmon Steaks, 122
dip
    Chicken Salsa Dip, 2
    Hot Spinach-Bacon Dip, 6
Double Cheese Fondue, 4
Double Chocolate Caramel Bars, 70
Double Dairy Salad, 214
dough
    Freeze Ahead White Bread
        Dough, 51
    Pizza Dough, 55
    Rye Bread Dough, 7
    White Bread Dough, 5
    Whole-Wheat Bread Dough, 11
doughnut
    Glazed Potato Doughnuts, 46
dressing
    Apple-Raisin Dressing, 136
    Creamy Garlic Dressing, 228
    Easy Blue Cheese Dressing, 215

Honey French Dressing, 212
dumplings
　　Chicken and Double-Corn
　　　Dumplings, 146
Dutch Pancake With Orange Sauce, 39
Dutch Potato Soup, 248

E

Easy Barbecued Fish, 123
Easy Blue Cheese Dressing, 215
Eggs, 106 - 114
　　Salmon-Egg Pie, 114
eggplant
　　Farm Garden Eggplant, 271
Extra-Special Mashed Potatoes, 275

F

Farm Garden Eggplant, 271
Fish and Shellfish, 120 - 126
fondue
　　Double Cheese Fondue, 4
Freeze Ahead White Bread Dough, 51
Freezer Coleslaw, 211
French Apple Pie, 98
French Rolls, 49
Fresh Fruit Bowl, 205
Fresh Fruit Slush, 204
Fresh Pumpkin Pie, 101
Frosty Pineapple Spritzers, 18
Frosty Tomato Cups, 216
Frozen Grapes in Lemonade, 89
fruit
　　Oatmeal-Fruit Cookies, 75
Fruit Salads, 204 - 209
Fruit Soup, 206
fruitcake
　　Glorious Golden Fruitcake, 59
Fruit-Nut Mix, 13
fudge
　　Minty Fudge Sauce, 81

G

Garden Club Sandwiches, 255
Garden Fresh Vegetable Salad, 217
gazpacho
　　Souper Gazpacho, 251
Georgia Peaches and Cream, 90
ginger ale
　　Summer Sparkle Punch, 21
Ginger Thins, 71
Glazed Potato Doughnuts, 46
Glazed Strawberry Cream Pie, 104
Glorious Golden Fruitcake, 59
Golden Autumn Salad, 207
Golden Carrot Cookies, 72
Golden Crunch Coffeecake, 42
Golden Delight Pancakes, 40
Golden Glazed Oven Chicken
　　　Barbecue, 148
Golden Parmesan Potatoes, 276
Golden Pecan Cinnamon Buns, 52
Golden Twice Baked Potatoes, 277
Gourmet Cheese Potatoes, 278
Grandmom's Apricot Squares, 87
grapefruit
　　Watermelon Grapefruit Fiesta, 23
grapes
　　Frozen Grapes in Lemonade, 89
gravy
　　Pork Steaks with Mushroom Cream
　　　Gravy, 192
　　Pot Roast With Vegetable
　　　Gravy, 176
　　Round Steak With Mushroom
　　　Gravy, 178
green beans
　　Dilled Beans and Carrots, 213
　　Dilled Green Beans, 164
　　Refrigerator Vegetable Salad, 223
green pepper
　　Frosty Tomato Cups, 216
Grilled Southwestern Steak, 177
ground beef
　　Bacon-Wrapped Beef Patties, 170
　　Meatball Stew, 174
　　Zucchini Beef Skillet, 183

gumbo
  Louisiana Gumbo, 241

H

ham
  Buelah's Ham, 195
  Country Crusted Ham, 196
  Potato-Ham Frittata, 112
  Quick Ham/Macaroni Skillet, 130
Ham and Broccoli Loaves, 5
Ham and Cabbage Soup, 239
Ham and Cheese Caesar, 256
ham hocks
  Split Pea Soup, 246
ham loaf
  Savory Ham Loaf, 198
hamburger (see ground beef)
  Old-Fashioned Hamburger
    Soup, 233
Ham-Pineapple Rings, 197
Hand-Painted Lemon Butter
  Cookies, 73
Harvest Lasagne, 128
Heirloom Raisin Muffins, 34
Herb Cheese Stuffed Cherry
  Tomatoes, 116
Herb Garden Bread, 54
Herbed Asparagus, 261
Herbed Carrots, 264
Holiday Potato Dish, 280
Homemade Sauerkraut, 165
Honey French Dressing, 212
Honey-Baked French Toast, 41
Honey-Citrus Glazed Veal Chops, 200
Hot Cross Buns, 53
Hot Spinach-Bacon Dip, 6

I

ice cream
  Crunchy Ice Cream Squares, 79
icing
  Hot Cross Buns, 53

J

Jam, 160 - 162
Jelly Roll, 62
Just-N-Trails Coconut-Topped
    Chocolate-Orange Muffins, 35

K

kabobs
  Marinated Beef Kabobs, 173
  Marinated Pork Kabobs, 189
kale
  Tortellini-Kale Soup, 247
Kidney Bean Salad, 218
Kulich
  Bread Machine Kulich, 47

L

lamb
  Simmered Lamb with Cabbage, 199
lasagne
  Harvest Lasagne, 128
Legumes, 117 - 118
lemon
  Banana-Lemon Loaf, 26
  Hand-Painted Butter Cookies, 73
Lemon Chiffon Cake, 60
Lemon Cod and Rice, 124
Lemon Cream Puffs, 91
Lemon Filling, 91
Lemon Glaze, 60, 91
lemonade
  Summer Sparkle Punch, 21
Lemon-Apple Sauce, 198
Lentil Sausage Soup, 240
lettuce
  Catalina Tossed Salad, 212
  Overnight Tossed Green Salad, 222
Light Chocolate Brownie Cupcakes, 66
Linguine with White Clam Sauce, 129
Louisiana Gumbo, 241

M

macaroni
    Quick Ham/Macaroni Skillet, 130
mandarin oranges
    Sparkling Fruit Cup, 95
marinade
    Sweet-Soy Marinade, 185
Marinated Beef Kabobs, 173
Marinated Corn Salad, 219
Marinated Pork Kabobs, 189
mashed potatoes (see potatoes)
    Glazed Potato Doughnuts, 46
Meats, 169 - 201
Meatball Stew, 174
Miniature Quiches, 109
Minty Fudge Sauce, 81
minute cube steaks
    Quick Baked Stew, 234
Mixed Vegetable Marinade, 220
mixed vegetables
    Cheesy Chicken Pie, 141
molasses
    Soft Molasses Drops, 77
Muenster cheese
    Garden Club Sandwiches, 255
Muffins, 30 - 36
Mulligatawny Soup, 238
mushrooms
    Spinach-Mushroom Vinaigrette, 226
    Round Steak with Mushroom
        Gravy, 178
    Veal Paprikash, 201
mustard
    Dill Mustard, 172

N

National Watermelon Promotion
    Board, 1
navy beans
    Pressure-Cooker Baked Beans, 117
    Sweet and Sour Baked Beans, 118
New England Sweet Potatoes, 283

nut
    Fruit-Nut Mix, 13

O

oats
    Pumpkin Oat Muffins, 36
    Pumpkin Pie Squares, 102
oatmeal cookies
    Amish Oatmeal Cookies, 74
Oatmeal Spice Cake, 61
Oatmeal-Fruit Cookies, 75
Old-Fashioned Beef and Biscuits, 175
Old-Fashioned Hamburger Soup, 233
Old-Fashioned Jelly Roll, 62
omelet
    Potato-Bacon Omelet, 111
Onion Rolls, 50
onions
    Baked Onions, 273
    Bratwurst and Onions, 187
orange
    Cabbage-Orange Slaw, 210
Orange County Rice Pudding, 82
orange juice
    Spicy Holiday Brew, 14
    Tropical Fruit Shake, 22
Orange Sauce, 39
Orange Sugar Ring, 43
Orange Walnut Bread, 28
Orange-Coconut Apple Crisp, 83
Orange-Glazed Carrots, 265
Orange-Pecan Salad, 221
Oriental Stir-Fried Vegetables, 272
Overnight Tossed Green Salad, 222
Oyster Stew, 242

P

Pancakes, 37 - 40
Parsleyed Chicken Chowder, 237
parsnips
    Butter-Glazed Root Vegetables, 270

Pasta, 128 - 133
 Old-Fashioned Hamburger
  Soup, 233
Pasta and Bean Soup, 245
peaches
 Georgia Peaches and Cream, 90
peanuts
 Peanut Cookie Balls, 76
Pear Melba, 92
peas
 Salmon-Egg Pie, 114
 Split Pea Soup, 246
pecan
 Orange-Pecan Salad, 221
 Range-Top Pecan Dressing, 137
peppers
 Frosty Tomato Cups, 216
 Salami and Sweet Pepper Loaves, 8
pickles
 Cucumber Refrigerator, 163
Pies, 97 - 104
pilaf
 Barley Pilaf, 138
Piña Colada Flip, 19
pineapple
 Frosty Pineapple Spritzers, 18
 Ham-Pineapple Rings, 197
 Marinated Beef Kabobs, 172
 Sparkling Fruit Cup, 95
 Sweet and Sour Baked Beans, 118
 Sweet and Sour Turkey, 155
pineapple juice
 Piña Colada Flip, 19
Pineapple Upside Down Cake, 63
pita bread
 Chicken Waldorf Pockets, 253
 Curried Smoked Turkey in a
  Pocket, 254
 Ham and Cheese Caesar, 256
pizza
 Breakfast Berry Pizza, 78
 Super Supper Pizza, 182
Pizza Dough, 55
Popovers, 29
Pork, 186 - 198
Pork Chop Skillet Dinner, 190

Pork Chops en Casserole, 191
Pork Steaks with Mushroom
  Cream Gravy, 192
Pot Pie, 149
Pot Roast with Vegetable Gravy, 176
Potato Puffs, 279
potato salad
 Sour Cream Potato Salad, 227
potato soup
 Dutch Potato Soup, 248
 Cream of Potato Soup, 249
Potato-Bacon Omelet, 111
Potatoes, 274 - 280
 Cheesed Mashed Potatoes, 274
 Cheesy Chicken Pie, 141
 Cream of Potato Soup, 249
 Extra-Special Mashed Potatoes, 275
 Golden Parmesan Potatoes, 276
 Golden Twice Baked Potatoes, 277
 Gourmet Cheese Potatoes, 278
 Holiday Potato Dish, 280
 Meatball Stew, 173
 Pork Chop Skillet Dinner, 190
 Savory Beef Casserole, 180
 Sour Cream Potato Salad, 227
 Stefado, 235
Potato-Ham Frittata, 112
Poultry, 140 - 157
Preserved Foods, 160 - 168
prunes
 Fruit Soup, 206
Pumpkin Oat Muffins, 36
Pumpkin Pie, 101
Pumpkin Pie Squares, 102
Pumpkin-Nut Cake Roll, 64
punch
 Sparkling Citrus Punch, 20
 Summer Sparkle Punch, 21

Q

Quick Baked Stew, 234
Quick Clam Soup, 243

Quick Coffeecake, 44
Quick Ham-Macaroni Skillet, 130

R

raisins
    Apple Raisin Dressing, 136
    Heirloom Raisin Muffins, 34
    Fruit Soup, 206
Ranch-Style Eggs, 113
Range-Top Pecan Dressing, 137
raspberry
    Cranberry-Raspberry Pie, 99
    Rhubarb-Raspberry Jam, 162
Raspberry Cheese Cups, 93
Refrigerated Pizza Dough, 55
Refrigerator Vegetable Salad, 223
relish
    Potpourri Relish, 166
Reuben Casserole, 180
Reuben Loaves, 7
rhubarb
    Rosy Spring Salad, 208
Rhubarb Crunch, 94
Rhubarb Surprise Pie, 103
Rhubarb-Raspberry Jam, 162
ribs
    Barbecued Country-Style Ribs and
        Kraut, 186
    Sweet and Sour Beef Ribs, 179
rice
    Chicken Rice Skillet, 143
    Lemon Cod and Rice, 124
    Turkey Curry with Rice, 156
rice pudding
    Orange County Rice Pudding, 82
risotto, 134
    Spinach Risotto, 135
Rosy Spring Salad, 208
rotini
    Three Times Three Rotini and
        Cheese, 133
Round Steak with Mushroom
        Gravy, 178
Rye Bread Dough, 7

S

Salads, 204 - 230
Salami and Sweet Pepper Loaves, 8
salmon
    Dilled Salmon Steaks, 122
Salmon-Egg Pie, 114
Salmon-Parsley Log, 9
salsa
    Chicken Salsa Dip, 2
Sandwiches, 253 - 257
sauce
    Lemon-Apple Sauce, 198
    Minty Fudge Sauce, 81
    Spaghetti, 132
sauerkraut, 186
    Barbecued Country-Style Ribs and
        Kraut, 186
    Homemade Sauerkraut, 165
    Sausage-Apple-Sauerkraut
        Supper, 193
Sauerkraut Slaw, 224
sausage
    Lentil Sausage Soup, 240
Sausage-Apple-Sauerkraut Supper, 193
Savory Beef Casserole, 181
Savory Ham Loaf, 198
Savory Potted Cheese, 10
Seafood Chowder, 244
shake
    Tropical Fruit Shake, 22
shrimp
    Louisiana Gumbo, 241
    Seafood Chowder, 244
    Sweet Spiced Shrimp, 12
Shrimp Creole, 125
Simmered Lamb with Cabbage, 199
slaw
    Cabbage-Orange Slaw, 210
    Sauerkraut Slaw, 224
Sliced Tomatoes with Sweet and
        Sour Dressing, 225
slush
    Citrus Slush, 16
    Fresh Fruit Slush, 204

Smoked Turkey-Stuffed Shells, 131
Soft Molasses Drops, 77
sole, 126
soup
    Fruit Soup, 206
Souper Gazpacho, 251
Soups and Stews, 232 - 252
Sour Cream Potato Salad, 227
Spaghetti Sauce, 132
Sparkling Citrus Punch, 20
Sparkling Fruit Cup, 95
Spice Cake, 61
Spicy Applesauce Cake, 65
Spicy Barbecue Sauce, 186
Spicy Holiday Brew, 14
Spicy Tea, 15
spinach
    Hot Spinach-Bacon Dip, 6
    Overnight Tossed Green Salad, 222
Spinach Risotto, 135
Spinach-Cheese Loaves, 11
Spinach-Filled Steak Rolls, 182
Spinach-Mushroom Vinaigrette, 226
Split Pea Soup, 246
squash
    Curried Squash Bisque, 252
    Yellow Squash Casserole, 282
steak
    Grilled Southwestern Steak, 177
    Spinach-Filled Steak Rolls, 182
Stefado, 235
Stir-Fry
    Sweet Hot Chicken Stir-Fry, 151
strata
    Broccoli and Cheese Strata, 106
strawberries
    Rosy Spring Salad, 208
    Glazed Strawberry Cream Pie, 104
Strawberries and Cream Spectacular, 96
Strawberry Hill Farms, 57
Strawberry Swirl Coffee Cake, 45
Stuffed Sole, 126
Sunday Special Chicken, 150
Super Supper Pizza, 183
Sweet and Sour Baked Beans, 118
Sweet and Sour Beef Ribs, 179

Sweet and Sour Turkey, 155
Sweet Corn Relish, 167
Sweet Hot Chicken Stir-Fry, 151
sweet potatoes
    Candied Yams With Pecans, 285
    New England-Style Sweet
        Potatoes, 283
Sweet-Soy Marinade, 185
Sweet-Spiced Shrimp, 12
Swiss cheese
    Double Cheese Fondue, 4
    Swiss Chicken Pie, 152

T

Tandoori Chicken, 153
tea, 15
Three Times Three Rotini and
    Cheese, 133
tomato juice
    Zippy Tomato Lemon Cocktail, 24
tomatoes
    Basil Beans and Tomatoes, 262
    Blue Cheese Stuffed Cherry Toma-
        toes, 115
    Broiled Tomatoes Parmesan, 284
    Frosty Tomato Cups, 216
    Herb Cheese Stuffed Cherry Toma-
        toes, 116
    Quick Clam Soup, 243
    Sliced Tomatoes with Sweet and
        Sour Dressing, 225
    Spaghetti Sauce, 132
    V-4 Tomato Juice Cocktail, 168
Topping for French Apple Pie, 98
Topping for Muffins, 36
Tortellini Salad, 229
Tortellini-Kale Soup, 247
tortillas
    Ranch-Style Eggs, 113
Tropical Fruit Shake, 22
Turkey, 155 - 157
    Curried Smoked Turkey in a
        Pocket, 254
    Smoked Turkey-Stuffed Shells, 131

Sweet and Sour Turkey, 155
Turkey Bow Tie Casserole, 157
turkey breast
    Garden Club Sandwiches, 255
Turkey Curry With Rice, 156
turnips, 270
    Butter-Glazed Root Vegetables, 270

U

Unfried Chicken, 154

V

V-4 Tomato Juice Cocktail, 168
veal
    Honey-Citrus Glazed Veal
        Chops, 200
Veal Paprikash, 201
vegetable gravy
    Pot Roast with Vegetable
        Gravy, 176
Vegetable Salads, 210 - 227
    Garden Fresh Vegetable Salad, 217
Vegetables, 258 - 286
    Chicken Vegetable Soup, 236
    Chinese Chicken with
        Vegetables, 142
    Creamy Vegetable Soup, 250
    Mixed Vegetable Marinade, 220
Vinaigrette, 221

W

Waldorf
    Chicken Waldorf Pockets, 253
Waldorf Variation Salad, 209
walnut
    Banana Walnut Bread, 27
Warm Chicken Salad, 230
Watermelon Grapefruit Fiesta, 23
White Bread Dough, 5
Whole-Wheat Bread Dough, 11
Whole-Wheat Pizza Dough, 55

Y

yams
    Candied Yams with Pecans, 285
Yellow Squash Casserole, 282

Z

Zippy Tomato Lemon Cocktail, 24
zucchini
    Colorful Vegetables, 269
    Marinated Beef Kabobs, 172
Zucchini Beef Skillet, 184
Zucchini Skillet Medley, 286